TARGET

ENGLAND

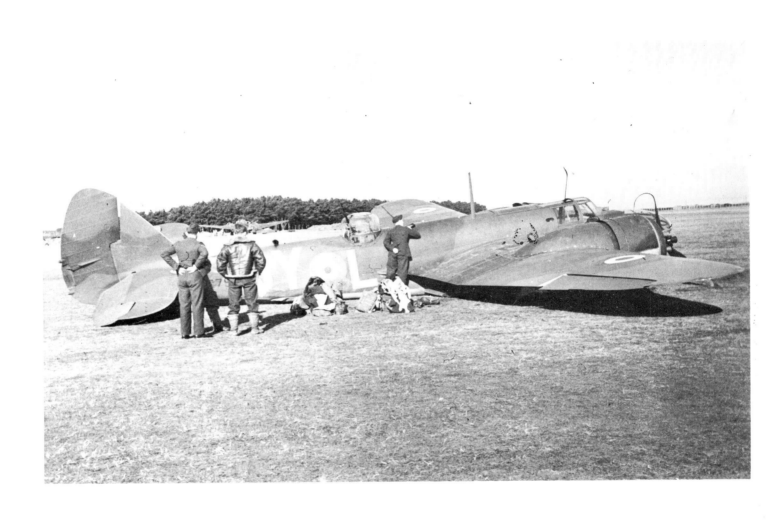

DEREK WOOD

TARGET ENGLAND

THE ILLUSTRATED HISTORY OF THE BATTLE OF BRITAIN

JANE'S

LONDON · NEW YORK · SYDNEY

First published in Great Britain by
Jane's Publishing Company Ltd,
238 City Road, London EC1V 2PU

ISBN 0 7106 0049 6

Design — Bernard Crossland Associates

Printed in Great Britain by
Netherwood Dalton & Co Ltd,
Huddersfield

Page 1: A Luftwaffe photographer took this picture from the ventral gun position of a Ju 88. He claimed that he had shot down the Hurricane which is seen diving away between the two gun sights. Ironically, this Ju 88 crashed in the Channel and the crew, including the photographer, had to be rescued by a seaplane. **Page 2:** A Blenheim IV of No. 235 Squadron crash-landed at Lossiemouth early in 1940. **Page 3:** A group of pilots from No. 303 (Polish) Squadron flying Hurricanes confer before take-off. **Page 4:** A line up of No. 65 Squadron Spitfires at Hornchurch in July. The fuselage serial numbers have been scratched out by the wartime censor. **Page 5:** A Ju 88 of KG 30 brought down in the sea at Pagham, Sussex, September 1940 after being attacked head-on. **Page 6:** Rescuers dig in the rubble of a bombed house in East London.

ACKNOWLEDGEMENTS

Many people have helped in the search for material. Miss Freda Tomlin permitted the use of her remarkable diary, while Derek Saunders provided the orders of the Crookham Home Guard and other documents. R D Cooling provided hitherto unpublished photographs as did Wing Commander E C Wolfe, Wing Commander R P Beamont and Robert Wright who also gave most valuable help. A W Gregg gave a unique insight into the armament position. Mrs. Aileen Clayton advised on the 'Y' service and Observer Commander Tony Lardner loaned the unique casualty log book kept by a 1940 member of the Observer Corps. Other photographs were kindly provided by John W R Taylor, Alfred Price, John Dyer and Jack Bushby. My thanks are also due to John Blake, Derek Ballington and Geoffrey Squire for maps and diagrams. Finally, I owe a particular debt of gratitude to my wife, Lin, and my daughter, Nicola, who typed the text and the captions at all times of the day and night.

PICTURE CREDITS

Associated Newspapers: Nos. 242, 273, 305 **P. Chevalier:** No. 138 **J. W. R. Taylor:** No. 90 **Evening News:** No. 339 **Wing Commander R. P. Beaumont:** Nos. 227, 252, 253, 254, 255, 272 **W. S. Jackson:** No. 72 **J. E. Sanders:** No. 231 **Imperial War Museum:** Page 4; Nos. 60, 69, 70, 83, 91, 117, 133, 149, 170, 180, 181, 183, 184, 185, 186, 192, 197, 201, 205, 213, 249, 275, 286, 289, 292, 293, 294, 297, 298, 299, 334, 350, 367, 368, 376 **Press Association:** Nos. 54, 113, 114, 126, 152, 375, 381 **Fox Photos:** Nos. 61, 268, 335, 345, 346 **Via Col. Terlinden:** Nos. 106, 107, 110, 111, 112, 116 **R. D. Bird:** No. 67 **Kent Messenger:** Nos. 59, 99, 115, 145, 146, 147, 148, 159, 162, 172, 173, 174, 215, 218, 234, 286, 318, 331, 369, 382 **Royal Armoured Corps Tank Museum:** Page 55; Nos. 97, 144, 150, 151, 152, 153, 314 **Bundesarchiv:** Page 7; Nos. 100, 127, 154, 171, 177, 178, 190, 194, 195, 198, 203, 208, 236, 237, 238, 249, 250, 251, 274, 279, 282, 283, 284, 295, 303, 311, 312, 313, 330, 336, 343, 347, 348, 349, 363, 364 **Crown Copyright:** Nos. 196, 243, 300 **Group Captain W. Maydwell:** 56, 65 **Group Captain Havercraft:** 101, 157, 301 **Central Press:** Page 6; Nos. 92, 108, 109, 142, 188, 191, 240, 260, 262, 267, 319, 320, 321, 322, 323, 324, 325, 326, 359, 360, 366, 371, 372, 385 **Via Alfred Price:** Nos. 248, 257, 258, 352, 353 **Dennis Knight:** Nos. 189, 220, 233 **Lufthansa:** Nos. 1, 2, 7, 8, 10 **Hull Daily Mail:** No. 163 **Sir Matthew Slattery:** No. 17 **Associated Press:** Nos. 202, 217 **J. Bushby:** Nos. 26, 41, 50, 135 **Museum of British Transport:** Nos. 97, 219, 384 **P. Moyes:** Nos. 306 **Wing Commander E. C. Wolfe:** Nos. 31, 32, 33, 34, 35, 355, 356 **G. F. Whitworth:** No. 103 **R. D. Cooling:** Page 2; Nos. 36, 37, 38, 128, 129, 130, 131, 165 **Robert Weylit:** Nos. 302, 380 **Group Captain J. Kent:** Nos. 42, 47, 271 **M. W. Payne:** No. 306 **Air Commodore J. Greswell:** No. 55 **Air Commodore P. M. Brothers:** Nos. 57, 58, 354 **Topix:** Nos. 221, 239 **Barratts' Photo Press:** Nos. 307, 327 **T. H. McLellan:** Nos. 308, 309 **R. T. Reeves:** No. 378 **E. Walters:** No. 245

Acknowledgements for quotations:

The Eyes of the Few, Daphne Carne, P. R. Macmillan Ltd., 1960
Nine Lives, Group Captain Alan C. Deare, Hodder and Stoughton, 1959
Spitfire Pilot, Flight Lt. D. M. Crook, Faber and Faber, 1942

CONTENTS

FOREWORD

1940 was the year that changed the course of mankind. Between April and June Nazi Germany with lightning speed crushed and occupied five European and Scandinavian nations, having already engulfed Austria, Czechoslovakia and Poland.

The rest of the world waited for the sole European survivor, Britain, to surrender or be overrun. Neither event took place and to the surprise of all, including Hitler, at the end of the year the islands still stood, battered and defiant but growing in strength. This is the illustrated story of that year, together with the background that led up to it. It is an attempt to recapture in text, documents and photographs the extraordinary atmosphere of the time and the victory that was won by the RAF as the shield of a mobilised and united nation.

THE RISE OF THE LUFTWAFFE

Heinkel He 111H releasing a two and a half ton bomb over England. The prototype for this aircraft first flew in 1935, the year the Luftwaffe came into the open.

In June 1940 the Luftwaffe was the master of the skies of continental Europe. It had destroyed the air forces of five nations and apparently nothing could stand in its path. Its strength was an integral part of the blitzkreig formula which had brought Adolf Hitler to the summit of power and there seemed to be no end to the fields for conquest. Only Britain's Royal Air Force barred the way to total victory and resolution of this problem was, obviously, a matter of time.

Yet, surprisingly, it had been only twenty-one years since the Treaty of Versailles had been signed, with the avowed intention of ending military aviation in Germany for all time. If June 1919 represented the nadir of German military hopes in the air, June 1940 represented the summit of its achievement. In fact the German Air Force was never completely destroyed at the end of the First World War. Some 1500 military aircraft were surrendered to the allies but an air embryo lived on.

The German Defence Ministry was allowed to remain in being and it was here that the Commander-in-Chief of the Reichswehr, General von Seeckt began to set up an air section with men whose ranks and titles appeared to bear no relation to 'air' forces. Von Seeckt envisaged the eventual setting up of an independent German Air Force and he was prepared to wait patiently. It is remarkable that all three of the Luftflotten commanders who faced Britain in the summer of 1940 had been employed by von Seeckt in the early 20's, namely Kesselring, Sperrle and Stumpff.

In February 1922 the regulations regarding German aircraft construction were relaxed and manufacturers got back into business making small transports and light sports machines. Much more significant, however, was the arrival in Russia at the end of 1921 of two of von Seeckt's envoys. They came to discuss the building of aircraft and the military training of German pilots in the Soviet Union.

The Soviet leaders were interested and two years later a clandestine pact was signed allowing the Reichswehr Ministry of Defence full facilities. At Lipetzk, two hundred miles south east of Moscow, a complete training complex was set up with men, aircraft and equipment smuggled out of Germany. By mid-1924 some 200 men on forged passports had arrived at Lipetzk and the first fighter pilot course had begun. With the active assistance of the Red Army, bombing and ground co-operation exercises were organised. A network of air services from Germany to Russia ensured that communications were maintained for important matters, while the hardware and supplies were shipped by a variety of illegal means and with the full support of the Kremlin.

The Lipetzk centre operated for ten years and during that time key personnel were fed through it, including engineers and mechanics. As a result of the experience gained, specifications were established in Berlin for a range of warplanes ultimately to be built by the new German aircraft industry. While Lipetzk functioned secretly behind Russia's iron curtain, Germany in the late 20's and early 30's became the most air-conscious nation in the world.

Captain Kurt Student (later General and head of parachute troops) was largely responsible for the formation of the Deutscher Luftsportverband which gave glider training to large numbers of youngsters. Aircraft companies sprang up with later well-known names like Junkers, Messerschmitt, Heinkel, Dornier and Focke-Wulf. When they encountered restrictions, these firms had subsidiaries established abroad, where research and development could continue unhindered.

The greatest boost, however, to the future Luftwaffe came from the founding in January 1926 of the airline Deutsche Lufthansa, amalgamated from two existing smaller operations. At the helm as Chairman was Erhard Milch (later Inspector General of the Luftwaffe), an extremely shrewd man who had been a flier in the First World War and had subsequently worked as salesman for Junkers. Through Lufthansa it later proved possible to train large numbers of aircrew, order and test civil prototypes of future service aircraft and experiment with a variety of electronic navigation and landing aids which were to become standard in the German Air Force. The airline was also to provide the means for a great deal of clandestine photography of the air forces and industrial potential of future enemies.

In 1928 Lufthansa suffered a setback when its Government subsidies were reduced by half. One Reichstag deputy, who successfully persued the cause of Lufthansa, was the 1918 Commander of the famous Richthofen Circus, Hermann Göring. The corpulent, loud-mouthed, politician and the short, astute, businessman worked closely together and out of their mutual interests emerged the Luftwaffe. On January 30, 1933, Hitler was made Chancellor of the Third Reich and with him to the top went Göring. In April 1933 the Reich Air Ministry was formed, with Göring as Minister and Milch as Secretary of State.

Göring was extremely busy with a variety of other offices he had acquired and the task of creating a new air force devolved upon Milch. He assembled a skeleton air staff, an administrative section, a technical and production office and a department to look after civil aviation—which only served to bring Lufthansa and other civil concerns closer into the defence orbit.

Light bomber, fighter and reconnaissance biplanes had been tested and were ready for production while several hundred trained crews were available. Everything connected with the air force was shrouded in secrecy as the idea of an air war and mass bombing were, to the civilians of the 1930's what the H-bomb is to those of the 1980's; Hitler wished to arouse no suspicions abroad or precipitate the re-armament of other nations.

Milch, ever cautious, wanted the Luftwaffe to come to a peak of strength and efficiency by 1942/43, with ample reserves to meet any contingency. He was not, however, allowed to carry out his plans as both Hitler and Göring wanted air power quickly, whatever corners had to be cut in the process. Milch's first production order for the German aircraft industry was placed in 1934, for 4021 aircraft of twenty-five different types, to be built in two years. These equipped six fighter, six bomber and six reconnaissance Geschwader which formed the basis of the air force. Milch organised a major expansion of factory capacity and brought in heavy industrial works such as Henschel and Blohm und Voss.

Expansion on all fronts was so rapid and the political climate so propitious that Germany was able to announce to the world that the Luftwaffe was already in existence on March 1, 1935—Hitler's decree having been issued on February 26. The Luftwaffe was 20,000 strong, with 1888 aircraft. Göring, naturally, was made commander-in-chief with Milch as Secretary of State for Air, and a brilliant officer, General Wever, as Chief of Air Staff. From that moment on the expansion was ceaseless. Lufthansa crews were put on the military reserve and more and more Luftwaffe personnel were trained with the airline, while airfields were built in many parts of the country. When the Luftwaffe was unveiled to an amazed world in 1935, its air fleet for the Battle of Britain five years later was already settled. In the fighter field, the prototype Bf 109 single-seater was nearing completion and the first two-seat Bf 110 Zerstörer (Destroyer) was under construction. Of the bombers, the Heinkel 111 was rolled out in the month before the Luftwaffe announcement, the Dornier 17 'Flying Pencil' had flown in the autumn of 1934 and the Ju 87 was also ready to be pushed out of the hangar doors. This represented a remarkable achievement but it also meant that there could be no deviation from the programme and, as it turned out, no more advanced types before the outbreak of the Second World War.

There were considerable arguments over the actual military role of the Luftwaffe but it was finally accepted that its tasks were air superiority, close support of ground troops, interdiction and reconnaissance. Wever wanted to build up a strategic bomber force as well but he encountered opposition and his untimely death in an air crash in 1936 meant the abandonment of the whole concept. Göring was not interested in any long-term investment in a multi-engined long range bomber, he wanted to 'darken the skies' with mass-produced light, medium and dive bombers and provide the fighter escorts to surround them.

The precision dive bomber idea was propagated by Ernst Udet, a noted fighter pilot of the First World War Richthofen Circus and one of the best known of the inter-war stunt pilots. Udet managed to purchase two Curtiss Hawk dive bombers in America and from trials with these emerged the requirement for the 'Stuka' (Sturzkampfflugzeug, literally—falling, fighting flying apparatus). Udet was appointed head of the Air Ministry Technical Branch where he was free to press his views. In the summer of 1936 Junkers was awarded the contract for the Ju 87 which became universally known as the Stuka. Göring became obsessed with the idea and thereafter almost every bomber specification called for dive-bombing to be incorporated in the design. Even the later lumbering and ill-fated heavy bomber, the Heinkel 177, was supposed to be able to power dive onto its target.

In general Hitler, Göring and the Air Force staff wanted strike power in the shape of bombers. The fighter programme was secondary and it remained so until 1942/43. This was one of the fundamental errors which was to lose Nazi Germany the Battle of Britain and, ultimately, the war. Without a Fighter Comand, the Luftwaffe fighter arm could not develop and expand on its own account and it suffered accordingly.

Göring gradually realised that Milch, not he, was building the air force and jealousy played its part in the service's ultimate fate. Göring stripped Milch of most of his appointments and turned the procurement side over to Udet. This was a fatal mistake; just when the bitter rivalry of the industrialists required a man of great discernment and toughness it was offered a happy-go-lucky, very brave aerobatic pilot with a loathing for organisation, decisions and paper.

The Luftwaffe was rapidly expanding but it needed operational experience. The great opportunity came with the outbreak of civil war in Spain. Here was the proving ground where tactics could be perfected, pilots blooded and the administrative organisation refined. The initial contribution to General Franco's war effort consisted of 85 volunteers, twenty Ju 52 bomber-transports and six biplane He 51 fighters. By late 1936 it was realised that this force was inadequate and obsolescent. In November the 'Condor Legion' was formed under General Sperrle and gradually more men and more modern machines gave the Legion air superiority. Many RAF pilots were to lose their lives in 1940 for lack of the experience that the Luftwaffe had gained in Spain.

The country was used as an operational combat training area where essential modifications for aircraft could be produced and tested and aircrew could learn their trade under real shooting conditions. Two of the many significant names from the Spanish War were Mölders and Galland, later to become the best known fighter pilot leaders of the Luftwaffe.

From 1935 onwards the Nazis indulged in a massive propaganda campaign designed to impress the world with Germany's prowess in the air and frighten the populations of other European nations. It represented a form of psychological warfare which built up in people's minds the idea that the Luftwaffe was invincible.

At rallies in Germany itself, wave upon wave of bombers (many of them obsolescent) flew over and were filmed from every angle. At air displays abroad, streamlined and hotted up versions of new German warplanes stole the limelight. In 1937 at the International Military Aircraft Competition at Zurich, a prototype Do 17 'Flying Pencil' won the circuit of the Alps and outran all the fighters put up against it. At the same meeting the Bf 109 fighter, in various modified forms, broke record after record and swept the competition board. The reputation of the 109 was further enhanced in November 1937, when a prototype aircraft with a specially boosted engine gained the world landplane air speed record at 379.38 mph.

A very clever piece of deception was used during the visit of the French Chief of Air Staff to the Messerschmitt works at Augsburg in August 1938. The Bf 110 two-seat fighter had hitherto been a carefully guarded secret but during the visit General Vuillemin was allowed to view a section of the production line and was able to watch a steady flow of take-offs by what were purported to be aircraft from the line. In fact they were a handful of 110's which took off, landed out of sight and then taxied back to take off again. The 110 had yet to be produced in numbers sufficient to equip even a first Luftwaffe unit.

Vuillemin was also shown, at Oranienburg, a prototype of the sleek and powerful looking He 100 fighter and was given the impression that it was in full production. Early in 1940, propaganda photographs flowed out of Berlin showing He 100's (with the phoney designation He 113) apparently in squadron service in the field. These were, however, just nine works machines posed in suitable surroundings and with a variety of specially concocted squadron markings and emblems. The 113 never saw service with the Luftwaffe. The ruse worked, nevertheless, as every aircraft recognition manual in Britain in 1940 contained silhouettes and/or pictures of the '113' and many RAF pilots in the Battle of Britain claimed to have been in combat with the type. Even as late as 1942, the 113 was 'identified' as taking part in the escape up the Channel of the battleships *Scharnhorst* and *Gneisenau*. Such are the effects of well-organised propaganda.

When the Munich crisis came in September 1938, the Luftwaffe was completely unprepared to go to war. Four months after Germany had occupied Austria in April 1938, on August 1, there were only 1669 serviceable aircraft available, with front-line types broken down into 582 bombers, 159 dive-bombers and 453 fighters. In no way were these numbers sufficient for a European conflict to be embarked upon. Hitler relied on the fears of war and the unpreparedness of Britain and France and in this he was quite correct.

Germany began the Second World War with too few aircraft and insufficient production. The industry had made tremendous strides in the early and mid-thirties but it was not turning out enough combat machines particularly fighters. Production of all military aircraft in 1939 was 8295 but it should have been several thousand more, plus a further major expansion to come in the crucial year of 1940. Udet must bear the blame for not pushing the industry harder and sorting out the constant squabbling between the manufacturers.

On the operational side, the Luftwaffe, at the beginning of September 1939, was an extremely well-trained and well-organised force with 600,000 personnel, not including those in the Flak or anti-aircraft branch which was part of the air force itself. Over 60,000 aircrew were available with a large number in training. The flying schools were turning out over 12,000 pilots per year from 100 schools.

The accompanying table shows the aircraft strength of the Luftwaffe on September 1, 1939, with a breakdown of the types involved. In all there were 3750 aircraft of all categories, of which 1170 were twin-engined bombers.

Milch was back in favour as the Luftwaffe Inspector General, while the Chief of Air Staff was General Jeschonnek. Three Air Fleets (Luftflotten) had been established No. 1 with HQ in Berlin, under General Kesselring; No. 2, HQ Brunswick, under General Felmy; No. 3, HQ Munich, under General Sperrle; and No. 4, HQ Vienna, under General Löhr—formerly of the Austrian Air Force. Each of the

Luftflotten was completely self-contained with fighter, bomber and reconnaissance elements. It was administered and supplied by a Luftgaue (air district) and had air transport units available for the provision of ammunition, bombs petrol and food during an advance.

Usually there were two Fliegerkorps or Fliegerdivisionen to a Luftflotte and these were, in turn, broken down into Geschwarden of 90-120 machines and Gruppen each of about 30 aircraft. Within a Gruppe the basic unit was the Staffel of about nine aircraft, which was smaller than its opposite number, an RAF squadron. Backing the Air Fleets was an excellent signals organisation under General Martini. Radio techniques were advanced, and well proven, although little was known of a radar based air-defence system such as that operated by Fighter Command.

Essentially, the Luftwaffe was a tactical air force designed to support and exploit the advances of the German Army. The bomber force was built for the overland role with fighters to clear the way for it and maintain air supremacy over the battlefield. Once the air was clear the fighters were to go over to ground attack. It was an efficient and well-oiled machine that was to change the face of Europe completely in nine short months.

Luftwaffe first line unit equipment 1st September 1939

	Medium Range bombers	Dive bombers	Single-engine fighters	Twin-engine fighters	Long range recce	Short range recce	Coastal	Grand Total
He 111	780							
Do 17	470							
Ju 88	20							
Ju 87		335						
Bf 109D			235					
Bf 109E			850					
Ar 66			5					
Ar 68			35					
Bf 110				195				
Do 17					280			
Hs 126						195		
He 46						100		
Miscellaneous						45		
Coastal types (various)							205	
Total	**1270**	**335**	**1125**	**195**	**280**	**340**	**205**	**3750**

1 Germany's first post-First World War aircraft was a very advanced all metal six-seater cantilever monoplane, the Junkers F-13. Over 300 F-13's were built, the type being later converted for military use in Japan and Russia. The method of construction employed in the F-13 was later adapted to the Ju 52.

2 Communications with Russia were vital for the German secret air force in the 1920's while the military training facility at Lipetzk was developed. The photograph shows a Rolls Royce Eagle-engined Fokker F.III transport, used by the Soviet-German airline Deruluft, landing at Moscow in May 1924.

3 Before the new Luftwaffe saw the light of day in 1935, training of aircrew was conducted in great secrecy. Here, future Luftwaffe officers are seen being inspected at the Schleissheim Flying School by Hermann Göring—as yet unable to don one of his fancy uniforms.

4 This photograph of the Dornier 19 four-motor heavy bomber was issued by the German Air Ministry Press Office in July 1937. The release was purely designed to impress the outside world, as the Do 19 and its competitor, the Ju 89, known unofficially as 'Ural Bombers', had already been cancelled. In developed form the Do 19 was intended to carry a substantial bomb load as far as the Urals or the North of Scotland. Göring wanted greater numbers of twin-engined bombers, not smaller forces of four-engined types and a large German bomber was not to see service until half-way through the war in the shape of the very unreliable Heinkel 177.

5 A first-class brain, Generalleutnant Wever was the first Luftwaffe Chief of General Staff who was killed in an air crash in 1936. With him died the concept of the 'Ural Bomber', a four-engined strategic aircraft which was to be missing in the Battle of Britain.

6 The first of the real dive bombers, the Henschel 123, deliveries of which to the Luftwaffe began in 1936. It proved remarkably robust and was used for dive bombing/ground attack in Poland, the Western campaign of 1940 and in Russia.

7 The corrugated fuselage, tri-motor, Junkers 52 transport played a major part in the build up of the Luftwaffe and in all its wartime operations. Lufthansa used the Ju 52 in large numbers and many Luftwaffe bomber pilots were trained on the type. This Ju 52/3mce powered by BMW Hornet engines was the first to enter service with Lufthansa and went on the German civil register in 1932.

8 The Diesel-engined Junkers 86 was first flown as a bomber but was subsequently developed as a 10-passenger transport. Some 800 military Ju 86's were built and the type was in training and small-scale operational use on the outbreak of war. This Ju 86 was one of a batch flown by Lufthansa.

9 The Ju 87 Stuka dive bomber spearheaded the Luftwaffe's Blitzkrieg on land in 1939 and 1940 and became known as a terror weapon. In the Battle of Britain the type suffered severe losses and was withdrawn from operations. In later campaigns, particularly in Russia, it again proved its worth in a number of rôles. The photograph shows the tenth production Ju 87A-1 in 1937.

10 The Fw 200 Condor achieved fame with Lufthansa in 1938 when it flew non-stop from Berlin to New York. In the Second World War the type was used as a VIP and general transport and for reconnaissance. It was best known, however, in maritime form where it played a major part in the Battle of the Atlantic.

11 Bf 109's of the Condor Legion fighter squadron 2./J88 at Saragossa, Spain, in March 1939. After the Civil War had ended the aircraft were taken over by the Spanish Air Force.

12 Heinkel 111E bombers used in the Spanish Civil War by the four Staffeln of K/88 of the Condor Legion. The light losses incurred by the Heinkels misled the Luftwaffe into thinking that speed would suffice without good defensive armament. This theory was disproved during the Battle of Britain.

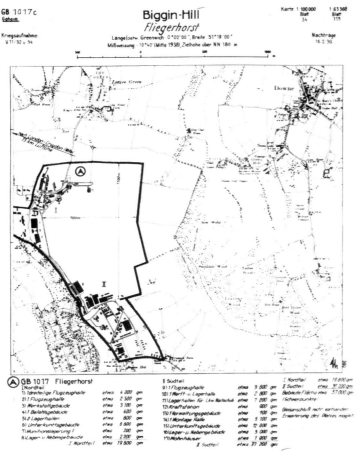

Größe: 700 × 1100 m

13 Two pages from the Luftwaffe airfield handbook for Britain showing Biggin Hill in Kent. The photographs were taken in January 1939 by a Luftwaffe airliner on its way to Croydon, while the map was based on a British Ordnance Survey sheet with additional details from the photographs. These illustrations were used by the Luftwaffe in 1940 as aids during the bombing of the Biggin Hill Sector Station.

14 This photograph of the Ju 88 bomber production line was intended for propaganda purposes. Despite the impressive line-up, the Ju 88, like other German first-line types, was in short supply in 1940.

15 The Heinkel 100 fighter was produced in very small numbers but it was represented by the Propaganda Ministry as a major weapon and in operational use. Although He 100s (allotted the cover designation He 113) never served in an operational unit, they were reported in action over the Channel and Britain on many occasions. That the type was taken seriously is shown by this page from Air Publication 1764 'Aircraft Recognition', issued in 1940.

16 The standard close-reconnaissance aircraft of the Luft-waffe on the outbreak of war and in the summer of 1940 was the Hs 126. Powered by an 850 hp Bramo Fafnir radial engine, the Hs 126 had a crew of two and a maximum speed of 193 mph. This picture was taken at Schonefeld in 1938 before delivery to units. Some Hs 126's were operated tentatively in the Channel area in 1940 but the majority were held back pending invasion.

17 The airship *Graf Zeppelin* carried out the first electronic warfare reconnaissance flight in history. An aerial array was fitted under the gondola and high frequency receivers instal-led, in 1939, in order to survey strange, tall aerial masts that were sprouting up all along the east and south coasts of

England. The Luftwaffe was aware that Britain had a radio-detection (radar) device similar in concept to the sets being developed in Germany, known as Freya and Wurzburg. Gen-eral Martini, head of Luftwaffe Signals, wanted to know what wavelength the British CH (Chain Home) system operated on and also whether it was already operational. Elaborate trials were carried out in Germany, on one of which the aerial engineer, Dr Sailer, slipped on the underside ladder and fell into a pine forest without time to open his parachute; he was seriously injured. At the end of May, *Graf Zeppelin* flew from Frankfurt to East Anglia to interrogate the CH Chain. At the RAF end, the vast blip of the Zeppelin was seen, first by Bawdsey and then by the rest of East Coast Stations. The airship went on its way north, the crew wrestling with dials and switches and fondly imagining that they were unde-tected. *Graf Zeppelin* transmitted position fixes to Germany which were picked up by the 'Y' service station at Cheadle and relayed to Fighter Command. As Flight Lt. (later Air Marshal) Pretty recalled: 'We were sorely tempted to radio a correction message to the airship but this would have revealed we were actually seeing her position on radar, so we kept silent'. In August a second flight was carried out but it was equally unsuccessful and, even worse, was inter-cepted off Scotland by two RAF fighters from Dyce. The operation was a total shambles and the real reason for its failure has never been revealed. General Martini refused to discuss the matter after the war and it can only be assumed that either the aerial did not work or that the *Graf Zeppelin* operators were searching on the wrong frequencies.

Before the war the Luftwaffe conducted a systematic aerial survey of Britain using Lufthansa aircraft and a special high altitude reconnaissance unit with Heinkel 111's. The picture below is one of the high-grade pictures thus taken.

18 Orfordness, where radiolocation was proven, the masts being denoted at 5). Photo taken April 9, 1939.

19 Stanmore, Middlesex, the home of headquarters Fighter Command. Photo taken May 5, 1939. The remarkable thing is that the balloon and supply depots are noted but Bentley Priory, which is clearly visible, is not even marked or referred to.

20   When a Luftwaffe delegation, including General Milch, visited the RAF in 1937, one of the factories included on the tour was Rolls Royce at Derby. The general impression formed was that the RAF was somewhat obsolescent in terms of equipment. This, however, was just before the monoplane fighters and bombers began to come into service and the major expansion of the RAF took place. Milch saw through the 'camouflage' but was completely unable to persuade Göring of the obstacle that an expanding RAF represented.

21   Herman Göring, head of the Luftwaffe. In the First World War he flew with the Richthofen Geschwader and then undertook test, commercial and stunt flying. In 1923 during a Nazi march in Munich he was injured in the groin and, prescribed with pain-killers, subsequently became a morphine addict. Although later pronounced cured, there is no doubt Göring continued to take drugs of one sort or another. As one of Hitler's closest supporters he was the obvious choice to run the Luftwaffe. When the Nazis came to power Göring began to acquire a whole series of titles and he left the planning of the new air force to others. Göring lacked technical knowledge and recent flying experience—he was so fat he could not get into any ordinary aircraft let alone pilot it. Göring had no experience of military staff planning and his overall understanding of the war machine, of which he was titular head, was very limited. He had an enormous opinion of himself which did not help in dealing with his subordinates.

22   Ernst Udet, brilliant pilot and one of the highest scorers in the First World War in the Richthofen Geschwader. His life was devoted to flying and he hated administration and paper work, this made him a poor director of the German Air Ministry technical department where a very tough character was needed to keep German industry in line and undercurrents and jealousies affected both development and production. In November 1941 Udet committed suicide.

23   General Martini head of Luftwaffe signals who built up a complete radio navigation and signals network and later was responsible for the German radar complex. Martini clashed on a number of occasions with Milch and had great difficulty in putting over technical matters to Göring.

24   One of the officers who originally worked in the secret airforce department in the Reichswehr Ministry after the First World War was Hans Jeschonnek. He became Chief of the General Staff of the Air Force in February 1939, a post he held until his suicide in August 1943.

25   Erhard Milch, one of the sharpest brains in the Luftwaffe. After service in the Flying Corps 1914-1918, Milch went into commercial business and by 1926 was chairman of Lufthansa. He was the original architect of the Luftwaffe but his detailed plans were upset because of Göring's jealousy. From 1939 Milch was Inspector General as well as Secretary of State for Air. In 1940 he was promoted Generalfeldmarschall.

BRITAIN PREPARES

From 1938 No. 19 Squadron at Duxford flew Gloster Gauntlet biplane fighters. Having been the first to use Gauntlets, No. 19, in August 1938, became the first to re-equip with the Supermarine Spitfire.

Following the First World War, Britain's air defences were swept away and virtually nothing remained. After the war to end all wars, nobody was interested in military activities; Britain had lulled itself to sleep. At the Armistice in 1918 there were 200 fighters, 286 anti-aircraft guns and 387 searchlights ready each day. By 1920 two squadrons of aircraft made up the whole of the home defence. The RAF itself had been reduced from 188 squadrons to 12.

Air Chief Marshal Sir Hugh (later Marshal of the RAF Viscount) 'Boom' Trenchard became the first Chief of Air Staff and he laid the foundations of a small but highly professional air force which was ultimately capable of rapid expansion in emergency. Above all he provided the continuity of experience, the discipline and the established chain of command so essential for any air force to maintain its morale and its efficiency.

The Cadet College at Cranwell trained the would-be officers, while the technical colleges like Halton produced some of the finest all-round servicemen/mechanics/engineers seen by any Service. The staff college was established to sort out the future senior officers and the highest possible flying standards were laid down by the Central Flying School.

Beyond this the RAF Short Service Commission Scheme was introduced with officers joining for five years and, on September 15, 1925, the first Auxiliary Air Force Squadron No. 602 (City of Glasgow) was formed. Finally, the first University Air Squadron at Cambridge came into being on October 1, 1925, followed by the Oxford UAS on October 11.

The RAF, for a period, lived dangerously as both the army and the Royal Navy were anxious to see its demise and its resources shared out to them. In 1923 the position of the air force was confirmed and it was also given control of the naval air squadrons. This latter was a pity as it stultified independent Fleet Air Arm thinking and did little towards producing modern naval aeroplanes.

The Steel-Bartholomew plan of 1923 recommended the establishment of an air defence belt across the south and south-east, with fighters, guns, sound locators and an observer network. The area was divided into eight sectors with two squadrons apiece. At the same time the Government agreed to a Committee of Imperial Defence scheme for a Home Defence Air Force of 52 squadrons—an increase of 18 squadrons over the then existing force.

All this, however, was so much wishful thinking as the Government had by then instituted the 'ten year rule' which foresaw no general war for ten years and thus required no major expansion of the air force due to Germany having been disarmed. Trenchard's thinking was also orientated towards the bomber which, in the twenties and thirties, appeared to be the weapon that would be all powerful and could punch its way through regardless of fighter opposition. The Battle of Britain was to finally disprove this theory but much had to change before then.

One ray of light was the establishment, in 1925, of the Air Defence of Great Britain (ADGB) including a fighting area and three bombing areas. Also, following aircraft reporting experiments in Kent in 1924 and 1925, the Observer Corps was officially created in October 1925 with two groups manned by Special Constables covering Kent and Sussex. The man who master-minded the Observer Corps was Major General E B Ashmore who had commanded London Air Defence Area in the First World War. The reporting and intercept network that he created in 1918 eventually formed the blueprint for the scheme adopted by Fighter Command under Dowding.

Trenchard went on planning for the fifty-two squadron air force and completed much of the basic work but the Government refused to implement it completely right up to 1934. The League of Nations and the Disarmament Conference seemed to assure peace and even the accession of Adolf Hitler to the post of Chancellor did little to arouse ordinary people from their stupor.

Winston Churchill spoke out strongly over the state of the RAF and the secret and rising power of the German Air Force. His sources of information were numerous and included air force officers and Whitehall officials whose protestations to the Government had fallen on deaf ears.

In July 1934 it was announced that the RAF at home would be increased to 75 squadrons, an increase of 33 squadrons over the number then in being. Aircrew training was to be the key to expansion. To achieve the numbers, the RAF Volunteer Reserve was formed in 1936 and thirteen civil flying schools were approved for RAF basic training. Advanced training was to be carried out at five service flying training schools. In addition, Australia and New Zealand began training schemes for their own nationals. Canada did not participate until the Empire Air Training Scheme was inaugurated in 1939.

It was clear that ADGB could not control 75 squadrons and all the facets of air defence, bombing, army co-operation etc. Accordingly the Air Staff, in 1936, took the momentous step of creating separate commands, Fighter, Bomber, Coastal and Training, each with an Air Officer Commanding. Thus the RAF moved in a completely opposite direction to the Luftwaffe. While the latter integrated all forces into single Luftflotte, the RAF concentrated on specialisation for the Commands. It was this above all else that gave Britain the chance to build a unique air defence system in time to meet the German onslaught in 1940. To Fighter Command went Sir Hugh Dowding, a man with a great deal of experience and an understanding of technical matters. There could not have been a better choice.

When Dowding moved to his new headquarters at Bentley Priory in 1936 his Command mustered two Fighter Groups, Nos. 11 and 12, which only covered the south-east and east and it was distinctly under strength in terms of fighter squadrons. Dowding also controlled the anti-aircraft defences, the balloon barrage and the Observer Corps. From this point on the whole set-up began to expand at an unprecedented rate. New squadrons and observer groups were formed and the structure was completely reorganised.

One thing Dowding had to have was advanced warning of attack. The Observer Corps could plot those aircraft that crossed the coast but in order to have any hope of getting his fighters into the right position at the right time he needed something else. That something came, like manna from heaven, in the shape of RDF or radar.

The army had been building a highly complex sound locator/Observer Corps network with remarkably advanced and automated plotting and reporting, known as the 'Fixed Azimuth System' it was brilliant in concept but its acoustic sensors only gave a possible range of 21 miles, an approximate bearing and no height.

The situation was so critical that a special committee was set up under Henry Tizard, a brilliant physicist. In the course of its investigations, the committee was presented with a report by Mr A F Wilkins which concluded that radio beams might be bounced off aircraft and thereby be used for detection. Wilkins worked for the Radio Research Station at Slough and its superintendent was Robert (later Sir) Watson-Watt. Between them they produced a document entitled 'Detection and location of aircraft by radio methods' which was submitted in February 1935.

Using Daventry radio transmitter as an 'illuminator', an experimental receiver lash-up in a van clearly indicated, in the same month, that a radio detection system was possible. Thereafter events moved very rapidly. A team under Watson-Watt was formed at Orfordness in Suffolk and an aircraft had been detected out to 58 miles by September

1935. On the basis of these few months of hectic work, it was decided to go ahead with a chain of detection stations from Southampton to the Tyne. To improve facilities and speed development, the team was moved to Bawdsey Manor on the coast south of Orfordness.

Thus, when Dowding took over Fighter Command in 1936 he not only knew all about radar but he had a chain of 20 stations approved and in hand. Many problems remained to be overcome but by 1938 five stations were operating in time for the crucial air exercises in August and a full chain was ready when war broke out. For Dowding the task was to integrate radar, the Observer Corps, the Groups and Sectors and Fighter Command in such a way that a continuous flow of prepared data could be converted into a moving picture on the operations tables showing the position in the air at any moment of the day or night. In this he was completely successful.

At the time of the Munich crisis in 1938, neither the RAF nor the Luftwaffe was ready for war. The RAF had only 93 monoplane fighters (Hurricanes) available out of a total force of 759 fighters, including reserves. What Munich did, together with Chamberlain's famous piece of paper, was to buy time, time to get more squadrons, pilots, radars, observer posts and communications.

While the air defence system was being built up, the aircraft industry had been called upon to build the necessary airframes, engines, armament, radios and a multiplicity of other modern equipment. The industry managed to keep going through the lean years of the twenties and provide such biplanes as the RAF needed for its various tasks. By 1934 it was on the verge of mass expansion and the building of a host of new monoplane types for every conceivable task. In 1935 Lord Swinton became Secretary of State for Air. He ordered aircraft off the drawing board instead of waiting for years of trials and he inaugurated the 'Shadow factory' scheme which provided state sponsored factories which could turn out everything from aircraft to ancillary equipment and thus change the overall production potential from hundreds into thousands.

By 1936-38 all the basic types to open the fight in the Second World War were either in development or full production. The Spitfire, Hurricane and Defiant for day fighting, the Blenheim for day and night fighting and bombing, the Battle as the single-engined light bomber, the Wellington, Whitley and Hampden as medium bombers and the Beaufort as the torpedo bomber. Beyond this were coming the Beaufighter and Whirlwind fighters and the heavy bombers, the Stirling, Halifax and Manchester.

When it went to war in 1939, the RAF still needed time but it had the potential behind it. The service was, however, lacking in certain key respects which were to cost it dear in pilots and machines. Its bombers were too poorly armed and protected to operate in daylight against modern interceptors and the squadrons of Fighter Command were using outdated interception methods and had had poor gunnery training.

The fighter attack formation manual might well have been written on the parade ground at Aldershot. As drill it was brilliant but as a means of fighting an air war it was useless. Close-knit stereotyped formations invited slaughter. These facts had been learned by the Luftwaffe in Spain and they flew loose formations which allowed great flexibility and saved squadrons from getting 'bounced'.

In the field of gunnery also, German fighter pilots were better trained. Many of the RAF squadron commanders in the Battle of Britain were Pilot Officers, Flying Officers or NCO Pilots in the 30's. They were tutored by CO's who were PO's and FO's in the twenties. As the Commanding Officers of 1940 had to tutor the pilots for the Battle—the continuity of First World War training philosophy and of weaponry was thus established and underlined.

Throughout the twenties and thirties the training methods neither varied nor improved to any degree and the general attitude of peacetime fighter pilots was hardly conducive to the acceptance of serious training. The fighter squadrons of those years were regarded as little more than a means of getting some exhilerating flying.

For just one concentrated period in the summer, someone would be sent up in a dual Siskin to fly boringly up and down as a target whilst some of his fellow pilots loosed off camera gun film after camera gun film at him in rapid succession. It was known that some flight commanders put all the films in a heap in their desk drawer without even marking names on them. The films were later brought out in batches at intervals, marked with names and convenient dates, developed and assessed for 'hits' and the appropriate periodical return made to HQ.

Once a year the Siskins, Gamecocks, Bulldogs, Gauntlets or Furies went for three weeks of practice camp operation. Here they flew day after day on air to ground firing at targets on the marshes. The results were pretty deplorable in view of the simplicity of the exercises. If a man got an exceptionally good score overall he was, for some strange reason, regarded as good material to mould into an armament specialist.

Later in the thirties the practice camps progressed so far as to include air-to-air firing, using flag or sleeve targets. These were towed behind slow tugs which flew straight and level courses. Even under these circumstances the average scores were appallingly low and a score of 2% hits was commonplace. Still no change occurred in the training or in fighter sighting devices.

Right up to the war no adequate ground instruction aid was in common use and the squadron commanders had to rely on the small minority of armament specialists devising their own methods and gadgets. Explanation and theory were however, useless without some installation in the aircraft that would remove the element of guessing range, deflection angle, target speed and the resultant position in the sight.

26 The Gloster Grebe, was one of the first post-World War 1 replacement fighters. The first unit to receive Grebes was 111 squadron at Duxford in 1923. The type remained in service until 1929. Armed with two Vickers machine guns, the Jaguar-engined Grebe had a top speed of 152 mph. These two Grebes were from No. 25 squadron.

27 Annual air exercises carried on through the late 1920s in somewhat unrealistic fashion. During a simulated night attack on London in August 1927, this Handley Page Hyderabad of No. 99 squadron developed engine trouble and force-landed at Mistley, Essex in a sugar beet field. There is no record of how the aircraft was recovered.

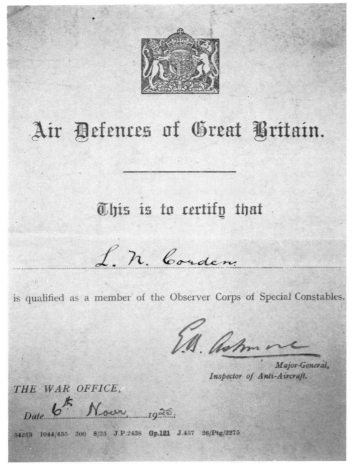

28 In 1925, after the official formation of the Observer Corps in October, special certificates were issued to special constable members who had learned their trade in the first air exercises. This document was issued to the 'Head Special' of the Pulborough, Sussex, post. It was signed by the founder of the Corps, Major-General EB Ashmore.

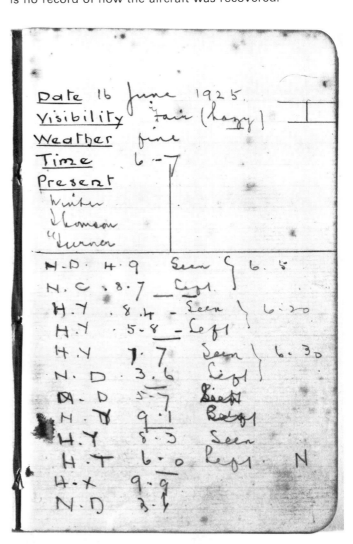

29 The logbook of 1/G.3 Observer post Tenterden, Kent during the first full-scale air exercises using two Observer Groups, Maidstone and Horsham, in 1925. The left-hand letters and figures denote grid references.

30 Britain produced a series of monoplane bomber prototypes in the second half of the thirties, one of which was the Vickers B.9/32, the forerunner of the Wellington, shown at Brooklands in 1936. During diving tests the elevator horn balance failed and the aircraft was thrown on its back. The pilot, Flight Lt Hare, was thrown through the roof and parachuted to safety but the flight engineer was killed. Accidents were, perforce, frequent during the large scale production of new aircraft in the thirties. In the case of B.9/32 good flying qualities had already become evident and development of the Wellington went ahead at a rapid rate.

A series of photographs taken at No. 9 Flying Training School at Thornaby in 1936.

31 Gloster Gauntlet 2 fighters. These aircraft were delivered in error and should have gone direct to an operational squadron; the C.O. at Thornaby retained them. **32** A line-up of Hawker Audax. **33** The spectacular result of a collision between left, a Turret Demon and right, a Hart Trainer, and **34** The 8th production Avro Anson which called in at Thornaby for FTS pupils to look over before delivery to No. 48 squadron. The general reconnaissance Anson was the RAF's first monoplane and the service's first aircraft with a retractable undercarriage. Nearly 7000 Ansons were produced in Britain and the type remained in RAF service until 1968.

31

32

33

34

35 Future pilots of the RAF on a short course at No. 4 Elementary and Reserve Flying Training School at Brough Yorks in 1935. The pupils had already gone solo elsewhere and, after successful completion of the Brough course, the majority went on to FTS as acting pilot officers.

Scenes at a typical flying school as young men flocked in to learn to be pilots and ultimately to gain coveted RAF wings. This was No. 4 Elementary and Reserve Flying Training School at Brough, Yorkshire in 1938. **36** From left to right, two Blackburn B.2s and a Hawker Audax. **37** A Fairey Battle light bomber pays a visit. **38** A Hind which was tipped on its nose.

36

37

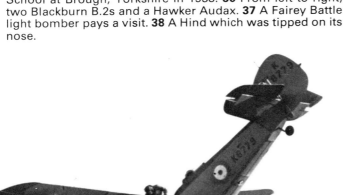

38

A.M.R.D.
D. of T.

With reference to minutes 1 and 22 on this file, the question of the location of the school for training Service personnel in R.D.F. has been under consideration by the Superintendent of the Bawdsey Experimental Station and Squadron Leader Hart, who was posted to take command of the school. Their recommendations are that the school should be located at Bawdsey since it will then be in close touch with the development work which is now proceeding, which may produce considerable changes in apparatus from time to time.

I agree with this recommendation and have asked for proposals to be put forward stating what accommodation will be necessary at Bawdsey to provide for the school. Such proposals must necessarily be delayed until it is known what the future policy regarding R.D.F. stations is to be, but in the meantime we must proceed with the training of personnel to man D.F. stations in accordance with the policy laid down in enclosure 23A.

The staff required to man the 4 stations at Canewdon, Great Bromley, Dunkirk and Dover will be:-

    12 N.C.Os.

    12 Wireless Operator Mechanics.

    24 Wireless Operators,

and these should begin training on April 1st.

39 A remarkably simple and cheap piece of machinery which was to play a major part in the Battle of Britain. The prototype Observer Corps all-metal post plotting instrument on test at Uxbridge in 1934. With small modifications it was to be standard throughout the Second World War and on into the 1950's.

40 An Air Ministry memorandum of early 1937 agreeing to the setting up of the world's first radar training school at Bawdsey. This was run by Squadron Leader (later Air Marshal Sir) Raymund Hart.

41 Summer camp at Royal Naval Air Station, Ford, Sussex, for B flight, No. 601 squadron Auxiliary Air Force, 1939.

42 First put into service in 1933, the Avro Tutor was a standard trainer for many years.

44

Before the advent of radar, total reliance was placed on sound locators for 'long range' warning. These devices proved to be very unreliable and subject to every sort of acoustic interference. **43**A massive concave sound locator on test in the late twenties and **44** a giant 200 ft long concrete locator erected by the army at Greatstone, nr. Lydd, Kent and still standing. Multiple microphones were fitted in the vertical surface and a man with headphones walked round the base trying to detect the bearings of aircraft noises.

43

46 The prototype Bristol Blenheim light bomber which first flew in June 1936. It was considered to be very fast when first produced but by 1940 it was too slow and poorly armed to resist single-engined enemy fighters. The Blenheim IF fighter was equipped with a four gun belly pack and served by both day and night in the Battle of Britain.

45 The Schneider Trophy resulted in major advances in aerodynamics and engine performance which had an effect on aircraft development for the Second World War. This is the Supermarine S.6B seaplane which won the Trophy in 1931.

47 The last of the RAF's big biplane bombers, the Handley Page Heyford operated continuously from 1933 right through to 1939. The type was in use as a trainer until 1941. With a crew of four, the Heyford carried 1600 lb of bombs and its maximum speed was 142 mph.

48/49 Probably the most important prototypes ever built in Britain, the Hurricane and the Spitfire. Without the rapid development and production of these eight-gun fighters, the Battle of Britain could not have been won. The Hurricane first flew on November 6, 1935 and was an immediate success, achieving 315 mph during its trials at Martlesham Heath. Even before an official order was received for 600 Hurricanes in June 1936, Hawkers had put in hand production planning and tooling for 1000. By Christmas 1937, No. 111 squadron at Northolt had one flight of flying Hurricanes. In the Battle of Britain 31 squadrons operated the type. The Spitfire was first flown in March 1936 and its performance was quite exceptional. No. 19 was the first squadron to receive them in 1938 and, in the Battle of Britain, there were 19 Spitfire squadrons.

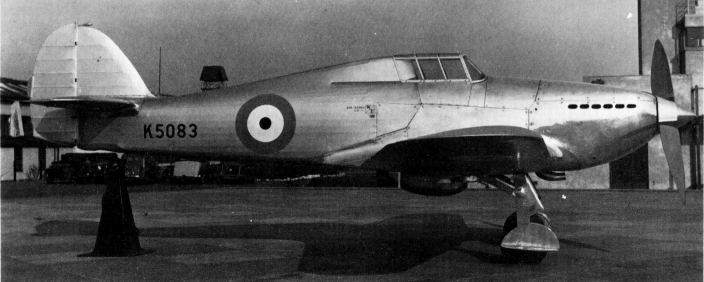

K5083

50 Newly equipped with Blenheim 1 fighters (minus the belly gun pack), a section of No. 601 squadron from Hendon flying over north London in July 1939.

The Vickers Wellington was one of the main types of medium bomber in the RAF when war broke out. It was unique, in this class, in having a geodetic criss-cross structure. The photographs show **51** L4317, a production Wellington 1 takes off at Brooklands over the Merlin-engined Wellington II prototype L4250. The Brooklands factory was severely damaged by the Luftwaffe on September 4 and **52** The Wellington Mk. 1 production line at Brooklands in 1939

51

52

53 The last of the RAF's biplane fighters, the 250 mph Gloster Gladiator seen here in the colours of No. 79 squadron. In the Second World War Gladiators operated in Norway, in the Battle of Britain, and in the Middle East. Sea Gladiators with deck hooks flew with the Fleet Air Arm.

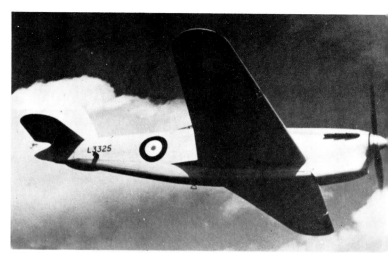

56 A wasted aeroplane, the Hawker Henley two-seat Merlin-engined monoplane which was designed as a high performance dive-bomber. Up to 550 lb of bombs could be carried and a top speed of nearly 300 mph was possible. It would have been an excellent and very manoeuvrable light bomber but instead it was arbitarily relegated to target towing. The light bombing task was left with the slow and vulnerable Fairey Battle which suffered extremely heavy losses in France in 1940.

57 A typical fighter station scene during one of the annual air exercises of the late thirties. Pilots of No. 32 squadron wait beside a Gladiator at Biggin Hill in 1937. **58** A line-up of the No. 32 squadron Hurricanes which replaced the Gladiators. These had fabric covered wings and two blade wooden propellers.

54 Twelve Hawker Furies from Biggin Hill on patrol during the period of the Munich crisis. The machines have been hastily camouflaged.

55 A Handley Page Harrow high-wing bomber of No. 215 squadron pictured at Odiham in 1938. The unit had the type until it was converted to Wellingtons in 1939. Thereafter the Harrow did yeoman work as a transport and was also used to drop aerial minefields in the winter of 1940/41. As an interim heavy bomber the Harrow had three gun turrets and a 3000 lb bomb load.

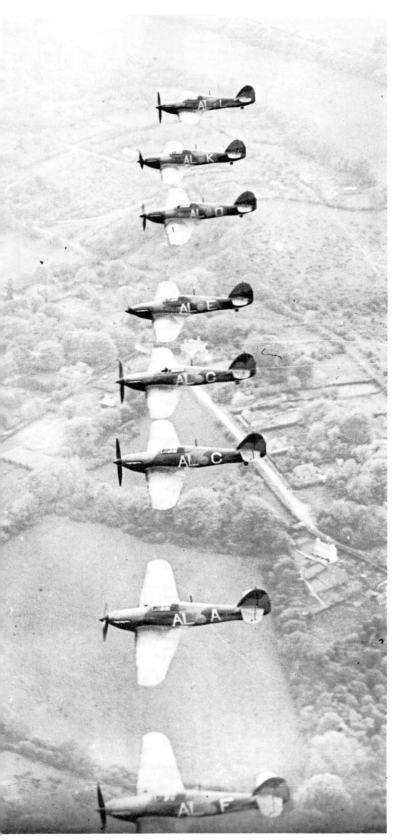

59 Eight Hurricanes of No. 79 squadron practising for the Empire Air Day display at Biggin Hill in May 1939.

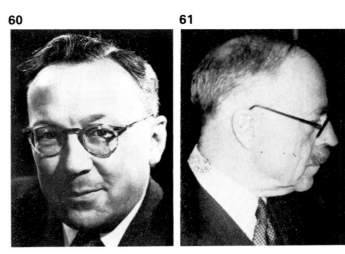

60 Mr (later Sir) Robert Watson-Watt who started the British radar story and made a major contribution to its coming to fruition.

61 Sir Henry Tizard, one of the most practical and far-sighted scientists associated with the development of air defence. Tizard clashed with Professor Lindemann (later Lord Cherwell) who became Churchills' scientific advisor and this nearly had a disastrous effect on science applied to the war effort.

62 Bawdsey Manor, south of Orfordness, where the budding RDF (radar) team moved in February 1936. Bawdsey not only provided the site for all the experimental work but was itself built as one of the first stations in the operational radar chain. It was here that the first radar training school was set up and the first filter room.

FLYING WITHOUT NAVIGATION LIGHTS

6. EASTLAND Bombers are not to switch on their navigation lights
whilst over the defended area or within 5 miles of the coast
line of WESTLAND except:-

(a)   when having attacked a target and then proceeding to
Home Station located in Westland.

(b)   when proceeding from Home Station located in Westland
territory until clear of Westland. (i.e., when first
proceeding to rendezvous).

(c)   In emergency.

NOTE.   Except for reasons of safety and as outlined in sub-
paragraphs (a) and (b) above, it is important that Eastland
bombers should not fly with navigation lights over Westland,
even when picked up by searchlights. Eastland bombers will
therefore ensure, on approaching Westland territory, that
they have switched off their navigation lights and keep them
off whilst over Westland until they have made their final
attacks on their objectives.

63 Operational instructions issued to the RAF for the Home Defence Exercises of August 1938 when radar was first used operationally. The main threat at the time came from Germany itself to the east. Five radars, and three squadrons plus one flight of monoplane Hurricanes were operated. The opposing forces included twelve Blenheim, nine Battle and four Whitely squadrons. The page from the instructions for the exercise clearly indicates how unrealistic they were. Also there was a chronic lack of camera guns on fighters.

64 Squadrons of Ansons escorted by Hawker Demon biplanes flying at the Hendon Air Display in 1937. Photographs of these formations have been used in several books and labelled as Dornier 17s and Bf 109s over Biggin Hill in the Battle of Britain.

65 The standard two-seat fighter from 1931 was the Hawker Demon, a fighter development of the Hart. The rear gunners' cockpit was originally equipped with a Scarff ring and Lewis gun. Late in 1936 Demons were fitted with a 'lobster-back' shield turret and this version became known as the 'Turret-Demon' as shown here. Demons were replaced by Blenheim fighters.

66 Spitfire 1, K9791, converted to take the Rotol constant-speed propeller. A major improvement in performance was possible with CS propellers. In 1940 de Havilland CS propellers based on American Hamilton-Standard patents were fitted to most Hurricanes and Spitfires.

64

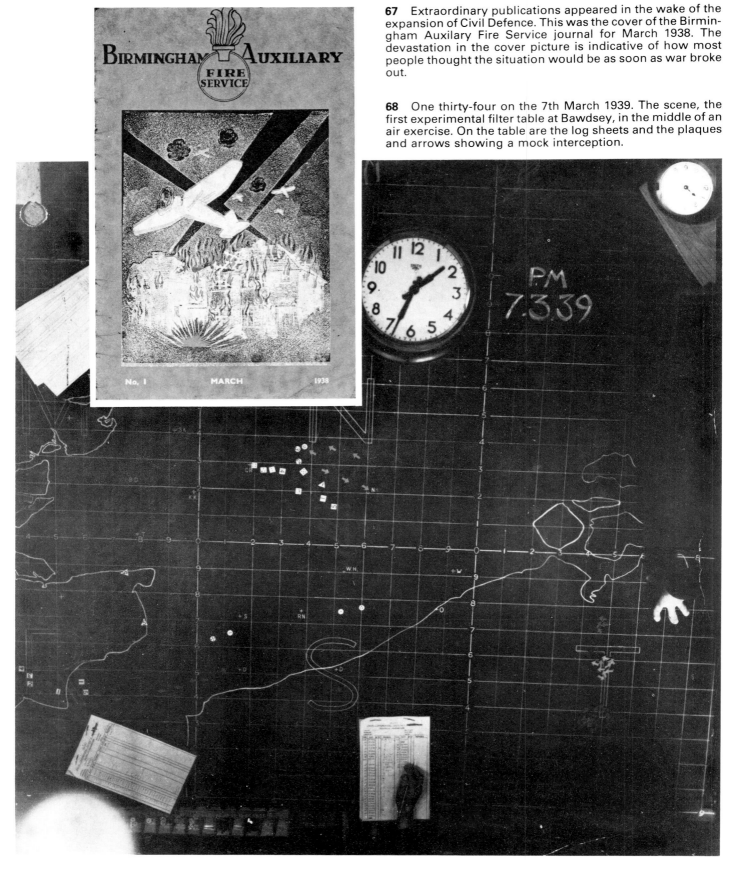

67 Extraordinary publications appeared in the wake of the expansion of Civil Defence. This was the cover of the Birmingham Auxilary Fire Service journal for March 1938. The devastation in the cover picture is indicative of how most people thought the situation would be as soon as war broke out.

68 One thirty-four on the 7th March 1939. The scene, the first experimental filter table at Bawdsey, in the middle of an air exercise. On the table are the log sheets and the plaques and arrows showing a mock interception.

THE RAF DEFENCE SYSTEM

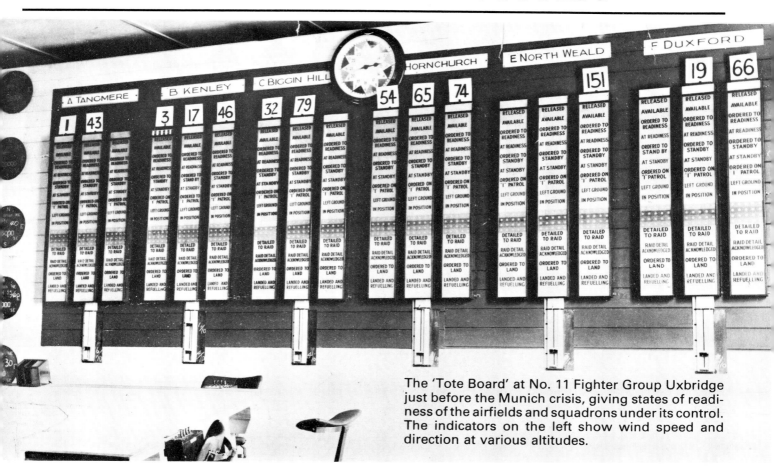

The 'Tote Board' at No. 11 Fighter Group Uxbridge just before the Munich crisis, giving states of readiness of the airfields and squadrons under its control. The indicators on the left show wind speed and direction at various altitudes.

The greatest achievement of Hugh Casswall Tremenhere Dowding, Commander-in-Chief Fighter Command, was not his prowess as an aircraft pilot but his ability as an organiser.

From 1936, when the Command was inaugurated, Dowding worked day and night to create the world's first modern air defence system on which planners still base their thinking, albeit with advanced computer technology.

He realised that if an enemy air force was to be defeated, he had to devise a highly complex network which would present a continuous, clear and up-to-date picture of all activity direct the interceptors to the target and maintain and resupply the defending squadrons involved. Throughout his tenure of command, Dowding never deviated from these principles, whatever the opposition. In the course of his years at Bentley Priory he incurred the wrath and enmity of ambitious officers in the Air Ministry and the dislike of some politicians. To all this he was impervious and his life was devoted to the one cause—defend Britain come what may. Dowding had to put his sensors, his fighting arm and his back-up organisation to best possible use, bearing always in mind that something had to be kept in reserve in case the enemy resorted to a full seaborne invasion.

Information was, and is, the primary material on which any battle is fought. Dowding threw away old fashioned concepts of control by rank and created a centrally organised flow of information plugged in at all levels. Wherever it was needed, a 'picture' could be produced of sufficient quality to allow the local commander to dispose of his forces down to unit level.

With interceptor closing speeds of up to 700 mph and only the Channel between Fighter Command and the enemy, Dowding's picture had to be continuously and accurately up-dated. In addition, he needed as much general intelligence and forewarning of enemy intentions as he could be provided with.

Great emphasis has been laid by writers in recent years on the breakthrough in the decoding and reading of signals from the German Enigma encoding machine by the British intelligence operation code-named 'Ultra'. In mid-1940, translated messages from 'Enigma' were sparse, erratic and very often late. In addition, most of the key Luftwaffe signals were transmitted over landline and could not be dealt with by the dedicated listeners at the Government Code and Cipher School at Bletchley Park, Bucks. A lot of supply and administrative information was forthcoming but very little that pointed the way to German operational planning and intentions.

Dowding had built a flexible network capable of rolling with the storm and recovering from heavy blows. His conduct of the battle was based, not like Montgomery in later land campaigns, on instant reading of the enemy's most secret signals, but on actual German methods of attack as they occurred. Dowding's first line of information was the RAF's 'Y' intelligence listening service which was established in the early 1930's. This yielded most valuable information and materially helped in the ultimate establishment, by Air Ministry Intelligence, of a very accurate Luftwaffe Order of Battle. It was on this basis that Dowding reckoned that he could wear the Luftwaffe down and survive the summer air war of attrition. The Y-service was far more important to the RAF in 1940 than was 'Ultra'. The original station was at Cheadle (No. 61 Wireless Unit) which intercepted medium and high frequency wireless telegraphy (W/T) from German bombers, long range reconnaissance, transport, and training aircraft. No. 62 WU was at Chicksands and it concentrated on as many channels as possible of Enigma-coded information between Luftwaffe ground formations.

The subsidiary stations, first at Fairlight, Sussex, and then at Hawkinge, Kent, concentrated on intercepting enemy radio-telephone (RT) transmissions from fighters, fighter bombers, channel reconnaissance and dive-bomber aircraft, Hawkinge being also responsible for listening-watch on German Navy E-boats. Flying Officer Scott Farnie set up the RT side of the 'Y' service using American Hallicrafter receiving sets purchased on the open market.

As Hawkinge was vulnerable, the main RT centre was moved first to a garage and then to Hollywood Manor at Kingsdown, Kent, as 63 WU. Hawkinge became a listening post for 'Noise', particularly traffic on short and ultra short wave. The system expanded rapidly during and after the Battle of Britain with many subsidiary units being set up, and the whole organisation owing its success to a handful of enthusiasts and many dedicated young WAAF's.

The primary line of sensors for watching and reporting actual enemy activity was the RDF or radar chain with 21 Chain Home (CH) and 30 Chain Home Low (CHL) stations plus a mobile reserve which could be used to plug gaps made by enemy attack. CH equipments had a range of 120 miles while CHL could 'see' for 50 miles at lower levels but gave no indication of height. The radars saw only out to sea and had no ability to look over the land behind. Where the radar vision finished at the coast, the Observer Corps took over, each of nearly 1500 posts being equipped with a triangulation instrument giving a position fix on a gridded map once a height had been estimated and the aircraft positioned in the sights. Some Coastguard stations also gave aircraft reports and fed them through the Observer Corps network.

Fighter Command was split into four Fighter Groups, Numbers 10, 11, 12 and 13, with each Group sub-divided into up to four sectors. In essence, Fighter Command maintained overall strategic control, the Groups fought the battle in their own areas (with some assistance from adjacent Groups if necessary) and the actual tactical operation of fighters was carried out by the Sectors. Each Sector had an operations room and emergency stand-by based on or near the main Fighter Sector station, such as Tangmere, and forward/satellite airfields on which squadrons were either maintained permanently or dispersed as required.

Each Sector in 11 Group differed; for instance, Tangmere was so far forward that it only had an adjacent satellite, Westhampnett; Kenley had no forward airfields; Biggin Hill and Hornchurch had one satellite each; while Hornchurch had no less than four subsidiary airfields.

Each Sector could deal with up to four squadrons using the 'Pip-Squeak' device in the aircraft which gave periodic radio emissions from which the ground direction finders could triangulate their position.

To understand the overall system, let us look at a typical, but imaginary, beginning to a day in the life of Fighter Command in that long hot summer of 1940. At Bentley Priory, the underground Operations and Filter Rooms has been working all night dealing with nocturnal raids. A new shift has moved in to cover yet another morning's activity. In the offices, analyses of the previous day's fighting and an assessment of the Command's situation are complete and ready for Dowding to read. Replacement Hurricanes and Spitfires have been flown out from maintenance units to the squadrons by the unflagging ferry pilots.

The Armaments Branch has checked on ammunition supplies, the Engineering Branch has dealt with a stream of requests for replacement parts, tools and equipment, while the communicators have been ensuring that telephone lines have been repaired and tested. Anti-Aircraft Command has been going through the same process.

Airfield state reports have been digested and every effort made to repair damage and replace lost personnel. A constant flow of messages has poured into the headquarters through the night by teleprinter and despatch rider. Intelligence reports at every level have been digested and vital information passed onto Groups and Sectors—changes of tactics, movements of enemy units, Luftwaffe armament improvements and results of POW interrogations to name only a few. Apart from the Fighter Command flow of information, there is a continuous input of messages from Air Ministry and Whitehall in general and overall intelligence assessments of the enemy's intentions, particularly on the invasion front. At Groups, Sectors, fighter airfields, radar stations and Observer Corps posts and operations rooms, personnel await the inevitable attack.

The 'Y' service begins to report a flow of messages emanating from across the channel; enemy radio and wireless testing on a large scale and the usual meteorological reports from Luftwaffe long range reconnaissance aircraft.

At each CH station in the 'R' or receiver hut sits the operator watching the cathode ray tube and another, the 'converter'. By 8 am the tube is showing a build-up of aircraft over northern France and then bombers with escorts move out over the Channel. The operator assesses a blip at 50+ and calls for the WAAF on the converter to 'read'. The grid position and height come up in glowing figures on the 'fruit machine' computer. The operator tells Stanmore that they have 'Track two—range 45—Sugar 3694—height 20,000 ft'.

The Stanmore plotter relays the information to the Filter Officer in the underground Filter Room. He assesses the situation and the call goes back to the CH operator, Track two is now Hostile 39. Further formations are seen and plotted and a steady flow of information is pumped into the Filter Room. The 'picture' on the operations table there is cleaned up and anomalies, such as confusion with friendly aircraft, are removed. The filtered picture is continuously told to the Fighter Command operations room in the same bunker and simultaneously the radar tracks with their prefix numbers are told on to the Groups who, in turn, pass them on to Sector Operations Rooms and to coastal Observer Corps centres. In the last mentioned case, they are received by the Sea Plotter and the Observer posts are warned to be on the look-out.

By the time the raid crosses the coast it has been reassessed as 100+ and it appears to be heading for a Sector airfield inland. The Group Controller has already ordered off squadrons of Spitfires to deal with the Bf 109 escort and Hurricanes to attack the bombers. The orders are relayed to the appropriate Sector controllers who are now getting a flood of position, height and strength reports from adjacent Observer centres.

At a Sector the controller has his own map table and WAAF plotters, albeit the area covered being smaller than that at Command and Group. The 'Ops A' WAAF or airman next to him is told by Group to scramble certain squadrons to intercept Hostile 39. A serial number for the operation is given and a form A handed to the Controller for him to conduct the operation. An Army officer on the dais monitors the air situation and informs the anti-aircraft guns.

Ops 'B', with the telephone switchboard, calls the squadrons and orders them to scramble, giving preliminary information on position to fly to and height to gain. The squadrons climb away and their leaders call the sector on R/T. Each squadron has a code-name which is changed frequently to confuse the enemy; some are simple like Tennis while others are made-up words like Keta and Caleb.

Watching the tracks moving across the map table, the Controller talks the fighters into position, the fighter position being checked and triangulated using direction-finders and 'Pip-Squeak', to meet the raid. As the enemy formations approach, one section splits off and heads for another airfield and this is duly reported by the Observer Corps and noted by the Sector Controller.

The Spitfires and Hurricanes have now sighted the main force and call 'Tally-Ho' to the Controller. Thereafter the fighter leaders conduct the battle themselves and the controllers can only listen. Group has ordered more fighters up to intercept the section that divided from the main force. A general air battle ensues as squadron after squadron attacks and formations are split. A number of bombers, however, fly on towards the targets.

All flyable aircraft on the airfields are ordered to take off and the guns are alerted as are the rocket-propelled parachute and cable systems designed to throw up a screen in front of bombers which come in low. All personnel on the fields are ordered into the shelters, while at Sector tin-hats are donned.

As the anti-aircraft defences open up, the bombs come raining down. Hangars and dispersals and fuel dumps are hit, water and gas mains burst and telephone lines are severed. The runways are pitted with bomb craters and delayed action bombs are lying around.

As the raid recedes, the Controller recovers his squadrons to a satellite airfield until the delayed action bombs have been dealt with and craters filled. On the Sector airfield the damage is being assessed and reports are going through to Group and Command on the situation. Local fire services send through appliances to help put out the blaze and GPO engineers start to reconnect the all-important telephone lines.

The squadrons meanwhile have landed and the Intelligence officers are assessing the claims and the losses. Aircraft are refuelled and re-armed ready for the next sortie. Away from the stations, bombers have jetissoned their loads on towns and villages. The police, Home Guard and Civil Defence are investigating and clearing. Aircraft crashes are being reported by the Observer Corps and the police. Some Luftwaffe aircraft have come down reasonably intact. They are camouflaged with branches or netting wherever possible and await the attentions of a qualified Intelligence officer while under guard. Injured RAF pilots have been transported to hospital, while others who have baled out make their way back to their stations by a variety of means. German airmen have been captured and are in police stations or at military units awaiting transport to the RAF's clearing cage where they can be interrogated.

While this particular raiding force has occupied this Sector's attention, Command and Groups have been dealing wth similar incursions to the West with a series of feints by small formations, designed to draw fighters away from the main streams and stretch the defending forces to the maximum. Some of these are at low altitude and are first seen by CHL operators while others get through to the coast undetected.

There is a lull for an hour or two as both sides draw breath and then the whole performance starts again—more plots on the radar scopes, more tracks from the Observer Corps, more dog-fighting, incidents, damage and casualties. A launch goes out to rescue a pilot down in the Channel, engineers complete the setting up of a mobile station to replace a CH knocked out by earlier bombing. By evening Fighter Command has assessed its damage, its losses and its achievements. Preparations are being made for any night raiders and the system is being geared up again to meet the threat of another day.

Luftwaffe tactics changed, not only from one phase of the Battle to another, but from one day to another as the Luftflotten sought to gain the upper hand. Fighter Command's system had to be capable of adaptation to meet situations which could not be foreseen and for which no precedent existed in the annals of warfare.

The system was by no means perfect but this is understandable considering that nothing like it had ever been created before. One of the biggest snags lay in the provision of fighters with radio. Sectors were limited in the number of squadrons they could control, far too few VHF radios were available and squadrons found themselves in battle alongside others that they could not communicate with or warn of impending danger as they were not on the same frequency.

The CH/CHL network was also very basic compared with modern radars and strength assessments depended on the skill and experience of the operator. Likewise, both the CH stations and the Observer Corps had problems with height estimation, the latter particularly on cloudy days. To overcome this deficiency, Controllers invariably added a few thousand feet to the fighters' instructions when raids were reported at 20,000 ft or above.

69 WAAF personnel operating teleprinters at an RAF Sector Station in 1940. The whole of the RAF was linked by the Defence Teleprinter Network which carried every form of communication from combat reports to indents for spares and equipment.

70 The scene at the Duxford Sector Operations Room in September 1940. Three squadrons are being operated, No. 302 call-sign 'Caleb', No. 310 'Calla' and No. 242 'Lorag'. No. 19 squadron is shown as on detachment to Luton. At the centre of the dais with the telephone to his ear, sits the Controller, a Volunteer Reserve Flying Officer who has clearly been a pilot in the First World War. To the Controller's right hand is an airman acting as 'Ops A' and prepared to take action messages from Group. At the extreme right is an officer working as an 'Ops B' and operating the communications keyboard to the parent and satellite airfields. In front of the dais is a dead reckoning navigator, receiving D/F fixes on the Sector's fighters from the direction finding room and working out courses to steer for the Controller. To the Controller's left hand is an army lieutenant, the gun control officer. Typical of the period are the aircraft recognition charts and the posters exhorting everyone that 'Careless talk costs lives' and to 'Keep it Dark'.

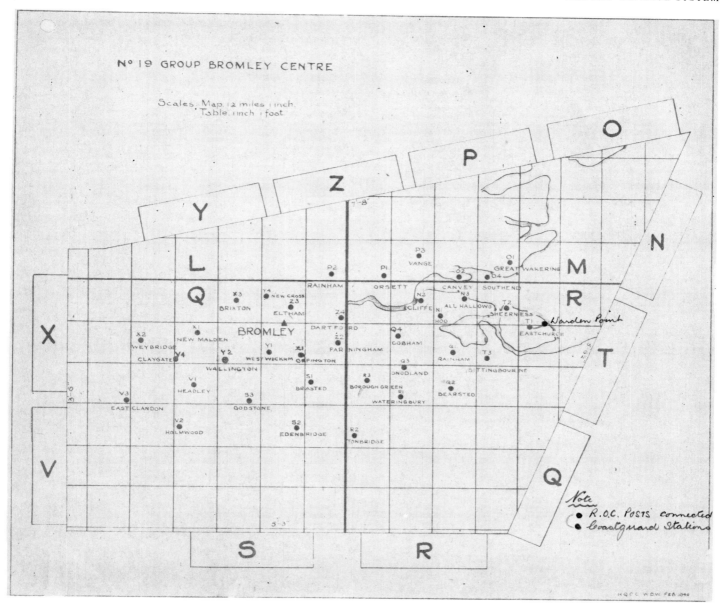

71 The Centre map of No. 19 Group Bromley, Observer Corps in 1940. The 1 inch to 1 foot scale table shows the positions of the eleven plotters, each connected to a 'cluster' of three/four Observer posts. Every post on an individual cluster was known by its prefix letter and a number e.g. Y4, N1, T3. The maximum number of posts on any one cluster was four and they could all hear the others in the same cluster, which allowed forewarning of incoming attack and the possibility of getting corrected heights from two or more posts on a raid. One post in this group was linked by telephone to a Coastguard station which reported any aircraft seen.

72 Inside the hut on a typical Observer Corps post in 1940. In this case the hut was home-made with one side fabricated out of an old pub sign and the other of a church packing case. The walls are festooned with recognition silhouettes and photographs and the kneeling observer is wearing the standard pattern head and breast telephone set.

73 The giant transmitter masts of a chain home RDF (radar) station.

74 The underground operations room at Fighter Command Headquarters, Bentley Priory. The Controller, his staff, officers from Anti-Aircraft Command and other officials sat on a balcony looking down on the main map table. The small white rectangles under the edge of the table were telephone jack positions for plotters. The 'croupier' rakes were for moving raid plaques into position. The plotters received filtered radar information from the Filter Room and Observer Corps information via the Fighter Groups.

75 A flight of three Bf 109Es passing the cliffs at Dover with the CH station towers on top. On the left are the transmitter masts and on the right the receiver masts.

76 The underground Filter Room at Bentley Priory with its crescent-shaped map table showing the coastal CH and CHL stations and the large circles radiating from them. Each plotter was connected to an operator in the receiver hut at a CH site. The filter officers checked the plots, whether they were hostile or 'X' (unidentified) and generally tried to avoid double tracking on targets. The track information was then passed to the Operations Room for display on the main table. Without the filter room the 'picture' in the operations room would have been chaotic with a mass of conflicting information cluttering up the table. The binoculars on the hand rail, upper left, were to allow the controller to get a close-up on raid plaques where necessary. The colour clock hanging from the balcony was of vital importance. Each five minutes in every quarter of an hour was denoted by a different colour: the first five minutes red, second five minutes yellow and third five minutes blue. These colours corresponded to the colours of the plotting counters in use on the table. Plotters removed stale counters when the next colour but one commenced. For instance red counters were removed as soon as the first blue counters went down on the map. This was standard procedure in all operations rooms and it ensured that tables were not choked with out-of-date information.

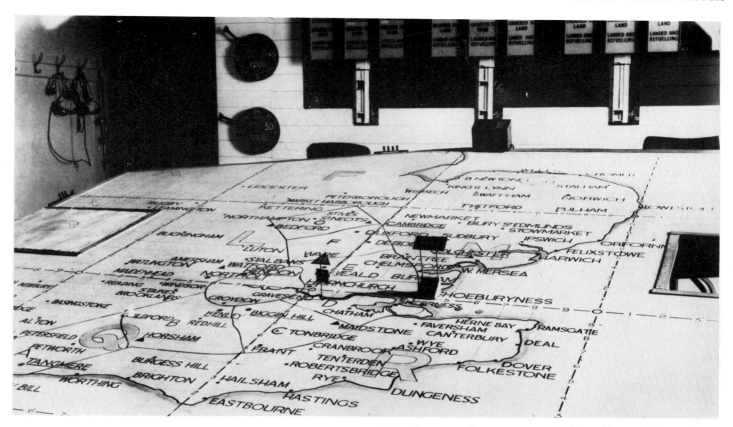

77 The operations room map table at No. 11 Fighter Group Uxbridge as it was before the Munich Crisis. CH radar stations were not yet operational but the map shows the then sector boundaries with designation letters, the sector stations and the Observer Corps centres (denoted by a black triangle). There are two plaques on the table, one referring to No. 74 squadron from Hornchurch.

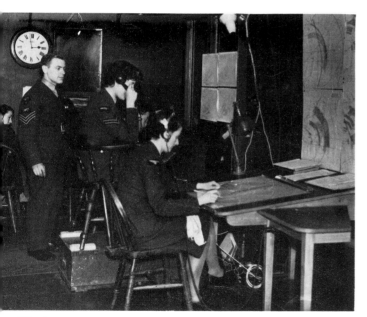

78 Interior of the 'R' or receiver hut at Dunkirk CH station in Kent in 1940. An airman towards the far wall is acting as the 'operator' and is seated watching the face of the cathode ray tube. To his right, in the chair on the raised box, sits the 'Converter' who reads off the actual position over the ground of the plot and the height. In the foreground is the recorder keeping a record of all the tracks. On the far wall is mounted the PBX telephone switchboard handling all incoming and outgoing lines. The operator reported the station's plots direct to a filter room plotter at Bentley Priory.

79 The transmitter room at a CH radar station.

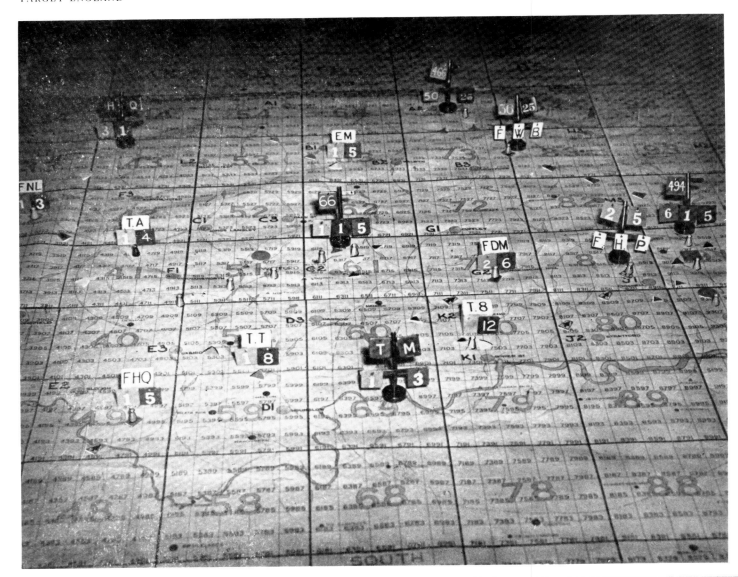

80 The Centre map table of No. 17 Watford Observer Group as it appeared at one period during the later stages of the Battle of Britain. On the so-called gallows arms, plaques carry details of the tracks while arrows and 'halma men' indicate the seen and heard progress of the tracks themselves. At the top of the table 50 hostiles at 25,000 ft are being engaged by fighters from North Weald, the F on the Gallows arm being friendly fighter, W standing for North Weald and B indicating the formation has split. To the right, raid 494 consists of six hostiles at 15,000 ft, with two fighters from Hornchurch climbing through 5000 ft in pursuit. There are a variety of other aircraft on the table, including trainers and single fighters, FNL being a fighter from Northolt at 3000 ft and FHQ another fighter from Hornchurch at 3000 ft. The line of the River Thames can be clearly seen and an idea of scale can be gained from the fact that the lettered squares (eg 78) have sides of 10 km and the smaller squares (eg 7383) have sides of 2 km. The 5 mile sound circles of all the posts in the group are also shown and the post designations, eg K.1 which was on the roof of the London University Building in Gower Street.

81 CHL rotating aerial.

82 Observer Corps No. 38 Group, Aberdeen, the Centre of which was situated in the Old Infirmary Building, Wool-manhill. The Controller is standing on the left of picture watching the table display. Down the sides of the recorder's box are recognition photographs and rows of raid designation plaques. All the Corps members present are wearing their badges and the striped police-type brassards over-printed 'Observer Corps'. A typical tellers report from an Observer Centre in 1940 would read 'Visual-Raid 5-*North-West-R for Robert 7592-7592* -8 at 10'.

83 WAAF plotters seated in their wicker chairs round the map table at Duxford Sector Operations Room. In front of each of them is a telephone jack, trays of plotting counters and raid plaques and a rake for putting them in position. On the left hand side are further trays of counters. The WAAF in the foreground has her telephone connected to a teller on the dais at No. 18 Observer Group, Colchester.

84 Houses in a small village dwarfed by the lattice receiver masters of a Chain Home RDF station.

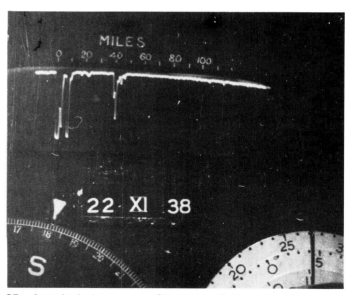

85 A typical picture on a CH station Cathode ray tube. The very long descending echoes on the left hand side were caused by the station's own ground ray and permanent echoes which were always present. Further to the right, at 40 miles range, is an echo made by 24 Blenheim aircraft flying in from the North Sea. The photograph was taken on the 22nd November 1938 in the course of a counting exercise. It was the first large formation ever dealt with using the prototype CH at Bawdsey. During the Battle of Britain operators were coping with formations of 100+ which produced massive echoes on the tube.

THE MICKLETHWAIT HEIGHT CORRECTION ATTACHMENT
STORES REF. No. 6E/339

THE THREADS OF THIS SCREW SHOULD
BE PAINTED WITH SHELLAC BEFORE
BEING SCREWED INTO POSITION.

Plan I
WITHOUT FIXTURE

Plan II
WITH FIXTURE

INSTRUCTIONS.

Part I.

HOW TO FIT TO OBSERVER INSTRUMENT

1　Withdraw four screws "A" (Plan I) and remove the two Brackets "K".

2　Withdraw the four screws "B" (Plan I) and remove the two clips for torch.

3　Screw the height corrector on to the Instrument by means of the four screws "A" (Plan 2).

4　Refix the two torch clips by means of the four screws "B" (Plan 2).

5　Release thumb-screw "E" (Plan 2); slip the bracket "D" behind it; then tighten up thumb-screw "E".

6　Fix upright arm of height corrector to top of sighting arm by means of screw "C" (Plan 2).

Part II.

HOW TO USE THE HEIGHT CORRECTOR.

1　Before starting to plot an aircraft it is necessary to see that the pointers "H" and "L" are aligned.

2　When the Post overhears another Post on the same circuit plotting the same aircraft, Number Two of the Post Crew joins up, by means of a straight edge, the positions on the Post Chart of the other Post and the plot given by that Post.

3　Number Two of the Post Crew moves Pointer "H" (Plan 2) to the straight edge.

4　The corrected height is then shown on the scale "P" (Plan 2) at the point at which it is intersected by the upper edge of the moving arm "G" (Plan 2).

5　Until the aircraft is out of sight, plotting can be continued without further adjustment by utilising pointer "H" instead of pointer "L".

6　Pointers "H" and "L" must be aligned before starting to plot another aircraft.

NOTE.—When the Instrument is dismantled and placed in the transit case, thumb-screw "E" must be replaced by thumb-screw "J" in order to keep bracket "D" in position.

R.B.P. & Co. Ltd. 2438K

86 Manufacturer's instructions for modifying the standard observer post plotting instrument Mk 11B, issued by R B Pullin and Co in July 1940. The Micklethwait attachment, which allowed for heights to be corrected between two posts, was invented by a Corps member and bore his name. With the basic instrument shown here the height was estimated and set on the vertical height bar. Thereafter, by viewing the aircraft along the sighting arm, the was pointer moved out to a position on a 2 km numbered square. A typical report of the period would be—B.3 calling, six Dorniers seen 7592, flying north, height 15,000 ft.

87 Each Post in the Observer Corps had a chart table on which the plotting instrument was mounted. The map was a small section of that at Observer Centres, and RAF Sectors and Groups. The basic plotting unit was a 2 km-sided square. This is the chart of post 1/E.1 Oare, Kent, with its centre at Maidstone. The 2 km squares of the grid are shown, together with circles for sound plotting purposes. Nearby posts are marked, together with an arrow which was aligned on Oare church spire and was used in setting up the instrument.

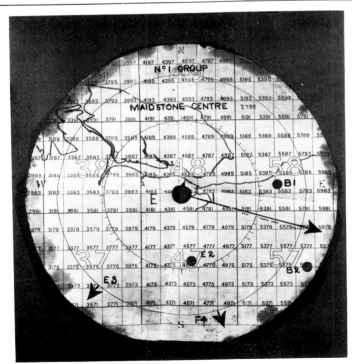

WAR-THE BEGINNING

With tin-helmets and gas masks, members of the Royal Observer Corps man their post on the roof of a London telephone exchange early in the war.

On the morning of September 3, 1939, just after war had been declared, the sirens in the south-east of England wailed and many people rushed to whatever shelter they could find. It was all a false alarm caused by a friendly aircraft from the continent which had not filed a proper flight plan.

The attack on Poland continued but neither France nor Britain was prepared to provoke Hitler by doing anything about it. With all his best troops and most of the front-line air force units engaged in the east, the Führer would have found himself in a very difficult situation had air attacks begun on Germany and even limited ground operations begun in the west. By September 28, the last resistance in Poland had been crushed.

Britain had been expecting an onslaught as H G Wells predicted in 'Shape of Things to Come' with enormous damage to cities, tens of thousands of casualties and general panic. Everyone was very surprised when nothing actually happened. The official estimates of the effects of air attack had been grossly exaggerated by the Home Office and other authorities but this had had a beneficial effect in that civil defence preparations had been accelerated to a marked degree.

Britain, however, still needed time to build up and prove its defences. The Fighter Command system of reporting and control needed many months of practice to become really efficient while the 'Phoney War' continued.

The first real test came in the so-called 'Battle of Barking Creek' which occurred in September 6, 1939. A searchlight unit at West Mersea reported incoming high flying aircraft. The guns opened fire the sirens sounded and fighters were scrambled. Radar erroneously reported more aircraft coming in and additional fighters went up. In the end the RAF fought the RAF and there were casualties. When the dust had settled, there was an inquest which showed that a major overhaul was needed. Dowding moved in with an iron hand and the measures taken ensured that the system worked effectively in the summer of 1940.

The lack of direct assault lulled the Government and the population into a false sense of security. Production did not expand as it should have done and many aspects of defence were left in abeyance while the bureaucratic machine churned inexorably on.

The British Expeditionary Force with the cream of the British Army, its weapons and vehicles, settled down in France to long months of boredom. At home, people stumbled around in the blackout and put up with a certain amount of restriction but life did not change a great deal.

The Luftwaffe first appeared over the Firth of Forth on October 16, when Ju 88s bombed the fleet. Thereafter the east and north east coast sea areas had frequent minelaying and reconnaissance visits. On February 3, 1940, Flight Lieutenant (later Group Captain) Peter Townsend of No. 43 Squadron shot down a Heinkel into the snow near Sneaton Castle Yorks., the first German aircraft to be destroyed over England since the First World War.

The winter of 1939/40 was bitter, with snow, high winds, frost, ice and fog. Isolated AA gun and searchlight sites, observer posts and other units were completely cut off, while over large parts of the country flying was impossible.

Neville Chamberlain's Government lived in a sort of dream world, believing that the Maginot Line in France was impregnable and the French Army in good shape. In fact, the French army was poorly equipped for modern war, it was disorganised and its morale low. The French Air Force was also chaotic with many aircraft obsolete and an air defence network rudimentary in the extreme. Whitehall took no steps to ascertain the true situation and lived on in blissful but terrible ignorance.

Hitler took full advantage of the Phoney War. His army was well disciplined, extremely well trained and, together with the Luftwaffe, had proved itself in the Polish campaign. He was prepared to take risks and conduct a series of Blitzkrieg campaigns.

The first of these lightning assaults came on April 8, 1940, when German troops overran a totally unprepared Denmark and invaded Norway. By the evening of the following day all the key ports from Narvik to Oslo were in German hands. Subsequently, allied forces landed at Narvik, Namsos and Aandalsnes but were not evacuated from Narvik until the situation in France became critical late in May. On June 4, 1940, King Haakon of Norway and his Government departed for Britain aboard the cruiser *Devonshire*.

The German navy in Norway had however suffered crippling losses, losing three out of eight available cruisers, half of all its destroyers (10) and suffering serious damage to its only

two heavy battlecruisers *Scharnhorst* and *Gneisenau*) and one of the only two remaining 'Pocket Battleships'. Particularly ominous for the future of all surface ships was the sinking, by Fleet Air Arm Skua dive bombers, of the cruiser *Königsberg*— the first major warship to be sunk by air attack.

In Norway, the Luftwaffe and airborne troops were employed with considerable skill and the experience was to be used to good effect in the major offensive which was only weeks away.

On May 10, 1940, seventy-five divisions of the German army (with forty-two in reserve), together with over 3500 aircraft were launched in a massive attack in the west. Meanwhile, on the evening of that same day something happened in London which was to help ensure the survival of the British Isles in particular and democracy in general. Criticised on all sides, Prime Minister Chamberlain realised that he could not bring the Parties together to form a National Government in the time of supreme crisis. At six o'clock, Winston Spencer Churchill, First Lord of the Admiralty, presented himself at Buckingham Palace to see King George VI and was asked to form a Government. By ten o'clock Churchill had the full support of the Labour and Liberal parties and had submitted to the King five names for the War Cabinet. At last, at the eleventh hour there was unity of purpose and a leader who was to be more than a match for Hitler in both word and deed.

On the Continent, things were already out of control. With lightning speed, German airborne and ground forces were pushing into Belgium, Holland and Luxembourg, covered by the umbrella of the Luftwaffe. Neutrality meant little to Hitler and he regarded it as a sign of weakness.

In Holland, despite valiant efforts, the campaign was over in five days with the Royal family and Government transported to England and the city of Rotterdam wrecked by a completely unnecessary and brutal air attack.

In Belgium, as in Holland, daring airborne attacks and heavy air strikes against key points caused panic and upset any plans the defenders had. The 'impregnable' fortress at Eben Emael, was taken by a specially trained group of 80 men who landed on top of it in gliders and blasted out the defenders with hollow-charge explosives and flamethrowers.

French forces moved into southern Holland, while the BEF travelled rapidly into Belgium, but to the south and sweeping round behind came the German 12th Army and Panzer Group Kleist. The Maginot Line was by-passed and the tank columns were on the move.

For the RAF the campaign proved to be a disaster. The vulnerable Battle and Blenheim light bombers of the Advanced Air Striking Force were shot to pieces by Messerschmitts and concentrated anti-aircraft fire as they attacked bridges and troop concentrations. After five days of battle, the RAF in France had lost 125 light bombers and 71 Hurricane fighters.

By May 12, three extra Hurricane squadrons had been sent from Britain to reinforce the six already there and on the

12th the equivalent of two more squadrons were despatched. The French Government demanded more and yet more RAF fighters to fill the yawning gaps in the Armée de l'Air.

Dowding, at Fighter Command, watched his forces wasting away in a futile continental battle where there was no proper organisation and no reporting and control network worthy of the name. At least fifty-two squadrons were needed for the defence of Britain itself and Dowding saw the lifeblood of the Command dripping away. He appeared in front of the War Cabinet on May 15 and put his points quietly but forcibly. He showed that, if Churchill gave in and sent continuing reinforcements to France, Fighter Command would be completely ruined by the end of July.

Dowding followed up his plea with the now famous letter to the Air Ministry which ended with the words 'But, if the Home Defence Force is drained away in desperate attempts to remedy the situation in France, defeat in France will involve the final, complete and irremediable defeat of this country'.

Churchill still wanted a further ten squadrons sent to the continent but fortunately sense prevailed and reinforcement was limited to six squadrons rotating through France each day, three in the morning and three in the afternoon. It then became impossible for RAF fighter squadrons to continue operating from French airfields and, on May 19, units were withdrawn to fight from southern England. Only three Hurricane squadrons were left with the Air Component to retreat westward with part of the British Army. In eleven days the RAF had lost a quarter of its total fighter strength.

On the ground, the situation went from bad to worse and, by 24 May, the German Army had swung in a long arm right up to the Channel coast, capturing Boulogne and investing Calais. On May 28, Belgium capitulated and the only hope for the BEF lay in retreat to the area round Dunkirk and possible evacuation of some of the troops.

In London it was realised that the Dunkirk perimeter could in no way be maintained as a fortress to be defended against the whole might of the German Army and the Luftwaffe. As many troops as possible had to be evacuated by every means available although vehicles, guns, tanks, ammunition and equipment would have to be left behind. On the evening of May 26, Admiral Ramsay at Dover was instructed to begin operation 'Dynamo', an undertaking which was to go down in the history books as the greatest maritime rescue undertaking of all time.

Every sort of vessel became involved in the evacuation, from rowing boats to luxury yachts and paddle steamers, although the bulk of the task ultimately devolved upon the Royal Navy and its destroyers. Dunkirk and its surroundings became an inferno as guns and the Luftwaffe endeavoured to stop the embarkation.

Göring was convinced that the Luftwaffe alone could beat the British into submission and the method and scale of the sea operations does not seem to have occurred to him. He assumed that his task was to reduce the BEF to a state of surrender by aerial bombardment. Only gradually did it dawn on him that the self-same BEF was slipping through his fingers to the last haven across the Channel. In the upshot, 360,000 men were saved who came back to form the backbone for a new army to defend Britain.

Fighter Command threw in everything it had to protect Dunkirk from the Luftwaffe but it was simply not enough. Operating outside the radar and Observer Corps network and patrolling under extremely difficult conditions, No. 11 Group could not hope to meet all the attacks. The sixteen available squadrons, including, for the first time, Spitfires, flew and fought ceaselessly and caused the enemy heavy casualties. The Dunkirk period cost Fighter Command 100 aircraft and 80 pilots and reduced its strength to the lowest point in the whole of 1940. By June 5, Dowding had only 331 Spitfires and Hurricanes available for operations plus 36 in reserve.

One pilot, Flight Lt F J Howell, recorded his impressions of the evacuation after one of the air battles over Dunkirk on May 31:-

'Having lost everyone else, and being all on my own—(A most unpleasant position to be in, I thought), I whistled around at 0 feet for a bit about 15 miles off Dunkirk. I thought I saw a boat, just a speck on the water, so went to have a look. There were 8 or 10 Tommies and sailors rowing for dear life in a ship's lifeboat for England about 70 miles away!

The way they were rowing, they would miss England altogether, so I flew three times in the direction. They all stood up and waved and cheered poor devils. I only hope they were picked up alright, as I reported their position as soon as I landed . . . .all the way back to England I flew full throttle at about 15 ft above the water and the shipping between England and Dunkirk was a sight worth seeing. Never again shall I see so many ships of different sizes and shapes over such a stretch of water. Paddle boats, destroyers, sloops, tugs towing anything up to four motorless fishing trawlers, river launches— 15 ft motor boats—fire boats, cross-Channel boats, tankers, coal barges and anything with a motor towing anything without one.'

The rapid German advance across France and the crushing of Holland and Belgium shocked the British Nation out of its stupor. It was feared that the sky was about to be filled with waves of air transports and gliders and darken with thousands of German paratroops aided and abetted by fifth columnists and soldiers dressed as nuns. Rumours gained credence over almost every facet of everyday life. On May 14 Anthony Eden broadcast to the nation and called for men between the ages of 16 and 65 to come forward and offer their services for a new force to be known as the Local Defence Volunteers. The result was little short of miraculous; police stations were besieged with men wanting to join and the first patrols were operated in the Worthing area on May 15. Britain was on the way to becoming an armed camp with a population totally at war—and alone.

Headquarters, Observer Corps,
Bentley Priory,
STANMORE. Middlesex.

Circular No. 6.   16th November, 1939.

Dear Sir,

1.   Secrecy. Information obtained by members, in the course
of their duty, regarding the conduct of the war by H.M. Forces is
strictly confidential.
          No discussion on such information should take place in
the presence of strangers or with Officers who are personally
unknown, except during official visits.
          Notice is always given to Centres and Posts of the visits
of authorised Officers or civilians.

2.   There has been a moderate amount of enemy air activity
off the East Coast during the last fortnight but there have not been
many opportunities for obtaining Observer Corps tracks of a
continuous nature.

3.   On a few occasions some good tracks were obtained of
enemy aircraft circling over the East Coast. Records were also
obtained of a track which split and was immediately given the
appropriate symbols by the Centre concerned.

4.   A very good track was obtained for a period on November
10th. The cloud conditions were difficult and most of the plotting
was by "Sound". The Posts and Centres which tracked and "Told"

88 Observer Corps Commandant's circular for November
16, 1939.

89 The German Navy suffered severe losses during the
Norwegian campaign in April 1940 which left it in a poor state
to provide support for any invasion of Britain in the summer.
Among the ships sunk was the light cruiser Königsberg. On
April 9 she was damaged by the coastal batteries at Bergen
and moored alongside the Skoltegrund mole. Seven Blackburn Skua naval dive bombers of No. 800 squadron led by
Capt Partridge RM and nine Skuas of No. 803 squadron led by
Lt Lucy RN set out from Hatston in the Orkneys. Showing
exceptional navigational skill, the force flew 330 miles and
arrived at Bergen after dawn on the 10th. The Königsberg
was dive bombed with great precision and wrecked.

90 At some schools the pupils built their own air raid shelters. These are boys from Soham Grammar School, Cambridge in September 1939.

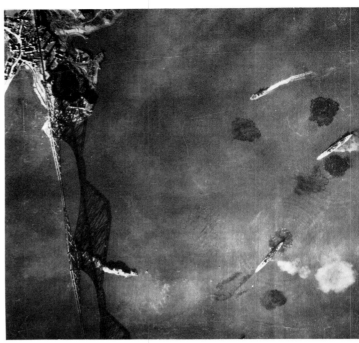

91 On October 16, 1939 nine Ju 88 bombers of KG 30
attacked the fleet in the Firth of Forth. This German photograph shows the cruisers Edinburgh and Southampton at
anchor during the raid. Both ships were hit. Two bombers
were shot down by No. 602 and No. 603 squadrons.

92 When schools returned from the summer holidays in
September 1939 war had been declared. One of the first tasks
was to give the pupils shelter drill. This photograph was
taken at a school in Southall, London on September 25.

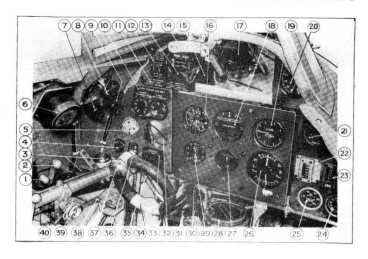

Reference:- OC/3.16.

GERMAN PARACHUTE TROOPS - INFORMATION CONSIDERED USEFUL
FOR DEFENCE ORGANISATIONS IN THIS COUNTRY.

From experience gained the following facts are known:-

AIRCRAFT.

The Ju.52 is used exclusively for carrying parachute troops and supplies.
This aircraft is a three-engined low winged monoplane with single fin and rudder, the
leading edge of the mainplanes being noticeably swept back.   The ends of the wings are
very square and it has a fixed undercarriage.

These aircraft contain approximately twelve parachutists who, prior to the
jump are lined up six a side on either side of a steel wire running through the centre
of the compartment.   A special type of parachute is used with an eighteen ft. cord
to the end of which is attached a spring hook.   On the signal being given by the
Observer to jump, the parachutists hook their cord on to this wire and jump from a
door on either side of the aircraft.   On jumping the cord pulls a covering envelope
from the parachute and the parachute automatically opens after approximately a hundred
and fifty feet.   The minimum height for jumping is three hundred feet and this height
is generally used.

The parachute itself is made of a light coloured silk and is about thirty-
two feet across.   Fourteen cords run right over the parachute and the twenty- eight
ends are fastened to a point a few feet above the parachutist's head.

It should be borne in mind that the time taken for the complete jump is only
about five seconds and the actual time when he is travelling comparatively slowly with
open parachute is little more than two seconds.

The object of dropping parachutists from this low altitude is to prevent too
wide a dispersal.

93 An information sheet on German parachute troops issued to defence organisations in late May 1940.

96 Cockpit photograph from RAF Pilots' Notes for the Hurricane 1 fighter.

97 A 11 Matilda 1 two-man infantry tanks in France in 1940. No German anti-tank could penetrate the front armour but the vehicle was very slow, had only a single machine gun and suffered from poor suspension.

94 On May 22, as the Germans turned their thrusts in France northwards towards the sea and Churchill conferred in Paris, the first British civilian organisation to be issued with arms was the Observer Corps. At lonely Observer posts up and down the country, officers arrived with a pair of Lee Enfield rifles and ammunition. This entry in the log book of 6/L2 post, Ripley, Derbyshire shows that the weapons were delivered at 9.30 that night with "Full instructions to follow".

95 French soldiers at Margate railway station after evacuation from Dunkirk, on June 4, 1940.

98 What would undoubtedly have happened to the ships of the Royal Navy if Fighter Command had been defeated in 1940. This French destroyer, its bows blown off by a bomb, lies high and dry on the beach at Dunkirk.

99 At Headcorn, Kent, the locals cut sandwiches day and night to feed the exhausted troops of the BEF returning from Dunkirk.

100 Harvesting goes on on the Somme in France around a wrecked British A.13 tank in the summer of 1940. The tank was from the ill-fated British 1st Armoured Division which was knocked out by German guns and Panzers.

101 A number of escaping French aircraft of various types appeared on British airfields at the time of Dunkirk. This one was a Potez 540, an obsolete bomber-reconnaissance machine which was put into reserve units when war broke out. In the background is an Avro Anson.

HEADQUARTERS, FIGHTER COMMAND,
ROYAL AIR FORCE,
BENTLEY PRIORY,
STANMORE,
MIDDLESEX.

Reference PC/S.19048.   SECRET

16th May, 1940.

Sir,

I have the honour to refer to the very serious calls which have recently been made upon the Home Defence Fighter Units in an attempt to stem the German invasion on the Continent.

2. I hope and believe that our Armies may yet be victorious in France and Belgium, but we have to face the possibility that they may be defeated.

3. In this case I presume that there is no-one who will deny that England should fight on, even though the remainder of the Continent of Europe is dominated by the Germans.

4. For this purpose it is necessary to retain some minimum fighter strength in this country and I must request that the Air Council will inform me what they consider this minimum strength to be, in order that I may make my dispositions accordingly.

5. I would remind the Air Council that the last estimate which they made as to the force necessary to defend this country was 52 Squadrons, and my strength has now been reduced to the equivalent of 36 Squadrons.

6. Once a decision has been reached as to the limit on which the Air Council and the Cabinet are prepared to stake the existence of the country, it should be made clear to the Allied Commanders on the Continent that not a single aeroplane from Fighter Command beyond the limit will be sent across the Channel, no matter how desperate the situation may become.

The Under Secretary of State,
Air Ministry,
LONDON, W.C.2.

-2-

7. It will, of course, be remembered that the estimate of 52 Squadrons was based on the assumption that the attack would come from the eastwards except in so far as the defences might be outflanked in flight. We have now to face the possibility that attacks may come from Spain or even from the North coast of France. The result is that our line is very much extended at the same time as our resources are reduced.

8. I must point out that within the last few days the equivalent of 10 Squadrons have been sent to France, that the Hurricane Squadrons remaining in this country are seriously depleted, and that the more Squadrons which are sent to France the higher will be the wastage and the more insistent the demands for reinforcements.

9. I must therefore request that as a matter of paramount urgency the Air Ministry will consider and decide what level of strength is to be left to the Fighter Command for the defence of this country, and will assure me that when this level has been reached, not one fighter will be sent across the Channel however urgent and insistent the appeals for help may be.

10. I believe that, if an adequate fighter force is kept in this country, if the fleet remains in being, and if Home Forces are suitably organised to resist invasion, we should be able to carry on the war single handed for some time, if not indefinitely. But, if the Home Defence Force is drained away in desperate attempts to remedy the situation in France, defeat in France will involve the final, complete and irremediable defeat of this country.

I have the honour to be,
Sir,
Your obedient Servant,

H.C.T.Dowding.

Air Chief Marshal,
Air Officer Commanding-in-Chief,
Fighter Command, Royal Air Force.

102 The famous letter from Air Chief Marshal Sir Hugh Dowding on May 16, which finally stopped the outflow of Fighter Commands' aircraft and pilots into the hopeless battle of France.

103 Early in 1940, an ARP post in Hull, Yorks with a cycle-shop owner, a builder, a clerk (who was later killed in an air attack) and the local doctor's sister. Gas capes and helmets were being worn. The message on the wall referred to the popular song, 'We're going to hang out the washing on the Siegfried Line'.

104 A posed scramble to its Hurricane aircraft by pilots of No. 87 squadron at Lille in the Autumn of 1939. One of the Hurricanes still has a two blade wooden propeller.

105 A Bf 109E-3 which was forced down at Amiens on May 2, 1940, appropriated by No. 1 squadron and then flown to Boscombe Down for flight evaluation. It was given the RAF serial AE 479.

106 A squadron of Hurricanes, the only really modern fighters in the Belgian Air Force. 2e escadrille, le Groupe, 2e Regiment d'Aeronautique at Schaffen, where nine of its aircraft were destroyed on the ground on the first day of the German offensive, May 10, 1940.

107 The Belgian Air Force fought hard but it was outnumbered and equipped with obsolete aircraft. These Fairey Foxes were based at Gossoncourt and at Neerhespen shown on May 10 after the Luftwaffe had left its visiting card.

109 Evacuation of children from the major cities started before war was actually declared. This group from London is shown on September 1, at a Surrey station, complete with gas masks and labels.

108 Masses of BEF troops stand, up to their waists in water, waiting for a boat to evacuate them from the beach at Bray near Dunkirk. Two rowing boats are pulling away with men from the heads of the queues.

110 Belgian Fairey Battle bombers of 9e Escadrille, II Groupe of the 3e Regiment before the German invasion.

111 An Italian Fiat CR 42 biplane fighter of 4e squadron, IIe Groupe, 2e Regiment Belgian Air Force. Fifteen CR42s were destroyed on May 10, 1940, alone.

112 Standing beside his Fiat CR 42 fighter early in 1940 is Jean Offenberg, 2 Groupe, 2e Regiment Belgian Air Force. He fought until Belgium capitulated and then managed to get to Casablanca and from there to Gibraltar and England. He joined No. 145 squadron RAF in August 1940 and fought through the Battle of Britain. He had shot down a Do 17 over Belgium and in 1940/41 got another six aircraft confirmed. He was awarded the DFC and was killed on January 22, 1942.

113/4 Recruiting was brisk when war broke out. Shown here are a recruiting desk for the Auxilary Territorial Service in Chelsea and an RAF mobile recruiting office outside Victory House, Kingsway.

115 The banshee wail of the siren became part of everyday life in Britain during the war. This siren, nicknamed 'Wailing Willie' was at Watling Street, Gravesend, Kent.

116 An RAF Hurricane of No. 87 squadron from Lille which force-landed in Belgium near Kurtrijk during the phoney war period.

117 Two Hurricanes from No. 111 squadron at Wick, Scotland refuelling in February 1940 and pilots from the same unit at readiness for a shipping patrol with the inevitable cup of tea coming up.

Aircraft recognition became a subject of vital importance. **118** the cover and one page of a booklet put out by the *Daily Mirror.* **119** the cover of the first identification handbook published by the trade journal *The Aeroplane.* **120** an assortment of cigarette cards, published pre-war, which were in great demand after war broke out. **121** a page from the *Hearkers' Bulletin,* a publication privately produced by a club formed in the Observer Corps in Surrey; ultimately the Hearkers' Club had branches up and down the country and it was officially recognised in 1941.

120

118

121

119

122 This instruction issued by Western Area Observer Corps just before the outbreak of war shows just how poor recognition standards were throughout the Services.

Reference SA/55/1.

CONFIDENTIAL.

Observer Corps,
Hillingdon House,
UXBRIDGE, Middlesex.

4th. December 1939.

Centre Controller No....Group;
Head Observer No.......Post;
O.G.O. No.....Group;
      Southern Area.
- - - - - - - - - - - - - - -

LIGHTING OF FLARES BY OBSERVER POSTS.

    In order to assist R.A.F. pilots when night-flying during black-out conditions it has been decided that certain Observer Posts will lay out and light flares at times and for periods required by R.A.F. Sector Station Commanders.

2. THE POSTS CONCERNED are as shown on list attached, which will be sent to Centre Controllers and Observer Group Officers only.

3. EQUIPMENT (i) One or more Money flares, and a paraffin container or drum, will be provided by the Sector Commander of the Sector in which the Post is located, together with the name of the local paraffin supplier

123 In order to assist RAF aircraft to find the way to their airfields over blacked-out England, many Observer Corps posts were called upon to light paraffin flares. It was a messy and tedious business which aroused the ire of local inhabitants who thought they would be bombed as a result. It was also dangerous as the Chief Observer of the Wolverstone, Suffolk Post found in July 1940. He lit the flares one evening and was set upon by a rather drunken naval Petty Officer who thought he was a spy. The Chief Observer was shot in the thigh and the finger for his pains.

HEADQUARTERS, (UNIT), FIGHTER COMMAND, BENTLEY PRIORY, STANMORE, MIDDLESEX.

No......3.

SCREENING OF LIGHTS ON MOTOR VEHICLES.

EXEMPTION PASS.

Vehicle, Registration No. F.X.XG.... is a Private Vehicle / Service Vehicle employed on Official Duty, and is not required to comply with the orders regarding the screening of lights.

Pilot Officer,
for Squadron Leader,
Officer Commanding, Headquarters (Unit),
Fighter Command,   Royal Air Force.

124 When war broke out vehicles on military service were for a time exempt from the orders which required headlights to be screened. Special certificates had to be issued for this.

125 Six Spitfires of No. 65 squadron on patrol late in 1939. The underside camouflage consisted of one wing black and the other azure blue.

126 Every night the population had to draw the blackout curtains or put screens in the windows. It became a ritual, with any infringements met by the Warden's shout of 'put that light out'.

127 Left on a French airfield after the invasion had passed, a Handley Page Hampden bomber from No. 61 squadron, Hemswell. It probably force-landed after a raid on Germany in May 1940. German military personnel are seen inspecting the aircraft.

A series of photographs taken early in 1940 at No. 15 SFTS, Lossiemouth where pilots were completing their training prior to being posted to squadrons. **128** A visiting Spitfire I from No. 603, City of Edinburgh squadron. **129** An Oxford 1 twin-engined trainer. **130** North American Harvard trainer. **131** Miles Master 1 trainer.

128

129

130

131

132 Winston Spencer Churchill, the man who forecast Nazi aggression and who fought it. When he was appointed Prime Minister in May 1940 he succeeded, on personality alone, in rallying the nation. He was probably the only person who could have gathered the reins together and inspired the populace to resist the German onslaught. His words exactly suited the mood of the time and in his later comment on the air battle 'Never has so much been owed by so many to so few' he mirrored British feelings on the subject. Efforts have been made to denigrate Churchill since his death but there is no doubt that Britain's chances of survival in 1940 would have been very slim without him. Where fighter defence was concerned, Churchill had already learned a great deal in the thirties and understood how the system worked. He was content to leave the direction of the Battle of Britain to Dowding as he knew his worth and despite the fact that they had crossed swords over reinforcing France with British fighters. Churchill was a realist as well as an orator and he actively pursued every cause that, in 1940, would resist invasion and keep the RAF in being. This photograph shows Churchill, second from right, walking along Cheapside past St. Mary-le-Bow church after one of the major night raids in 1940.

THE SCENE IS SET

Men from the Berkshire Home Guard manage to look business-like behind their hastily improvised armoured car, a Hudson saloon armed with Ross rifles and a Vickers .303.

As the last exhausted, hungry and bewildered remnants of the British Expeditionary Force were landed on the south coast on June 4, the realisation began to dawn on the island race that it was completely on its own. Nothing stood between the ill-prepared nation and the might of the Wermacht except the Channel and the forces that could be mustered by the Royal Air Force and the Royal Navy, both of which had already suffered severe losses.

As if given a massive electric shock, the whole of Britain was galvanised into activity. Instead of admitting that the odds were impossible and defeat almost certain, the people bent their backs to the task of providing some form of defence against an aggressor daily expected to appear from the sea preceded by waves of parachutists.

For the Germans it was a golden opportunity to throw in every paratrooper and improvise an immediate seaborne assault to capture a British port and an airfield before the defenders could draw breath. One division would have caused chaos and given a bridgehead which could have been expanded. Fortunately, Germany had no contingency plan

for the invasion of Britain. Hitler assumed the British would sue for peace and he was intent on completing the humiliation of the old enemy, France.

At Dunkirk the BEF had lost more than 1000 guns including light and medium anti-aircraft weapons. Vast quantities of mortars, ammunition, rifles, machine guns, lorries and every other form of equipment had been wrecked or left to the enemy.

After Dunkirk the sole British Armoured Division, the 1st, was smashed on the Somme, whilst the 51st Highland Division was captured at St. Valery. The remaining British units were finally evacuated by ship but with further losses in vehicles and weapons. By mid-June over 1200 tanks, the bulk of the armoured forces, had been lost.

The Royal Navy had also suffered severely, with six destroyers, five minesweepers and one gunboat sunk and 23 destroyers, one sloop, one corvette and four minesweepers damaged. To these figures had to be added eight passenger ships and a host of smaller vessels.

The last RAF unit to leave France was No. 73 Squadron

which took off from Nantes for Tangmere on June 18. Altogether, between May 10 and June 20 the RAF lost 931 aircraft, of which 453 were Hurricanes and Spitfires; some 915 aircrew did not return, of which 435 were pilots. As if to rub salt in the wound, France refused to hand over 400 captured Luftwaffe personnel; they were repatriated to Germany and subsequently flew against Fighter Command in the Battle of Britain.

When all that was left from the wreck of defeat in France had been safely gathered in, the Government and a large proportion of the British population on its own account, began to prepare for all-out war. The British, so long the disciples of do-as-you-like democracy in all its forms, submitted willingly to total central direction and order.

The first civilian organisation to be armed was the Observer Corps with two rifles issued, immediately after Dunkirk, to all posts in threatened areas. The police, for the first and only time, were issued generally with rifles and revolvers and the public got used to patrol cars with two Lee-Enfields neatly stowed between the front seats.

All over the country road-blocks, slit-trenches, pill-boxes, sandbagged emplacements and barbed wire blossomed like spring flowers. A series of miniature Maginot Lines began to creep across the fields and hedgerows. Many of the instant fortifications were badly sited or back to front but to Luftwaffe reconnaissance aircraft they appeared most impressive. In addition to the defensive sites, every field was ploughed up or sown with stakes or wire obstacles. Road blocks were improvised, first from farm carts and steamrollers and later by means of concrete 'Dragon's teeth' sunk into the asphalt. Whether they would have hindered the Germany army is doubtful but they certainly slowed the long columns of British army vehicles on manoeuvres.

In the counties most likely to face invasion, seaside resorts became ghost towns. Shops were closed and boarded up and many inhabitants evacuated. Within five miles of the coast, private cars were allowed to pass only if the driver possessed a special yellow police permit.

Every sort of place-name was removed, sign posts were dug up and station name boards painted over. Even small sub-post offices had the name of the village deleted. On June 13 the ringing of church bells was banned, except as a warning of airborne invasion.

Without official sanction motor vehicles could not get a fuel allowance. They were either put on blocks for the duration, or turned over to the authorities for use by the Services. Any vehicle left unattended had to be immobilised by removing the distributor rotor arm. Anyone who ommitted to do this was liable to be taken to court.

At the end of June, the Local Defence Volunteers, at Churchill's behest, were renamed the Home Guard. This vast organisation, ultimately nearly one and a half million strong, became a law unto itself. Every sort of weapon from assagai to crossbow, and twelve-bore to elephant gun was pressed into use. Platoons across the land made Molotov cocktails from wine bottles filled with petrol and equipped with sandpaper and matches, while others amused themselves with lengths of gas piping packed with weed killer and fitted with a fuse.

RAF stations tried desperately to arm themselves against paratroop landings. At the No. 12 Group Fighter Station at Duxford, the armaments officer, was particularly enterprising. Rifles, Lewis guns and revolvers were at a premium so he cast about for alternatives. As he put it 'Spurred on by necessity I found that the station workshop windows were protected by bars, some five feet long and half an inch in diameter. I had them all cut down and fashioned and ground in the blacksmith shop in the form of a spear. These I 'airtested' by hurling the prototype clean through a dustbin at 30 paces. Then I found, in a store, a large number of oddly-shaped pieces of wood about two feet long. By the simple expedient of having a length of barbed wire wound onto one end, I had them fashioned into the most frightening knobkerries. The troops didn't laugh when I had these strange weapon issued; they were plain grateful'.

Himmler's Reich Security Head Office in Berlin evolved elaborate plans for the total subjugation of occupied Britain. They intended to destroy every organisation that they thought presented a threat to the occupiers from all levels of Parliament and Whitehall, through the Public Schools and religious bodies, down to the Boy Scouts and the Church Lads Brigade. With hindsight it is clear that any Nazi occupation would have been accompanied by every form of 'frightfulness'. The excesses in occupied Europe were carried out on populations initially docile, whereas the whole of Britain was distinctly hostile.

The SS in particular would have exacted a heavy toll in reprisals as a result of the activities of an extraordinary clandestine organisation, the cover name for which was Auxiliary Units. Composed of a wide variety of people, but largely Home Guard personnel, these units would have formed Britain's stay-behind army. Well armed and well trained, these phantom soldiers were housed in underground bunkers with entrances that were well-nigh impossible to detect in the normal course of events. Their task in invasion was to lie low until the German advance had passed through. They were then to emerge and create as much havoc as possible behind the lines. Britain is probably the only country in the world to have formed a complete underground army before the country had actually been attacked.

It should not be imagined for a moment that an invasion of the islands in 1940 would have been conducted by the defenders according to the normal 'rules'. If Germany was prepared to use unpleasant methods, then Britain would more than match them. Acting on Churchill's 'You can always take one with you', many of the Home Guards in the threatened areas put their varied rounds of ammunition into bench vices and sawed the ends off, thus turning them into 'dum dum' soft nosed expanding bullets. A rifle round treated in this way would show a small clean puncture on the point of entry and a jagged hole the size of a saucer on the point of exit. It was, of course, officially banned by the Geneva Convention.

Even nastier were the last ditch plans for chemical warfare. If the German Army had gained a foothold and looked like breaking through, sixteen squadrons (5 Lysander, 4 Battle, 5 Blenheim and 2 Wellington) were to attack the bridgeheads with mustard gas sprayed from custom-built containers. Training on Battles, which began before the war, involved using practice tanks filled with water and special charts for height, airspeed and wind direction to calculate the angle at which the liquid was to be released.

Experiments were also carried out at Halton, using Tiger Moths as human crop sprayers. In the front cockpit a tank was fitted and powder dispensers were located under the wings. The tank contained 'Paris Green', an extremely poisonous bright green insecticide made up of arsenic, trioxide and copper acetate. The combined effects of a fine spray of mustard gas and a good dusting of arsenic on a soldier wading up a beach in Kent leaves little to the imagination—particularly as, for the Sealion invasion force, gas masks were stowed aboard the landing craft, to be retrieved later! Setting fire to the sea was also contemplated but proved not too successful when tested.

Fighter, Bomber and Coastal Commands arranged to have every possible aircraft available for attacking an invasion fleet and bombing and machine-gunning troops that actually landed. Coastal Command began to run anti-invasion patrols from far to the South West of Cornwall right up to north west of the Shetlands.

Training aircraft were to be used in large numbers for bombing and machine gunning. Late in May the newly titled Flying Training Command had revised orders to operate in emergency under the code name 'Banquet'. The aircraft involved numbered around 300 and included Whitleys, Hampdens, Wellingtons, Blenheims, Battles, Ansons and even Audax, Hart and Hind biplanes. In August this force was supplemented by 350 Magister and Tiger Moth trainers fitted with 20 lb bombs and to be used under the code name 'Banquet Light'.

There were many arguments over how an invasion warning communications network was to be established. Eventually it was perfected using all normal tri-service channels, the Coastguards, the Observer Corps and a WT/RT system called 'Beetle'. In the case of the Observer Corps, Dowding had already engaged in lengthy correspondence with the army in 1939. He fully appreciated that the Observer Corps might be the first to see parchute or glider landings but thought it unlikely if the force emerged from the sea. He told GHQ Home Forces in November 1939. 'The first news that the Observer Corps would get of invasion would be in the morning papers'. By mid-1940 this was not strictly true but above all Dowding tried to keep his 'eyes and ears' concentrated on the all-important task of aircraft reporting.

While every possible effort was being made to fight the land battle, the RAF was girding its loins for the crucial war in the air. As Dowding knew, unless the Luftwaffe could achieve air superiority, any form of invasion became a most perilous affair for the German Army. With slow vessels and a small and battered navy, the key had to be total unopposed air cover and a clear field for the bomber force to act as mobile artillery.

Under Lord Beaverbrook at the Ministry of Aircraft Production, a top priority scheme was evolved whereby production would be concentrated on the Spitfire, Hurricane, Blenheim, Wellington and Whitly. The first type to be given the top priority stamp was the Hurricane, on May 24. Similarly, priority was given to the power plants of the aircraft, namely the Rolls Royce Merlin, the Bristol Mercury and the Hercules.

Production which had languished in the phoney war, began to shoot ahead; 309 Hurricanes were turned out in June and 272 in July while the comparable figures for Spitfires were 135 and 140. Rolls Royce output of Merlins in April was 389, but in June no less than 839 engines came off the line. Workers in the industry toiled day and night and put in so much overtime that many fell asleep at their machines.

One of the keys to keeping Fighter Command flying was the supply of repaired and rebuilt aircraft. The Civilian Repair Organisation (CRO) had been set up by Lord Nuffield with a string of repair depots, working parties and transport provided by No. 50 RAF Maintenance Unit. Under Lord Beaverbrook it was to maintain a continuous flow of aircraft and equipment back to the squadrons. In February 1940 twenty repaired aircraft per week were being returned to service. By mid-July this figure had risen to 160 per week. Rolls Royce delivered 130 repaired Merlins in April 1940, whereas in June the figure went up to 292. Altogether, between July and December 1940, 4196 damaged planes were put back into service and 35 per cent of fighters despatched to squadrons between July and October were repaired machines.

Improvements were also made to the fighters themselves. Constant-speed propellers offered a marked improvement in performance for both Hurricane and Spitfire. The de Havilland company produced a private venture conversion kit, had it test flown and then proceeded, on a verbal say-so, to re-equip Fighter Command. Teams went from airfield and, by August 15, no less than 1051 aircraft had been converted. At the same time RAF Henlow was not only conducting a 'fly-in' out-patients department for damaged Hurricanes but every week it was converting .303 Browning guns from Mark II to Mark II* to give improved rate of fire.

Dowding, meanwhile, was engrossed in obtaining more pilots to get the Command up to strength, providing anti-aircraft defence for airfields and factories and in extending and streamlining the radar warning network and the Observer Corps. One hundred and twenty-eight pilots had been lost in the air fighting over Dunkirk and this gap had to be filled. The Royal Navy found fifty-eight first rate pilots for transfer to the RAF, while Bomber, Coastal and Army Co-operation squadrons were combed for suitable men.

Only a quarter of the anti-aircraft guns needed for the whole of Britain were available, with the RAF in the queue for batteries along with a host of other priority sites including aircraft factories, ports and cities. In July, No. 10 Fighter Group, with headquarters at Box, Wiltshire was set up and an Observer Corps Group was established in Cornwall, with headquarters at Truro. Exeter airfield was enlarged and two Hurricane squadrons despatched there.

For Germany it was a period of euphoria and indecision. Hitler had never expected the western front to collapse with the speed that it did. When France finally capitulated he was left without a strategy. He hoped—and even expected—that beleagured Britain would come to terms. Hitler neither knew nor understood the British race and he was in every sense a landlubber incapable of really assessing the problems of crossing anything larger than a river. He also believed that the United Kingdom was basically a feudal system in imminent danger of being overthrown from within.

From the High Command downwards there was a feeling that the Franco-German armistice, signed on June 17 by the Petain Government, marked the end of hostilities and that time alone was needed to bring Britain to heel. The vital adrenalin in the German armed forces temporarily stopped flowing as troops went home on leave to be greeted as heroes, some units were demobilised and war production lagged.

Germany now had large conquered territories to exploit and, if necessary, gear to the Nazi war machine. The most important outside supplier, however, was the Soviet Union under the terms of the German-Soviet non-aggression pact and trade agreement. Russia became Germany's main provider of grain and a key supplier of manganese, platinum, chrome and oil. Some idea of the quantities involved can be gained from the fact that between February 1940 and June 22, 1941, (the day Hitler invaded Russia) Stalin supplied Germany with one and a half million tons of grain.

Those toiling in British factories to keep Hitler at bay were regaled by the Communist Party of Great Britain with the usual propaganda on the brotherhood of the Proletariat. The purveyors of these glad tidings would probably have been lynched had British workers known that the Communists of Moscow were feeding the German armed forces and providing the raw materials to make the Luftwaffe's bombers and bombs.

The Luftwaffe slowly began to build up its facilities in the occupied territories. Heavy bombing had wrecked many of the airfields and buildings and these needed to be repaired. Stocks of bombs, ammunition and spares had to be built up, anti-aircraft guns provided and railway facilities extended. The signals organisation started to set up permanent ground and ground-to-air communications alongside navigation aids such as beacons. Along the coast intelligence listening stations were erected in an attempt to penetrate the secrets of the RAF's air defence system.

Three Luftflotten were established in a ring round the south and east of Britain:-

Luftlotte 2 under Kesselring; HQ Brussels; forward HQ, Cap Gris Nez

Luftflotte 3 under Sperrle; HQ Paris; forward HQ, Deauville

Luftflotte 5 under Stumpff; HQ Stavanger.

During June, Luftwaffe activity was widespread and almost exclusively at night. Small numbers of aircraft roamed across the country, keeping the sirens wailing and disturbing people's sleep. Bombs were aimed at fourteen ports, sixteen industrial plants and thirteen aerodromes. Damage was caused and there were casualties but none heavy. The raids were a nuisance but they proved invaluable in hardening the population to the prospect of air raids and in practicising all elements of the air and civil defence systems.

Measures for deception were also expanded, including the provision of more decoy airfields and dummy aircraft and the setting up of 100 special 'Starfish' fire sites to lure bombers away from key targets.

The decoy airfields were called K-sites while dummy flarepaths were designated Q-sites. A K-site often involved dummy aircraft made of wood and canvas, canvas buildings and a flarepath consisting of gooseneck flares. A small party of airmen, under the command of an NCO, ran the site. At night, when the enemy was in the vicinity of the nearby operational base, the personnel would be called upon to light the flarepath and even ride up and down on a lamp-equipped bicycle to simulate the taxying of aircraft on the ground. As some sites received regular loads of high explosive and incendiary bombs, posting to a K or Q site was not something to be looked forward to in the ranks.

One bonus of the June operations by the Luftwaffe was the discovery of the German beam bombing system known as 'Knickebein' (bent-leg). Luftwaffe pilots were able to get to within 500 yards of a target through signals received on the Lorenz beam approach landing receivers on the aircraft. A continuous note was heard in the pilot's headphones if he was accurately positioned on the beam directed at the target, deviation to one side or the other produced either dots or dashes and a last note indicated that the target area had been reached.

The puzzle was solved by Professor R V Jones using documents from crashed aircraft, interrogation of prisoners of war by Squadron Leader Felkin and use of a specially equipped Anson aircraft from the Beam Approach Aid Development Unit at Wyton which located the beams in the air.

No. 80 Wing, RAF, was formed in July to counter German bombing aids, including Knickebein. Nine transmitters were erected, the signals from which could 'bend' the beam away from the target. In addition, hospital X-ray sets were used to jam Knickebein and ensure that the pilots could not hear the signals. No. 80 Wing marked the beginning of electronic warfare as we know it today.

133 In June 1940 decorations were awarded to fighter pilots involved in the Battle of France and Dunkirk. At an investiture carried out by King George VI at Hornchurch, the King is shaking hands with Flight Lieutenant Deere of No. 54 Squadron. Behind the King is Air Chief Marshal Dowding.

134 Dummy airfield and factory sites sprouted up all over Britain in 1939-40. The major film companies and other firms mass-produced dummies known as 'target' aircraft fabricated out of wood and fabric. Many hundreds of 'target' aircraft were produced, those representing operational aircraft including Hurricane, Spitfire, Defiant, Blenheim, Whitley, Wellington and Battle. Shown here is the dummy factory and airfield site for the de Havilland Aircraft Company's works at Hatfield. Situated in open countryside some three miles east of the main plant, this dummy included frame and canvas buildings and an imitation Airspeed Oxford tied down to the ground. **135** A dummy Whitley at Driffield.

36

HOME GUARD
A HANDBOOK FOR THE
L. D. V.
By JOHN BROPHY

PARACHUTE TROOPS, ANTI-TANK WARFARE, OBSERVATION AND REPORTING, THE RIFLE, THE BREN GUN, THE LEWIS GUN, THE THOMPSON GUN, GRENADES AND 'MOLOTOFFS,' ROAD-BLOCKS, AMBUSHES, STREET FIGHTING, ETC., ETC.

HODDER & STOUGHTON   1/- net

135

136 Advice to the newly formed Local Defence Volunteers poured out in magazines and newspapers and anyone with experience of the Spanish Civil War was sought after as an expert. Reproduced here is the cover of a Hodder and Stoughton pocket book aimed at Britain's amateur army. Clearly the publishers put the book out when the name was in process of change from LDV to Home Guard.

137 Lines of old motor cars which would be drooled over by the automobile collector of the 1980's. This extraordinary collection formed the night runway obstruction force at Hatfield in June 1940 to deter enemy glider or transport landings. Every morning the cars were pushed off the runway and flying recommenced. In the right background is a Tiger Moth in the circuit.

138 A typical occupation for British army gunners after Dunkirk—a gun-less detachment of the Sussex Yeomanry sand-bagging the sea front at Hove, Sussex. Armament consisted of one rifle for every two men and a Lewis gun which refused to function. The unit, the 74th (Sussex and Surrey Yeomanry) Medium Regiment, Royal Artillery, was subsequently moved to Kent during the Battle of Britain as part of the anti-invasion forces. It was supplied, from Woolwich, with ancient 6-inch howitzers and 60-pounder guns; these had solid tyres and were towed by Thorneycroft Athey trucks and Scammel coal lorries. Down the roads of Kent young ladies fed the troops with plums of doubtful ripeness which resulted in a mass exodus to the ditches and bushes. As the maximum road speed of the column was only 4 mph, the soldiers were able to catch up 'at a leisurely jog'. The battery commander, of considerable girth, was wedged into a little Austin 7 motor car while the gun position officer's transport was a barely camouflaged fish van which continued to smell regardless of scrubbing with carbolic. The 60-pounders had massive recuperator springs, in tubes, to absorb recoil. The first calibrating round from one gun burst the tubes, the springs overtaking the shell and landing in an orchard.

139 One of the few American aircraft up to the warfare standards of the period was the Douglas DB-7 Boston light bomber. It was not available in sufficient numbers to equip squadrons during the critical period in 1940 but was later used in large numbers for bombing, night fighting and intruder operations. For all these roles it was far better equipped than the obsolescent Blenheim. This aircraft AH433, shown flying in the United States, was the third of an initial batch of 100 DB-7A Boston IIs ordered by the British Purchasing Commission in 1940. All Mk. IIs were converted at Burtonwood near Liverpool, into night fighters as Havoc Mk IIs. The first Bostons to arrive with the RAF consisted of a batch of 16 Mk Is aircraft ordered by Belgium and some contracted for by France which were diverted to Britain in 1940.

139

140 While Fighter Command was desperately building up its strength for the Battle of Britain, the new long range force for Bomber Command was beginning to materialise. Shown here in June 1940 is the second prototype Avro Manchester powered by two Vulture engines. The Vulture, which consisted of two Kestrel engines on a common crankshaft, was singularly unsuccessful and like the similar engine on the later Heinkel 177, frequently burst into flames. Re-equipped with four Merlins the Manchester became the Lancaster, one of the most successful and powerful bombers of the war.

140

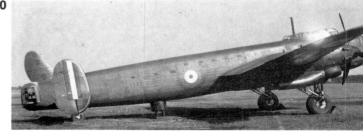

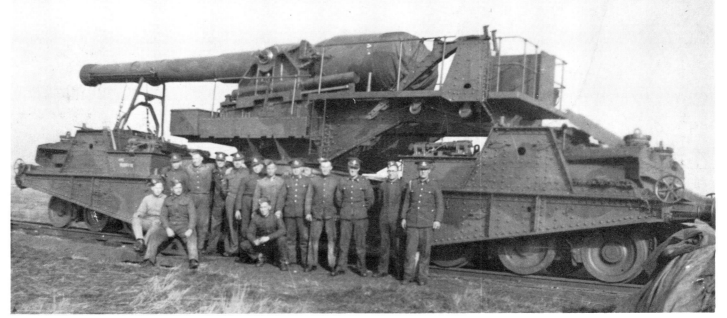

141 Railway guns became a speciality with the Royal Garrison Artillery in the First World War and the weapons lingered on to form a key part of Britain's defences in 1940. The BEF took a battery of these massive 9.2 inch guns to France in 1939 and they ended up firing horizontally from an embankment at an advancing German Panzer division. The guns were subsequently rolled over into a valley and the breech blocks thrown into a canal. The Territorial survivors returned from Dunkirk to man 9.2's operating on the Southern Railway networks in Kent and Sussex. This gun was based at Ashford and the final anti-invasion tally of 9.2's in the south-east was 26, representing tremendous fire-power capable of being aimed at the beach-heads.

142 Mobile guns were moved into position by rail but at the same time a number of naval weapons were converted into fixed emplacements. This heavy gun guarded a harbour approach area and is shown during practice firing in 1940, manned by a coastal defence gun crew.

143 The war produced all sorts of anomalies in the award of RAF pilots 'Wings'. In 1939 there were many hundreds of Civil Air Guard and RAF Volunteer Reserve pilots ready to go to Service Flying Training Schools for advanced flying. Because of the shortage of SFTS facilities a massive bottleneck developed and personnel were either held back or posted to do elementary training all over again. These would have been a godsend to Dowding in the summer of 1940. In marked contrast, some people with a civilian flying licence

walked into the Air Ministry as 'Mr' and walked out the other side as a pilot officer with wings. Probably the shortest wings course ever was achieved by Acting Squadron Leader (later Air Commodore) F R Banks. A leading civilian expert on aero engines and fuels, 'Rod' Banks had volunteered for the RAF in September 1939 and was sent to Boscombe Down to deal with engine problems. He had a private flying licence but could not put up RAF wings. Air Vice Marshal Roderick Hill arranged a 'fiddle' whereby Banks should go to Central Flying School Upavon for a 'refresher' course. He arrived on Sunday May 12, as the Germans poured into France and Belgium. On Monday he did 40 minutes dual on a Master and then went solo. After 4 hours he flew the Hurricane, the Spitfire and finally the twin-engined Blenheim. After five and a half days he finished the course and was awarded his wings—as promulgated in the letter shown here.

143

SINGLE-ENGINE AIRCRAFT				MULTI-ENGINE AIRCRAFT						PASS-ENGER	INSTR./CLOUD FLYING (Incl. in cols. (1) to (10))	
DAY		NIGHT		DAY			NIGHT					
DUAL	PILOT	DUAL	PILOT	DUAL	1ST PILOT	2ND PILOT	DUAL	1ST PILOT	2ND PILOT		DUAL	PILOT

6 - 6 - '40

C O P Y.

Acting Squadron Leader F. R. Banks

Sir,

I am directed to refer to your letter 24G/9740/39/Air 4. dated the 7th December, 1939 and to inform you that Acting Squadron Leader F.R. Banks is given authority herewith to wear the pilots Flying Badge with effect from the 17th May, 1940.

I am, Sir,
Your obedient Servant,

(Sgd) G. R. A. ELSMIE S/L

for Air Commodore,
Director of Training.

I concur in the award of Flying Badge to Squadron Leader (Acting) F.R. Banks.

Roderic Hill

Air Vice-Marshal.

Director-General of Research and Development.

17/6/40.

146 After Dunkirk, invasion was expected hourly. Road blocks appeared all over the country—albeit to a very haphazard pattern. The first to be erected consisted of farm carts and thereafter anything that came to hand. This road-block at East Peckham, Kent in June 1940, was made up of an ancient steamroller, two water carts and some steel rails.

147/8 To prevent glider landings, the open fields in the east and south-east were either ploughed up or scattered with obstacles including wooden poles. These photographs show steel hoops set in concrete blocks in a Kent field and a straight stretch of main road equipped with poles and wires.

144/5 From early June 1940 Britain became an anonymous island. Road signs and town signs disappeared and station name boards were painted over. Driving often became a nightmare as those with cars were treated with great suspicion if they asked where they were. The RAC and the AA did a roaring trade in providing detailed map routes for those who had to travel. Even the Army had to grope its way round unfamiliar country lanes.

149 One of the new types of aircraft entering RAF service in 1940 was the Bristol Beaufort torpedo-bomber. These aircraft were from No. 22 squadron (the first to receive Beauforts) which began life at Thorney Island in January 1940 and in April moved to North Coates-Fitties to undertake mine-laying operations. The Taurus radial engine on the Beaufort was plagued with problems, however.

One extraordinary result of the invasion threat in 1940 was the appearance on the roads of large numbers of home-made armoured vehicles converted from cars and vans. Built in garages and workshops, they showed great ingenuity but operationally could well have proved more lethal to the occupants than to the German army. These pictures show only a small selection of the 'one-offs'.

150 Local Defence Volunteers (later Home Guard) at Stroud, Gloucestershire, manning an armoured car built on a Morris chassis and named "The Eagle". Overhead fly three Spitfire Is.

151 A 1933 Sunbeam made unrecognisable by the addition of steel plate and a revolving machine gun turret. This unit of the Berkshire Home Guard had no uniforms, only a few steel helmets and a mixture of .303 Lee-Enfield and .300 American Kennington rifles.

152 A complete Home Guard armoured unit! A remarkable collection of armoured motor car conversions at Kings Lynn, Norfolk. From left to right; Ford, Hillman, Rover and 1934 Alvis 'Speed 20'. The idea for the chicken wire canopies came from early tanks of the First World War where netting was used to keep hand grenades out. On the two motor-cycles and one of the cars the louvered blackout covers for head-lights can be seen.

153 To give some anti-paratroop protection to airfields and aircraft factories, the Ministry of Aircraft Production ordered the 'Beaverette' which was a light armoured car based on the Standard 14 hp motor chassis. The army subsequently purchased Beaverettes in large quantities as light reconnaissance cars and altogether 2800 were built. The version shown here is the Beaverette Mk III with a fully enclosed body and a small turret mounting twin Vickers 'K' guns.

154 Your friendly British policeman meets the Luftwaffe. In this case a posed photograph taken in the Channel Islands after the Germans had occupied them.

155 Basic trainers like the Tiger Moth and the Magister were to be used in large numbers for bombing in the event of invasion. A scheme for fitting bombs on the Tiger Moth had been worked out for an Arab country in the mid-thirties. These plans were pulled out of the archives and in a very short time 1500 conversion sets had been produced for racks with eight 20 lb bombs. The bombs are shown here being loaded onto the racks under the rear cockpit of a Morris Motors-built Tiger Moth.

156 Some 40 armoured trains were improvised during the period 1939-1940. The engines carried armour plate as did the converted goods wagons. This wagon had a machine gun section using Bren guns and a second section mounting a 6-pounder Hotchkiss gun. This latter was retained from a First World War 'Male' tank and included the original curved shield.

157 The Hawker Henley two-seater carried 550 lb of bombs internally and its outer wing panels and tailplane were built on the same jigs as the Hurricane. Instead of being used for ground attack, the type was relegated by the Air Ministry to target towing, a total waste of a good aircraft and the Merlin engine. Some 200 Henleys were built but none was used in an offensive role. This Henley, L3286, was built by Glosters at Hucclecote and is shown, in mid-1940, ready for take-off. The pylon extending outwards from the rear cockpit was for air-towing the Mk III air towing sleeve for budding fighter pilots and air gunners to shoot at.

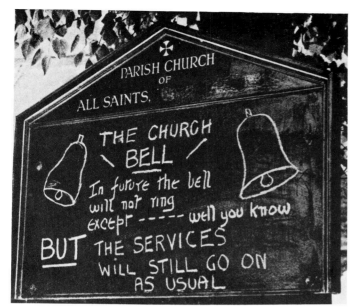

160 The sentinel at the gate, a German photograph of a barrage balloon floating over London before the blitz. The lower central feature of the picture is St Pauls Cathedral, later to stand out like an island in a sea of devastation.

158 On June 13, 1940, an order was issued prohibiting the ringing of church bells other than by the Army or the Police for the purpose of giving warning of airborne invasion. On this church board, the message was self-explanatory and the vicar had erased the parish name so that German paratroops should have no idea where they had landed. On the evening of September 7, the code-word Cromwell was issued to indicate an advanced state of readiness. Many thought it meant that invasion had started and the church bells were accordingly rung. Road blocks went up, roads were mined—killing some service personnel—and everywhere the Home Guard prepared for action. At one remote village in Sussex, following the bells, the local platoon was fully armed and ready to go but the only problem was that of communications. From the platoon commander's house the telephone hand crank was turned again and again. Finally the disgruntled voice of the elderly lady, who operated the exchange in the next village, was heard stating that she had been disturbed from her slumbers and that no-one was going to be connected to anyone, Germans or no Germans. It took 15 minutes persuasive talking to get her to connect the platoon with battalion headquarters in the nearest town and then leave the line plugged through.

159 A road block erected outside the Running Horse Inn on the Maidstone-Chatham road in June 1940. Holes were dug, wooden boxes put up, a girder sunk and concrete poured in. Later it was realised that to stop a tank, something a good deal thicker was necessary.

161 The Merlin engine assembly shop at the Rolls Royce Nightingale Road, Derby, factory known generally as 'The Glasshouse'. It was from here that the majority of all Merlins for Hurricanes and Spitfires emerged during the Battle of Britain. Production reached a peak of 100 engines per week with workers doing 72 hours per week.

162 During June 1940, the ARP organisation practised continuously to cope with the bombing that must come. The civil defence network was complex and well organised, covering the fire service, rescue squads, medical services, public utilities and the Air Road Wardens. Shown here is the control centre for the Borough of Gillingham ARP Organisation in Kent.

163 All over the country the call went out for aluminium to be re-processed into materials for making aircraft. Boy scouts, WVS, civil defence and many other organisations went round collecting saucepans, pots and kettles. These air raid wardens in Hull are viewing their salvage collection.

GASES USED IN WARFARE: WHAT THEY ARE AND HOW TO TREAT THEM

TYPES	NAME	SMELL	NATURE AND EFFECT		REMEDIES
I **Blister**	**MUSTARD**	VERY SLIGHT ONION GARLIC, OR HORSERAD -DISH	DARK BROWN OILY LIQUID	Most persistant-difficult to detect. Delayed action. Best Gas for spraying	*(Mustard)* Immediately apply bleach paste or bleach ointment. Then wash and scrub with soap and hot water (If bleach not available mop off before washing) Then (24 hours) Saline or Bicarbonate Dressing.
	LEWISITE	GERANIUMS, VERY STRONG	COLOURLESS VAPOUR	Quick action: Skin Stinging, Sneezing. (Leaves arsenic in blisters) Expensive and hitherto untried in Warfare	*(Lewisite)* Wash and Scrub with Soap and Hot Water. Break blisters (because of arsenic) Then treat as for mustard. But do not apply bleach paste or bleach ointment.
II **Lung** irritant (Choking)	**PHOSGENE**	MUSTY HAY	Powerful Lung irritants causing coughing, choking, with burning sensation in nose, throat and chest and irritation of eyes. Followed by Collapse and Acute Inflammation of Lungs.	*(Phosgene)* More deadly. Often followed by feeling of 'well-being' (Delayed Action) before Collapse	Stretcher Cases Keep warm. Treat as for Bronchitis and Collapse.
	CHLORINE	CHLORIDE OF LIME		*(Chlorine)* Collapse follows quickly (No Delayed Action)	
III **Nose** irritant (Sneezing)	DA DC DM	SCENTLESS	Intense depression general Influenza effects		Reassure Patient. Douche nose passages with Bicarbonate of Soda Solution In case of vomiting, drink Bicarbonate of Soda Solution
V **Tear** (Crying)	BBC KSK CAP	AROMATIC PEARDROPS SCENTLESS			Bathe eyes with Bicarbonate of Soda or Saline Then Oil or Vaseline No Bandage.

KEEP TO WINDWARD ~ WHERE THERE'S SMELL THERE'S DANGER

164 The possible uses of gas frightened both sides in the conflict. Following experience in the First World War, the British thought that it might be used by the Germans and were fully prepared to use it themselves in a last extremeity. Gas masks were issued to everyone and this poster shows the instructions issued for recognising the various types of gas that might be used. In the event, gas was not employed by any of the combatants.

165 A quiet smoke on a dump of bombs and fuel drums. A sergeant from No. 9 squadron lights up at Salon near Marseilles in June 1940. Hours before Italy declared war on June 11, six Wellingtons from No. 99 squadron flew to the South of France as a part of 'Haddock Force'. The French drove lorries onto the airfield to stop the Wellingtons taking off to bomb Italy, for fears of retaliation. One Wellington from No. 9 squadron was sent to Salon to do a recce in case the whole unit should be sent there but the situation deteriorated so quickly that the move never took place.

166 Circular to Observer Corps members issued from Bentley Priory in June 1940 by the Commandant, Air Commodore Warrington-Morris.

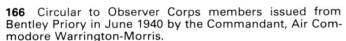

15. The following incidents have been reported by Posts crews:-

(a) An R.A.S.C. lorry arrived at an Observer Post with 1371 lbs of mutton. The mutton had been consigned to an R.A.F. formation in the district, and the driver assumed this to be an Observer Post. The address of the R.A.F. Unit was Wedlock Estate, Lovibond Road, and the "bit of meat" was delivered safely.

(b) At one Post a bomb dropped within 50 yards, but the Observers on duty were so busy plotting that they did not notice it. At another, where a bomb dropped closer I have been informed that I am to be asked to supply a new pair of trousers.

(c) A Coastal Post was much worried by seeing a red light at sea, and asked the Centre if any explanation could be suggested. The Centre replied that it might be a "Mermaids residence".

(d) A Posts crew were ordered to temporarily evacuate their Post on account of local gun practise as the shells were falling uncomfortably near. Another on the South Coast disturbed by a very violent nearby explosion were relieved when it was ascertained that it was only due to local quarry men blasting.

R.D. Warrington - Morris

Commandant,
OBSERVER CORPS.

PHASE I · JULY 10-AUGUST 7

By the beginning of July the brief Alice in Wonderland phase following Dunkirk had definitely finished. The two sides gazed at each other across the Straits of Dover and wondered what would happen next.

Britain's intelligence network on the continent had been ripped apart by the capture of two agents Best and Stevens in the 'Venlo' (Holland) incident of November 1939. The German occupation of France, Belgium and Holland had completed the intelligence rout. For the Germans, however, the situation was the same. There they sat, the victors of Europe, but the island on the other side of the Channel yielded nothing by the way of immediately useful information.

Because of accurate British code de-cryption and the turning of the German agents that were landed on the islands, the two German intelligence authorities, the Abwehr and the SD, could only get minimal information and most of this was false. Of great assistance to the British war effort—and the air war in particular—was Oberst 'Beppo' Schmid, head of Luftwaffe IC intelligence. A man of remarkably little ability, Schmid existed only to please his master Göring, which he did by telling him what he wanted to hear. He consistently underrated the RAF's resources, did not understand Britain's air defence system and misjudged target damage and losses.

Schmid felt that the RAF was easy meat and could be overwhelmed in a short space of time. For instance, by August 20 he estimated that the Luftwaffe had destroyed 664 RAF fighters between August 12 and 19 when the actual figure was 103. He also reported that forty-four RAF airfields had been attacked, of which eleven had been 'permanently destroyed' and twelve 'severely damaged'. Only five of the airfields 'destroyed' belonged to Fighter Command and of these one, Manston, was out of action for any length of time. With advice like that, it was hardly surprising that Göring could not understand why the RAF remained in existence.

To the British government, invasion appeared likely if not inevitable and the lack of knowledge of German intentions led the Army to split its main forces between the eastern and southern counties.

The Fighter Command Operational Diary for July referred to the 'Grand Assault on this country that was now overdue' and went on to report a conference of Group Commanders summoned by Dowding on July 3, to concert Fighter Command measures to repulse the 'Grand Assault' (ie the invasion). The Diary stated that the discussion was opened by the C-in-C who said that they were to discuss:

(a) the rearrangement of Groups caused by
   (i) the vulnerability of St. George's Channel and the North Channel
   (ii) by the alteration by the Navy of the main trade lines
(b) the tactics to be employed by fighters in the event of an invasion.

It was decided: (1) that the new No. 14 Group should include Aberdeen, Evanton and Wick.

(2) that No. 13 Group should include Turnhouse, Usworth, Catterick, Church Fenton, Squires Gate and Aldergrove; though conceivably, it might have been necessary to form an Irish Fighter Command or Group.

(3) that No. 12 Group should be split down the middle and have as its function the defence of a long narrow strip facing east.

(4) that No. 11 Group should now include Tangmere and Middle Wallop.*

(5) that No. 10 Group should include Ringway, Turnhill, Castle Bromwich and St. Evill, Barnstaple, Filton, Pembrey and Anglesey.

(6) that a new West Midland Group should be formed. The C-in-C thought it might be necessary to ask the Air Ministry for another Group on the South coast.

Turning to tactics the C-in-C thought that parachutists would begin the attack. Then troops might come by air transport, gliders and airborne tactics. Then would come fast motor boats. It seemed likely that barges carrying tanks would not arrive until the enemy had a foothold on our shores. The Germans would first push all they could into the air—transports, parachutists, gliders, tanks, flame-throwers; this glorified circus would be accompanied by bombers under an umbrella of fighters.

The Navy would have its part to play but could not expect much aid from fighters who were to have their own primary and overriding responsibilities.

Group Commanders would exercise more tactical control than usual and yet give liberty of action to sectors as far as possible. The squadron would be the smallest unit. For the first twenty-four hours everybody would have to work night and day. But as the attack proceeded, he wished everyone to be released for at least eight hours a day. Aerodromes were not to be abandoned except in the last resort.

The C-in-C also thought that the enemy might: (a) deal a battering-ram attack at one point (b) attack on a wide front and wait for an opportunity to break through.

*In the event, Middle Wallop became the main Sector Station for 10 Group.

He might push off expeditionary forces simultaneously from Norway, Denmark, Heligoland, Holland, Dunkirk, Ostend, Calais, Boulogne, Dieppe and Cherbourg.

A dispersed attack would be suitable for Fighter Command but not for the Army. The C-in-C thought that if only one squadron were sent up, one section should deal with fighters and two sections should deal with bombers. He would prefer the circus to arrive from one direction than that bombers should arrive from different directions. The Ju 90 was to be engaged in preference to other aircraft as it was a tank carrying machine.*

The C-in-C concluded with an emphatic repetition of his earlier remarks on the defence of aerodromes—the substance of which was stay and fight.

What both Churchill and Dowding had to have was an accurate Luftwaffe order of battle with some idea of reserves. From this could be calculated just how long Fighter Command had to survive in an air war of attrition.

Initially Air Intelligence grossly overestimated the forces available to the Luftwaffe, including its reserves. By early July, however, based on Ultra and straight Y-service information, Air Intelligence was able to reassess German front-line bomber strength at 1259—almost exactly right. Thereafter the staff at Air Intelligence, many of whom were volunteer reserve officers brought in from industry and commerce, built up a remarkably accurate picture of Luftwaffe strength, its re-supply capability and the composition of its units.

Air Intelligence was also able to tell the Air Staff that the long-range bomber units would complete refitting by July 8 and that the air offensive against Britain would begin at some point after July 1. That judgement was quite correct.

On the other side of the Channel, Göring had bestirred himself and, on June 30, issued preliminary instructions for the first phase of the battle. Air superiority over the English Channel must be established and the Channel itself denied to British shipping. This task was to be undertaken by Fliegerkorps II in the Pas de Calais under General Lörzer and Fliegerkorps VIII, near Le Havre, commanded by General Richthofen. Lörzer decided that no great force was necessary for his task and he allocated the job of closing the Straits of Dover to Johannes Fink commanding KG 2 equipped with Do 17s. With the resounding title of Kanalkampführer, Fink was given charge not only of the seventy-five Do 17s of KG 2 but also of sixty plus Ju 87 dive bombers and around 200 Bf 109 fighters. Two of the 109 units were commanded by pilots who had already achieved considerable distinction, namely Adolph Galland and Werner Mölders.

Richthofen only had Ju 87s, supported by fighters, to deal with his side of the affair, the area of which extended from Portland to Portsmouth.

The detailed orders for operations were issued on July 2 and thereafter small groups of bombers, with fighter escort, began attacks on shipping and ports. Over 30 Ju 87s hit

Portland on July 3 and found only AA fire barring their way. The forward airfield for Middle Wallop—Warmwell—had just been completed but fighters were not yet positioned there. The problem of air cover west of No. 11 Group's boundary was finally solved on July 13, when No. 10 Group, with HQ at Box, Wiltshire, came into being, its forces including No. 609 squadron at Middle Wallop and No. 87 squadron at Exeter.

During the first week of July raids were sporadic but it was clear that fighters had to be moved to forward airfields if cover was to be provided for the ships. With no steady long range build-up at altitude, the radar warning time was limited and squadrons tended to get bounced by the Luftwaffe escorts. In addition, the RAF was still flying in the ludicrous close formations laid down in the book, which made them very vulnerable to interceptors coming in from above, abeam and behind. Dunkirk had revealed the disastrous nature of these tactics but it was only gradually that the lessons began to sink in and, in most cases, loose formations were adopted as the result of clear thinking by individual squadron commanders.

One source of RAF losses at this period was the flying of offensive reconnaissance patrols over the Channel and France which could only result in the units involved being attacked by Bf 109s. Wisely these wasteful sorties were later discontinued.

Although July 10 was considered by the RAF to be the opening day of the Battle of Britain proper, there had been heavy skirmishing before that date and some extensive night raids. On the three days July 7-9, several sharp fights developed and there were significant losses on both sides, including 13 RAF pilots killed.

Gradually the population grew accustomed to the sirens, the noise and the damage. Initially it was fear of the unknown that had the greatest effect. The then editor of the Kent Messenger, H R P Boorman, recorded that, when bombs dropped on Lenham on July 4 'In a house nearby, an old lady of 80 was found sitting by herself downstairs with her gas mask on, a saucepan on her head, sobbing for all she was worth'. In complete contrast, at around the same time, a farmer driving a tractor was so absorbed in his work that he did not hear the fighting going on, or the crash of an aircraft. The first he knew, was the appearance of a German pilot who saluted and spoke to him in fluent English. The only thing the farmer could think to do was to take the pilot home, give him a cup of tea and send for the police.

The German attacks from July 10 onwards began in a somewhat haphazard fashion, with numerous small attacks by day and by night on a wide variety of targets, sharp attacks on certain ports and the main emphasis on convoys and shipping generally. In effect Luftflotten 2 and 3 were feeling their way, probing the defences and trying to destroy as many British fighters as possible.

In some ways the Luftwaffe had the advantage, as the raiding formations dropped their loads either over the

*There were only a handful of Ju 90s available and none of them could ever have carried a tank.

Channel or at the coast. On cloudy days the enemy was difficult to find and, if spotted, was very likely to have fighter escort close by and above.

The 'official' first day of the Battle of Britain, July 10, was typical of many to follow and is worth looking at in some detail. In the morning, off the north Kent coast, a Do 17P reconnaissance aircraft with a strong escort, discovered a large convoy code-named 'Bread'. The force was engaged by Spitfires and the Dornier was damaged, subsequently crashing in France. The convoy's whereabouts was however now quite clear and Luftflotte 2 prepared to attack it at lunchtime when it was off Dover. Some 25 Do 17s, escorted by 50 Bf 109s and Bf 110s took part in the action which was hotly contested by elements of three Hurricane and two Spitfire squadrons. Three Dorniers, one Bf 110 and two Bf 109s were destroyed while the RAF lost one Hurricane and suffered damage to others.

Away on the West coast, Luftflotte 3 tested the air defences and found them wanting—with patchy radar coverage and too little warning. Over sixty bombers attacked Falmouth and the area round Swansea. Sixty casualties were caused (of which 30 were deaths) and a Royal Ordnance Factory was hit. A reminder that anything that moved was considered fair game by the Luftwaffe came on this day when a train near Newhaven was bombed, the driver being killed and the guard injured.

For the next eight days the pattern of operations remained much the same with major convoys being attacked as they passed down the Channel and a variety of targets, including ports and airfields being subjected to raids by small bomber formations, plus extensive airborne mine-laying. The bombing attacks were not made to any consistent plan as the airfields did not belong to Fighter Command and the aircraft factory hit—at Yeovil on July 15—was not building fighters or bombers then operating with front line units.

Putting patrols over the convoys and reinforcing them when under attack was, however, wearing down Dowding's forces. Between July 10 and 18 inclusive, 34 fighters had been destroyed, more damaged and a number of pilots killed or injured. The Luftwaffe's losses were substantial considering the lack of real results but the units were being provided with invaluable experience.

It was evident that the fighter defences had to be strengthened to the West to curtail Luftwaffe incursions. On July 13, Dowding moved No. 152 squadron and its Spitfires from Acklington, Northumberland to join No. 609 squadron at Middle Wallop, Hampshire, while, for the defence of Plymouth, a flight of Gladiator biplanes from No. 247 was moved from the Shetlands to the small grass airfield at Roborough, Devon.

On July 16, unknown to Churchill and War Cabinet, Hitler issued his famous Directive No. 16, the opening paragraph of which stated: 'Since England, in spite of her hopeless military situation, shows no signs of being ready to come to an understanding, I have decided to prepare a landing operation against England and, if necessary, to carry it out.

The aim of this operation will be to eliminate the English homeland as a base for the prosecution of the war against Germany and, if necessary, to occupy it completely'.

This Directive was followed, on July 17, by a German Army High Command allocation of thirteen picked divisions to the Channel coast to prepare for ultimate embarkation as the first wave of the invasion.

On July 19, the two seat Boulton Paul Defiant fighter was finally shown to be unsuitable for the day battle. Newly arrived from Edinburgh, No. 141 squadron got airborne from Hawkinge at around midday. The nine Defiants were bounced out of the sun by twenty Bf 109s. Five Defiants fell in the sea and one on land; three returned to base covered by the Hurricanes of III squadron. What was left of a very sad unit moved to Prestwick in Scotland. It was on the 19th that Fighter Command flew more sorties than ever before—701—but lost eight machines to the Germans two.

On July 19, Hitler made his 'Last Appeal to Reason' speech in the Reichstag, Berlin, in which he claimed he was 'The victor speaking in the name of reason'. Thousands of English translation reprints of this were despatched to the Luftwaffe for air delivery on the apparently quaking population of England. They subsequently floated down, to be chewed by cows and sheep and auctioned by village communities for the Spitfire fund. As late as August 10, the Luftwaffe was still trying to get rid of this rubbish; it succeeded in unloading about one hundredweight directly onto the Barming Mental Hospital in Kent. There is no record of what the inmates thought of it.

Right up to August 7, the main effort stayed against shipping and ports and Dowding complained bitterly of the necessity to provide standing patrols over slow convoys up and down the coast.

Invasion plans across the Channel were progressing and it was significant that, on August 1, a high-wing two-seat Henschel 126 battlefield reconnaissance aircraft of 4 (H) 31 was being used off the south coast when it was intercepted by 145 squadron aircraft. The 126 succeeded in killing Sub Lt Kestin of the Royal Navy in his Hurricane but was, in its turn, destroyed by another aircraft of the same squadron.

The Luftwaffe felt they had the measure of the RAF despite the fact that, during July, they had managed to sink eighteen small steamers and four destroyers for the loss of 270 aircraft (due to all causes), compared with the direct British loss of 145 fighters. Göring and his staff had been preparing for 'Adlerangriff' or Eagle Day, which was to mark the opening of the real air offensive against RAF Fighter Command itself and its bases. The Reichsmarschall was confident that this new phase would bring the opposing fighter squadrons into an arena of his choosing, where they could be destroyed at will. The skies would then be clear for the bombers to pound down strategic and tactical objectives in southern England as they pleased, with only anti-aircraft gunfire to worry about.

It was likely, so Göring thought, that this phase, on its own, would lead to a British surrender, or at least a request for armistice terms. He would then be able to prove to Hitler that air power *was* the supreme instrument and that the failure to destroy the BEF at Dunkirk was a pure accident.

His assumptions were based on poor intelligence, lack of military knowledge and, above all, lack of personal experience. What had happened in the skies over France was, he believed, about to be repeated over the shores of England.

He did not know or understand Dowding, nor did he wish to . He also did not know that, despite a month of attacks and air combat, Dowding had succeeded in building up his forces from 587 aircraft operationally available and 1200 pilots on June 30 to 708 aircraft and 1434 pilots on August 3. There were fifty-five fighter squadrons available with more under training, including the Canadians and the Poles. Beyond this, the air defence system as a whole had been proved under battle conditions, many of the snags overcome and the whole network was working at a maximum pitch of efficiency.

Bomber and Coastal Commands had not been idle in this period. Twin-engined bombers roamed the skies of Germany at night just as did those of the Luftwaffe. The bombing was not very accurate but Göring was made acutely embarrassed by it. Light bombers also made several sharp attacks in daylight on airfields in occupied territory, while night bombing of Channel ports reminded the German Army that the RAF would strongly contest any invasion that might be launched. Coastal command flew far and wide reconnoitering the seaways and contributing its own bombs.

Anti-Aircraft Command steadily improved its accuracy in daylight and German crews developed a very healthy respect for British flak which claimed a number of victims. At night the story was different. The only glimmer of hope for a future antidote to the night raider came on July 23 when an AI radar-equipped Blenheim from the Fighter Interception Unit at Tangmere successfully located a Do 17 and shot it down into the Channel. With a combination of information from a coastal CH station and the crude blip on the Blenheim's cathode ray tube, the world's first successful radar-directed fighter interception at night had been made.

Ju 87s taking off past their unit's standard from a French airfield.

DIARY JULY 10-AUGUST 7

The losses shown in these diaries include write-offs through accidents on all Luftwaffe types in the war area and on RAF fighters. Losses by other RAF Commands are not included. Damaged aircraft not included.

July 10: Day: Battle over convoy off Dover. Serious raids on Falmouth and Swansea.
Night: Raids on Home Counties, east coast and western Scotland.
Losses: Luftwaffe 13: RAF 6.

July 11: Day: Many recce sorties. Portland, Portsmouth and south east convoy bombed.
Night: Scattered raids from south west and south east through to Yorkshire.
Losses: Luftwaffe 21: RAF 7.

July 12: Day: Shipping attacks off Isle of Wight, Norfolk-Suffolk and Aberdeen.
Night: Raids on Bristol and South Wales.
Losses: Luftwaffe 9: RAF 8

July 13: Day Shipping attacks, Dover and Portland.
Night: Thames estuary minelaying.
Losses: Luftwaffe 7: RAF 5

July 14: Day: Shipping attack off Dover.
Night: Scattered raids, Bristol, Isle of Wight, Kent and Suffolk.
Losses: Luftwaffe 3: RAF 1

July 15: Day: Norfolk coast and Channel shipping raids. Raid on Westland factory, Yeovil.
Night: Minelaying.
Losses: Luftwaffe 5: RAF 3

July 16: Day: little activity due to bad weather.
Night: North-east coast, minelaying.
Losses: Luftwaffe 3: RAF nil.

July 17: Day: Factory at Ardeer, Ayrshire, bombed, light attacks on south east coastal shipping.
Night: Light raids in south west: minelaying.
Losses: Luftwaffe 4: RAF 1

July 18: Day: Raids on Montrose, Aberdeen and convoys off south coast.
Night: Minimal activity.
Losses: Luftwaffe 5: RAF 6

July 19: Day: Dover, Folkestone area, Selsey and Portland.
Night: South coast, Thames Estuary and Harwich.
Losses: Luftwaffe 5: RAF 10

July 20: Day: Convoy battles off the south coast.
Night: Widespread minelaying.
Losses: Luftwaffe 16: RAF 7

July 21: Day: Channel convoys.
Night: Merseyside.
Losses: Luftwaffe 12: RAF 2

July 22: Day: South coast shipping.
Night: Minelaying down the east coast.
Losses: Luftwaffe 3: RAF 2

July 23: Day: Slight activity over east coast convoys.
Night: Widespread minelaying.
Losses: Luftwaffe 6: RAF 4

July 24th: Day: Channel and Medway convoys.
Night: No activity.
Losses: Luftwaffe 13: RAF 4

July 25: Day: Heavy fighting over Channel convoys.
Night: Reconnaissance, Bristol and English Channel and minelaying in Thames Estuary and Firth of Forth.
Losses: Luftwaffe 16: RAF 7

July 26: Day: Only slight convoy activity due to bad weather.
Night: Minelaying.
Losses: Luftwaffe 2: RAF 4

July 27: Day: Convoy off Swanage, destroyers sunk off Dover and Suffolk and raid on Belfast.
Night: Targets in the south-west.
Losses: Luftwaffe 4: RAF 3

July 28: Day: Attacks on Dover
Night: Widespread minelaying.
Losses: Luftwaffe 13: RAF 5

July 29: Day: Convoy off Dover, convoy off Portland.
Night: Limited activity.
Losses: Luftwaffe 13: RAF 4

July 30: Day: Small raids over Scotland and off east coast.
Night: Small scale raids and minelaying.
Losses: Luftwaffe 7: RAF 1

July 31: Day: Reconnaissance and limited convoy attacks.
Night: South Wales and Thames Estuary.
Losses: Luftwaffe 4: RAF 5

August 1: Day: Attack on Norwich, Boulton-Paul factory hit.
Night: South Wales and Midlands minelaying.
Losses: Luftwaffe 16 (plus 3 in RAF raid over Holland): RAF 2

August 2: Day: Shipping attacked in Channel and off east coast.
Night: Light raids on Midlands and South Wales. Minelaying.
Losses: Luftwaffe 5: RAF 2

August 3: Day: Shipping reconnaissance.
Night: South Wales, Liverpool, Crewe and Bradford.
Losses: Luftwaffe 4: RAF nil.

August 4: Day: Reconnaissance.
Night: Little activity.
Losses: Luftwaffe 3: RAF 2

August 5: Day: Shipping in Dover Straits.
Night: Minelaying on east and north east coasts.
Losses: Luftwaffe 2: RAF 2

August 6: Day: Little activity.
Night: Minelaying.
Losses: Luftwaffe 4: RAF 5

August 7: Day: Convoy off Cromer; reconnaissance.
Night: Widespread raids from the Thames to Aberdeen, from Poole to Cornwall and north to Liverpool.
Losses: Luftwaffe 6 (plus 2 in RAF bombing raid on continent): RAF 5

Reference No:-
OC/150.

Headquarters, Observer Corps,
Bentley Priory,
STANMORE,
Middx.

Circular No.25.   7th August, 1940.

1.   There has been nothing of special note during the last fortnight regarding enemy raids, but the Prime Minister has emphasised the necessity for all to be on their guard against a sudden attack.   The small amount of activity by the German Air Force indicates that their Air Force is being conserved for large scale attacks.

2.   Parachute dummies were successful in diverting the attention of defenders in Holland and Belgium, and might be used for a similar purpose in this country. All members of the Observer Corps should be on their guard against this and other ruses.

3.   Reports on a variety of subjects are called for from the Observer Corps and replies have in general proved to be very reliable.   Speed and accuracy in the reporting of aircraft are of the greatest importance.   One minutes delay in passing messages through to the R.A.F. causes an error of at least 4 miles in position.   This is not always fully realised by some members of Centres and Posts, especially when tracking by "Sound".   Particular attention should be drawn to this matter by those in charge.

167 Circular issued in early August by the Commandant, Royal Observer Corps, Air Commodore Warrington-Morris.

168 Instructions for an Observer Corps Centre on how to report airborne landings by enemy troops. These applied to the area of No. 9 York Group but similar instructions were issued to all Observer Groups in vulnerable parts of the country.

3. PARACHUTISTS.

(a)   Seen by Post crews. If parachutists, more than six in number, are seen by an Observer Post, a message is to be transmitted as above giving the estimated number of parachutes, and the approximate square in which they land.
Example of message:- To Army and R.A.F.
"16.30 hours 20 parachutes dropping V.8713."
        Repetition to Chief Constable (Northallerton) will read:-
"20 enemy parachutes dropping one mile East of Northallerton"
        It is to be noted that messages to Army and R.A.F. are given by grid reference, but those to Chief Constables must give the distance and compass direction from a place named on Ordnance Maps.
        Also it is necessary to state whether the parachutes are 'friend' or 'enemy', if this is known, when making reports to Chief Constables.

4.   The dropping of FEWER THAN SIX parachutes, and the dropping of parachutes from aircraft identified as our own, is to be reported to the O.C.L.O. only.

5.   LANDING OF TROOP CARRIERS OR GLIDERS.
        These are to be reported to the authorities given in Para:2.
Example:- To Army and R.A.F.
"16.55 hours 12 gliders landing A.3561"
        Repeated to Chief Constable (E.Riding)
"12 enemy gliders landing one mile South of Market Weighton".

169 Pilots of No. 92 squadron relax on the grass at Bibury, Gloucestershire waiting for the call to scramble. On the left is Flight Lt C B F Kingcombe, while behind is a Spitfire with the starter trolley plugged in. In the extreme right-hand is the nose of a Proctor communications aircraft.

170 The United States came to the aid of beleagured Britain in July 1940 by selling stocks of arms from its reserve arsenals. The deal covered 900 'Seventy-five' field guns of various types, including modified British 18-pounders and American-made weapons, and half a million .300 Kennington rifles with 1000 rounds of ammunition apiece. Top priority was given to the shipments which were made in fast liners escorted by battleships and cruisers. As they neared Britain, they were met by destroyers and flying boats and escorted into harbour. First shipments arrived towards the end of July. The photograph shows a No. 210 squadron Sunderland over the convoy, with HMS *Revenge* in the centre. The Sunderland proved to be a major asset in the maritime role and earned its nickname of the 'Flying Porcupine' with its eight machine guns.

171/2 Much attention was given by the Luftwaffe to air-sea rescue and Seenotflug-Kommando units operated from Brest, Cherbourg, Boulogne and Wilhelmshafen. In the main they used He 59 floatplanes plus some Do 18's, Do 24's and impressed French Bréguet Bizertes. As they were picking up aircrew which would return to fight another day, the British Government publicly announced that it would grant these machines no immunity even if they carried Red Cross markings. The white painted He 59 in the lower photograph was shot down by No. 54 squadron on July 9 and towed to the beach at Deal by the Walmer lifeboat. The camouflaged He 59 in the photograph left was from Seenotflug Kdo 3 based at Boulogne and is shown lifting a pilot from the sea. This particular seaplane, DA + WT, was lost in an accident on September 7.

173/4 The Kent hopfields in July were short of pickers who normally came in large numbers from the East End of London. Local army units stepped into fill the breach as shown right. The hopfields also became the recipients of bombs, machine gun bullets and wrecked aircraft. The second photograph shows an aircraftman and crowd of hop pickers examining the remains of a Do 17 from 8/KG 77 damaged by fighters and then shot down by anti-aircraft fire at Marden on July 1.

175 The burned-out wreck of a Do 17 shot down by fighters near Portisham, Dorset in July.

176 A No. 56 Squadron Hurricane ends up nose in the hedge on the Epping road after overshooting North Weald in July.

177 Fighter-reconnaissance patrols over France in July often led to RAF losses to Bf 109's. This Spitfire is believed to have been from No. 64 Squadron, Kenley, shot down near Rouen on July 5.

178 The ageing Swordfish naval biplane was used in a remarkable number of rôles throughout the Second World War. At the time of Dunkirk, numerous sorties were flown and thereafter No. 1812 squadron, under Coastal Command control, carried out minelaying and bombing operations against the invasion ports. The photograph shows an aircraft wrecked in France after a night raid over Dunkirk.

179 The high-wing Westland Lysander with its slots and flaps was the standard short-field capabilities army co-operation aircraft in 1940 and it was used later in the war for agent and saboteur dropping and pick-ups in Europe. The Lysander carried racks for bombs/supplies on the undercarriage legs. This very bent target-towing Lysander was at Southend in July.

180 Bomber Command began its night offensive against targets on the continent from May 1940 onwards. This Merlin-powered Whitley V Bomber was taking off from Linton-on-Ouse, Yorkshire for Germany in July.

181 A vital task was the calibration of the Chain Home (radar) system. In November 1939 it had been agreed by the Air Minstry that the Cierva Autogiro Company should undertake such work under the control of test pilot R A 'Reggie' Brie. Initially three and later five C.30A Rota autogiros were used to calibrate the stations from the Isle of Wight to the Orkneys. Brie was made a Squadron Leader and, on May 1, 1940, the unit became No. 1448 Rota Calibration Flight based at RAF Duxford, attached to No. 19 Fighter Squadron. The C.30's were fitted with special tail aerials and a calibrating radio transmitter. One C.30A so equipped is shown being wheeled across the grass at Duxford in July. The C.30A was powered by a 140 hp Genet Major radial engine and had a maximum speed of 100 mph.

182 As the bombing began, even animals were supposed to take cover! While families were busy with Anderson shelters, the RSPCA was recommending the 'Dustbin dugout' for pets. The instructions read: 'Constructed from an ordinary household dustbin, the RSPCA recommend this simple form of shelter for a dog or cat. The dustbin lid, pierced with a number of airholes, should be placed over the entrance, affording additional protection, and, within a few inches of the shelter, a fairly high mound of soft earth should be heaped. Alternatively, a dog could be secured inside the bin by a short chain, in which case the lid need not be used'. There is no record of how many, if any, of these remarkable contraptions were built or how pets felt inside them as the bombs crashed down outside.

183
184

185

183   Key people, the mechanics fitters and armourers, seen here working on a Hurricane 1 at a dispersal. Without the devotion to duty of the ground crews, the fighter squadrons would have ceased to operate.

184   The Boulton Paul Defiant was built to Air Ministry specification F.9/35 which called for a monoplane successor to the turret Demon biplane fighter. The basic concept was, however, wrong for an interceptor which had to live in the environment of fast, well-armed single-seaters like the Bf 109. The Defiant had the same Merlin power plant as the Spitfire and Hurricane but it had to carry the heavy weight of a four gun dorsal turret and an extra crew member. There were only two Defiant squadrons operational during the Battle of Britain, Nos. 141 and 264. No. 141 had a tough battle with 109's on July 19, lost six aircraft and was withdrawn north on July 21, while No. 264 suffered a similar fate in August and was taken off day operations. Both squadrons had much more success at night and the Defiant became the standard single-engined night fighter. Shown here is a group of No. 264's pilots and air gunners at Kirton-in-Lindsey, August.

185   Three Hurricanes of No. 151 Squadron just airborne from North Weald in July.

186   A further three No. 151 Squadron Hurricanes airborne at North Weald over another aircraft from the same squadron.

187 No. 32 Squadron on stand-by at Hawkinge in July. Five of the pilots are wearing Mae West life jackets.

188 Refuelling operation being carried out with a three-arm tanker vehicle capable of refuelling three aircraft at once if required.

189 In an attempted raid on Portsmouth in the early evening of July 11, He III's with Bf 110 escort, were mauled by fighters from Tangmere. This 2/KG 55 Heinkel crashed onto the beach between Selsey and Pagham, Sussex. Two of the crew were killed and three injured.

190 The crew of a Do 17 from IV/KG 3 based in Belgium stand in front of their aircraft. The cumbersome life jackets are noteworthy.

191 Reconnaissance was a major preoccupation of the Luftwaffe. Here, in a well-rehearsed session for the photographer, the pilot of a KG 53 Heinkel III hands a tin of film to a despatch rider.

192 The Air Council meeting at the Air Ministry in July 1940. From left to right, round the table, Air Marshal Sir Christopher Courtney (Air Member for Supply and Organisation), Air Marshal E L Gossage (Air Member for Personnel), Captain H H Balfour (Parliamentary Under Secretary of State for Air), Sir Archibald Sinclair (Secretary of State for Air), Air Chief Marshal Sir Cyril Newall (Chief of the Air Staff), Sir Arthur Street (Permanent Under Secretary) and Air Chief Marshal Sir Wilfred Freeman (Air Member for Development and Production).

193 A No. 92 squadron Spitfire at dispersal with the pilot in the cockpit and the starter trolley plugged in.

194 Used for detecting British convoys and tracking them for Stuka attack, this German Freya radar set was installed on the cliffs at Wissant in late July. It had no aircraft reporting function and therefore took no part in the air battle as such. Had Freyas been erected for air detection and the proper communications supplied, it would have been possible to watch RAF fighter movements and warn Luftwaffe formations of impending attack.

193

194

195 Göring in France with his personal Mercedes and staff. The battered forage cap hardly went with the rest of the uniform but the cigar box indicated a good dinner in view.

196 Pilot Officer M J Appleby of No. 609 squadron in his Spitfire at Middle Wallop. The motto under the deer and crown emblem reads 'Resurgam'.

197 North Weald in July; pilots from No. 151 Squadron in front of a Hurricane. Fourth from the left is Squadron Leader (later Group Captain) E M Donaldson, No. 151's CO. He had been shot down in the sea the previous day and was highly displeased, on return, to find that the squadron had a new but very temporary CO. Fifth from the left is Wing Comman-der F V Beamish, North Weald Station Commander who flew frequently during the Battle and was awarded the DSO, DFC and AFC. On the extreme right is Flying Officer R M Milne who, later in the war commanded the Biggin Hill Spitfire Wing.

198 The limited range of the Ju 87 was overcome, in the case of the Ju 87R (R = Reichweite = range) with increased internal tankage and 66 gallon underwing drop-tanks. These aircraft were first seen by the RAF over Hampshire in July and this example was from III/StG2 'Immelmann'. The fitting of drop tanks reduced the bombload.

199 Joint leader with Kesselring in the Battle of Britain, Generalfeldmarschall Hugo Sperrle commanded Luftflotte 3. Extremely tough and unpleasant, Sperrle had originally joined an infantry regiment in 1903. He flew in the First World War and ultimately commanded the front-line flying formations attached to the army. He was in the secret air force of the Reichswehr from 1919 onwards and commanded the Condor Legion in Spain.

200 Generalfeldmarschall Kesselring (second from right) was originally a gunner and served as a staff officer in the First World War. His association with the air force did not begin until 1933 when he was posted to the Air Ministry. For one year from June 1936, he was Chief of the air force general staff and then commanded Luftflotte 1 in the attack on Poland and Luftflotte 2 in the assault in the West. He was the head of Luftflotte 2 throughout the Battle of Britain. A very able officer, Kesselring is probably remembered more for his command of land forces in Italy and the West than for his air efforts against the British Isles in 1940.

201 Air Vice Marshal (later Air Chief Marshal) Sir Keith Park, AOC No. 11 Group throughout the Battle of Britain. A forceful and dedicated New Zealander, Park joined the army in 1911 and transferred to the Royal Flying Corps in 1917. He continued as a professional RAF officer and, as Senior Air Staff Officer, Fighter Command, was closely associated with the organisation and build-up of the fighter network. His command of 11 Group in 1940 showed a brilliant understanding of tactical requirements and he must be considered the key battle commander of 1940. Park understood Dowding's thinking and methods and there was considerable mutual respect between the two men.

202 Dover became a prime target for the Luftwaffe during July and suffered numerous raids of varying intensity. This photograph was taken at breakfast-time on July 29 at the height of an attack by 48 Ju 87s of LG 1, StG 1 and StG 4 escorted by some eighty Bf 109s. The force was met by No. 41 squadron Spitfires from Manston and No. 501 squadron Hurricanes from Hawkinge. Four Ju 87s were shot down while the RAF lost a Hurricane and Spitfire with several more damaged. Bombs can be seen bursting among the ships in the harbour while five Stukas wheel around amid the bursting anti-aircraft shells.

203 Generalmajor Theodor Osterkamp who commanded Jagdfliegerführer 2, with all the Bf 109 and Bf 110 fighter forces in the north-east France, facing England. His fighter Gruppen provided the escorts for many of the Channel attacks in July. Osterkamp is shown here conferring with other officers at his headquarters at Wissant.

204 Air Vice Marshal (later Air Chief Marshal Sir) Trafford Leigh-Mallory, who commanded No. 12 Fighter Group in 1940. Leigh-Mallory was extremely ambitious and disliked both Dowding and Park. He was the cause of considerable friction during the Battle of Britain and Dowding can perhaps be blamed for not either calling him to heel or removing him. Leigh-Mallory was in league with Air Vice Marshal Sholto Douglas (later Marshal of the RAF Lord Douglas of Kirtleside), at that time Deputy Chief of the Air Staff. It was hardly

surprising, that, after the Battle of Britain, when Dowding and Park were hurriedly removed from their commands, Sholto Douglas should become C-in-C Fighter Command and Leigh-Mallory should get No. 11 Fighter Group.

205 Air Chief Marshal Hugh Caswall Tremenheere Dowding, the architect and Commander of Fighter Command on whose shoulders rested the fate of Britain and of the British Empire in 1940. As a military strategic planner on the grand scale, Dowding has probably had no peer. First commissioned as a gunner in 1900, Dowding learned to fly at Brooklands in 1913 and subsequently gained his Royal Flying Corps Wings in the spring of 1914. He flew a wide variety of types and ended the war as a Brigadier-General. In 1930 Dowding became Air Member for Supply and Research and, later, Air Member for Research and Development. He had early shown a marked interest in and understanding of all

205 types of technical matters relating to aviation and his work in the first half of the thirties brought him into close contact with airframes, engines, armaments, radio and, eventually radar in embryo. Knowledge of these, plus his planning ability, enabled Dowding to produce an overall air defence system based on technology and capable of fighting a modern air war. It was the world's prototype and it withstood the full might of the Luftwaffe thrown against it in 1940. Dowding was an aloof and somewhat withdrawn man, characteristics which earned him the nickname 'Stuffy' at Staff College. He had, however, an abiding interest in those who worked for him particularly the fighter pilots whom Churchill christened Dowding's chicks. He could and did stand up against the Air Ministry or anyone else who wanted to interfere with the smooth and effective running of Fighter Command or inhibit its progress. In both brain and character, Dowding was the complete antithesis of Hermann Göring, which is one of the reasons why the RAF did not lose the Battle of Britain.

204

206 Generaloberst Hans-Jürgen Stumpff was one of the original group of German air force planning officers secreted in the German Defence Ministry in 1920. In the Thirties he became head of the operations staff of the air force general staff and in 1937, Chief of the Air Staff. On the outbreak of war, Stumpff was commanding Luftflotte 3. At the end of April 1940, Stumpff took over the air command in Norway as the head of Luftflotte 5, which position he held until January 1944. Luftflotte 5 was severely mauled in August 1940 and some of its units were transferred to the Channel coast.

207 By July the Home Guard was beginning to have some semblance of military organisation and over one million men were engaged in watching over and guarding their localities. Essentially a static force, the Home Guard was able to relieve the army of a multitude of duties. This duplicated sheet was part of orders and rosters issued by the Home Guard at Crookham, Berkshire.

Now that the moon is waning, it becomes possible to temporarily reduce Patrols. As from Monday, there will, therefore, be one Patrol (two men) only on each Watch, instead of two Patrols (four men). The single Patrols will cover only the main road between the "Volunteer" and "Travellers' Friend", and make one contact only, i.e. at Greenham. It will concentrate on the area ½ mile on either side of signpost. There is no objection to short spells of sitting, provided Patrols maintain effective observation.

Each Patrol to report at Crookham House 10 minutes before duty time, for latest orders, arms and ammunition.

Times of Watches remain unaltered.

Under no circumstances must arms and ammunition be left out by either Patrol. It _must_ be passed to relieving Patrol, or handed in at Crookham House.

Arms: The Short Lee-Enfield service rifles and ammunition have been called in, and replaced by a larger number of new American Rifles of the Springfield type. Each man should make himself familiar with the new arm as quickly as possible.

PHASE 2·AUGUST 8-23

The second week of August 1940 saw the beginning of a period of intense air warfare in which both sides made maximum efforts. Between August 11 and 18 more Sorties were flown and more actions took place than during any other comparable period.

Göring was now aiming to destroy the vitals of Fighter Command, including its radar stations and its airfields. In so doing he hoped to bring into combat, and crush, the bulk of Dowding's force of Hurricanes and Spitfires.

What the Reichsmarschall needed was a period of fine weather in the shape of a belt of high pressure approaching slowly from the Azores. Code-named 'Adlerangriff' and to be opened on 'Adlertag' (Eagle Day), the offensive was intended to achieve air superiority over Southern England in 'four days'. Thereafter the Luftwaffe could bomb land targets at will, lay the mine barrage in the Channel for the landing fleet and prepare to act as the mobile artillery for the invasion which bore the code name 'Seelöwe' or Sealion.

In fact Göring still imagined that not only would he achieve air superiority very rapidly but that this alone would suffice for Britain to come to terms. Hitler liked the idea as it seemed to him Britain was on its last legs and victory in the air would preclude the necessity for an opposed landing across the Channel.

Apart from the strength and organisation of Fighter Command, however, what militated against the Luftwaffe was overall lack of numbers, particularly Bf 109s. The 109 also lacked the essential range to penetrate deeply into England and then 'mix it' for some time before returning across the Channel.

August 8 showed a marked increase in activity with heavy raids on a Channel convoy 'Peewit' causing the loss of four merchant ships sunk and six damaged, plus six armed rescue vessels damaged. Before dawn the convoy had been attacked by German E-boats which sank three ships. This was the heaviest convoy battle to be fought during the summer of 1940 and its resulted in highest losses on both sides since Dunkirk.

The 9th and 10th were quiet due to the weather. It did not improve enough on the Sunday, the 11th, for the full-scale 'Adlertag' attack but did allow sufficient time for a very heavy attack on Weymouth and Portland by a force of 150 aircraft which was met by seven RAF squadrons. The Luftwaffe was using feints to draw British fighters away from the area of a main raid and, in this case, they were directed at Dover.

With the weather improving, 'Adlertag' was set for August 13, when the whole arena would be moved from the Channel to the British mainland itself. As a prelude, on the 12th, the Luftwaffe launched a series of attacks intended to put out of action the main radar screen and forward airfields.

Luftwaffe Signals Intelligence, under General Martini, had correctly deduced the importance of the giant towers strung out round the coast but all sections of German Intelligence failed to understand how the control and reporting system worked or that it was producing a total three-dimensional picture of the air situation, broken down into suitable sections for Groups and Sectors. As no such system had ever before been constructed—and certainly did not exist in Germany—it is easy to understand the Luftwaffe's lack of comprehension.

It was assumed that, if holes could be punched in the radar chain, then large areas would be without early warning and control would break down. Similarly, if certain coastal airfields could be rendered uninhabitable, fighters would have to operate from further back; they would thus be late in intercepting and would be at a disadvantage in height and position when attacked by the waiting Messerschmitts.

The radars, in fact, had overlap, they were difficult to destroy and mobiles were ready to plug in to fill any gaps. The most forward airfields, like Manston and Lympne, were too far forward for proper warning. They were to prove a liability to the RAF and should have been abandoned at an early stage in the battle.

The attacks on the 12th were aimed at Dunkirk, Dover, Rye, Pevensey and Ventnor CH stations. In her book 'The Eyes of the Few', Daphne Carne describes the raid on Rye as follows:-

'I passed another couple of plots, enough to make it quite evident that if they continued on the same course they would pass overhead. "Stanmore, is this track still unidentified? There's an X just been put on it". Syd was standing over Helen watching the track and F/O Smith was behind me, watching the tube. "Corporal, you'd better warn the guns and I think it would be a good idea if we had our tin hats he said"...... "Afterwards we were quite sure that we heard nothing between the distant sound of aircraft engines and the sickening whine of those same aircraft diving down on us".... "Suddenly the noise was unbelievable, diving aircraft, exploding bombs, guns, voices.... the very walls seemed to come at us and go out again!

My indignation gave way to fear and for a few moments I

was so frightened that I was beyond speech or movement. To an onlooker I've no doubt I appeared calm and unruffled while in actual fact I was numbed and incapable of expressing any emotion, in words or actions. A small far away voice in my ear brought me out of my near hypnotic state. "Rye what's happening to you? What's all that noise? Why don't you answer me?" . . . . "I tried to keep calm as in a voice I didn't recognise I replied "Your X raid is bombing us Stanmore, and it's no wonder you can't hear me, we can't hear ourselves either!'"

There had been heavy damage, as at other CH stations but, using a standby diesel generator Rye was on the air and plotting within ten minutes. Within six hours all stations except Ventnor were back in action.

What Daphne Carne had been watching on the tube was one section of Erprobungsgruppe 210, a specialised precision attack unit using bomb-equipped Bf 110s. Swiss-born Hauptmann Rubensdorffer commanded the unit with considerable success until he was killed on August 15. This was undoubtedly the right way to use the Bf 110 but Epr. 210 was the only unit of its type.

The attacks on this day moved across the coast like a scythe—radars, Lympne, convoys and Portsmouth, then back to the coastal airfield at Manston and Lympne and the forward airfield at Hawkinge, near Folkestone. At the end of the day the Luftwaffe began, in error, to write targets off its books—a process that was to lead to self-delusion as the battle progressed. The damage was, in fact, made good and in the course of the day German losses totalled 31 against the RAF's 22.

'Adlertag' should have commenced on the morning of August 13 but moderate to poor weather led Göring to postpone the effort until the afternoon. Seventy-four Dorniers of KG 2, already airborne, received no radio message but the Bf 110 escort did, and turned back. The Dorniers severely damaged the Coastal Command fighter/light bomber station at Eastchurch and Luftflotte 2 promptly wrote it off as a No. 11 Group airfield. To the West a series of attacks missed the targets allocated, to the extent that the bombers for a raid on Portland did not arrive but the Bf 110 escort turned up on schedule. They were severely mauled and six went down in a space of minutes.

'Adlertag' proper opened in the afternoon with waves of Ju 88s, Ju 87s, Bf 109s and 110s pouring in over Jersey towards Portland and Southampton. One Staffel of II/StG 2 was caught by the Spitfires of No. 609 squadron without its escort and six out of nine Ju 87s were shot down. The myth of Stuka invincibility was beginning to fade. Southampton was hard hit and Andover received some bombs intended for Middle Wallop.

Away to the east Detling airfield, near Maidstone, was badly damaged and bombs fell on a wide variety of targets. As evening came, Fighter Command had experienced its toughest fight since the battle opened. The Luftwaffe had flown 1485 sorties and the RAF 700, resulting in forty-five losses to the former and fourteen to the latter.

The 14th showed a much smaller effort by the Luftwaffe while it recovered from its exertions of the 13th but Middle Wallop was hit, although the German crews thought they had hit Netheravon.

The annual anniversary of the Battle of Britain is always held on September 15 but the day of greatest effort by the German Air Force was August 15 when no less than 1786 sorties were flown in the 24 hour period and it suffered its heaviest losses to date. That claims of the period for both sides were greatly exaggerated is evidenced by the RAF announcement of 182 Luftwaffe aircraft destroyed and the German communique which claimed 101. The actual respective totals were 75 and 34.

These figures however, in no way detract from the importance of the occasion or its effect on the future of the battle.

The aim of the Luftwaffe planning staffs was to carry out a series of attacks along the whole perimeter from Northern England to the West Country. During the course of these, holes would be punched at weak points, airfields and radars would be put out of action and RAF fighters brought to combat and destroyed in the largest possible numbers. The plan misfired.

The first raids developed over Kent and its airfields, with Lympne again, were hard hit. Shortly afterwards Luftflotte 5 from Norway launched two thrusts against the north and north-east where, if Luftwaffe intelligence was to be believed, the defences had been greatly reduced to reinforce the vital area in the south. Heinkel 111's with Bf 110 escort and Ju 88s set out to bomb what appeared to be a defenceless area. Warned by radar, no less than eight squadrons of Hurricanes, Spitfires and Blenheims intercepted the two wings of the attack. In the ensuing fighting, Luftflotte 5 lost sixteen out of its 123 available bombers and seven out of its 34 fighters. Thereafter its participation in the main battle was very limited.

In the south, raid followed raid, aimed at the airfields at Martlesham Heath, Manston, Rochester, Eastchurch, Middle Wallop, Worthy Down and Odiham. In addition bombs were aimed at the radar stations at Dover, Rye, Bawdsey and Foreness which, however, continued to operate. At Rochester the Pobjoy engine factory was hit but far more serious was the damage done to the Short Brothers factory where production of four-motor Stirling bombers suffered a serious set-back.

Epr. Gruppe 210, looking for Kenley, mistook its target and wrecked two factories at Croydon causing over 80 casualties. This was the first raid on the greater London area and it was a foretaste of things to come. Epr. 210 suffered the loss of seven of its aircraft, including that of the commanding officer.

While his aircraft had been ranging over Britain, Göring had been addressing his general staff and the Luftflotten commanders. He demanded closer escort for the Stukas and exclusive daylight operation against the RAF and its aircraft industry. He indicated that attacks on the vital radar stations were not worthwhile as, despite all efforts, they continued to operate. Of particular significance was his order of the 15th limiting each aircraft to one officer in the crew. Apparently the NCO's of the bomber fleets were expendable.

By the evening Göring had a great deal more to think about and he was not pleased; twenty-four of his Ju 87 and Ju 88 dive bombers had been destroyed along with twenty-six of his pet Bf 110 Zestöreren, quite apart from the other bombers and fighters lost and the damaged machines in need of repair. Hopes for the four day victory were beginning to fade.

It was a singular victory for Fighter Command, tempered by the knowledge that seventeen of its pilots were dead and a further sixteen wounded.

On the 16th, airfields were again the main targets, with Manston, West Malling, Tangmere, Lee-on-Solent, Gosport, Farnborough and Brize Norton bombed. For No. 11 Group, Tangmere sector station was the most important target; the damage done by Ju 87s was extensive, although retribution came within minutes from the guns of Nos. 43 and 602 squadrons which shot down nine Stukas and damaged others. Ventnor CH was again hit and this rendered the station unserviceable until the 23rd when a mobile radar set went on the air at Bembridge which at least gave the impression that the station was still operating.

The greatest Luftwaffe success of the day came at Brize Norton where Ju 88s wrecked no less than 46 aircraft, mostly trainers but also including maintenance unit Hurricanes. These losses were not included in the official record of 22 fighters destroyed and they considerably alter the accepted version of the day although no operational aircraft were involved.

It was on this day that Fighter Command won its only VC of the Battle. Flight Lieutenant J B Nicholson of No. 249 squadron intercepted a Bf 110 involved in the attack on Gosport. Bullets from the rear gunner set his aircraft on fire but he stayed with the aircraft long enough to put in another burst which shot the 110 down. Badly burned, Nicholson was shot at and further wounded by rifle fire from the Home Guard and the army.

On the 17th, both sides drew breath and Luftwaffe activity was limited to reconnaissance. On Sunday, August 18, however, the mass formations returned and a series of bitter battles were fought over airfields and radar stations. Nine Dorniers from 9/KG 76 hedge-hopped in from Beachy Head and flew up the London-Brighton railway to attack Kenley. Because the Observer Corps kept good tracks going, the station was on the alert and put up fierce opposition. Out of the nine Dorniers, only one returned intact to base. The high level raid then came in to add to the damage, while sixty

Heinkel He 111s of KG 1 were bombing Biggin Hill.

Luftflotte 3, meanwhile, was concentrating on the airfields at Thorney Island, Hants, and Ford, Sussex, together with the radar station at Poling, near Arundel. Neither of the airfields belonged to Fighter Command but a great deal of damage was done, particularly at Ford which was being used by the Royal Navy. The gunners and personnel had not been alerted at Ford and they paid dearly for this. Just why Ford was chosen for this heavy attack instead of a follow-up on Tangmere, has never been clear.

It would seem that German intelligence assumed that all airfields could operate fighters whereas this was not the case because of lack of suitable facilities and communications. Also the Luftwaffe was writing off airfields that had been heavily attacked whereas they were continuously patched up and put back into action.

Losses were severe on both sides, with the RAF having ten pilots killed and many more injured. For the Ju 87, it was a costly swan-song. On this day seventeen of the type were wrecked and, apart from sporadic sorties, they were withdrawn from the battle to re-group and await the invasion.

There were only isolated raids on the 19th and both sides took the opportunity to issue new instructions. Göring, at Karinhall, demanded 'the utmost damage possible on the enemy fighter forces'. He also wanted attacks on Bomber Command bases but without 'unnecessary losses'. The continuing efforts of RAF bombers were obviously annoying the Reichsmarschall but without escorts his own bombers stood little chance in deep daylight penetration. He criticised the fighter units when it was his own fault that there were too few of them.

Meanwhile Air Vice Marshal Park issued Instruction No. 4 to his controllers. To save pilots being lost at sea he wanted large formations engaged overland or within gliding distance off the coast. Mass attacks overland should have the main concentration on the bombers, not the fighters and No. 12 Group should be called upon to patrol Debden, North Weald and Hornchurch if all No. 11 Group squadrons were already in action.

Bad weather on the 20th led to only scattered small raids on airfields, Dover, a convoy and some inland cities and towns, while only one or two bombers were over during the night. The same pattern emerged on the 21st with isolated 'tip and run' raids, while on the 22nd convoy attacks were renewed, together with 100 shells from the German heavy batteries at Cap Gris Nez.

The period of poor weather was ending and, unknown to Fighter Command, it was entering upon the shortest but most critical phase of the Battle of Britain.

DIARY AUGUST 8-23

August 8: Day: Heaviest attacks on Channel convoy.
Night: Minelaying and small raids.
Losses: Luftwaffe 31: RAF 20

August 9: Day: Small scattered raids, mainly on convoys.
Night: East coast and minelaying.
Losses: Luftwaffe 5: RAF 4

August 10: Day: Shipping reconnaissance and single aircraft raids.
Night: Widespread minelaying.
Losses: Luftwaffe nil: RAF nil

August 11: Day: Heavy attack on Portland. Diversionary attacks on Dover.
Night: Merseyside and minelaying.
Losses: Luftwaffe 38: RAF 32

August 12: Day: Sharp attack on Portsmouth. Raids on Dover, Pevensey, Rye, Dunkirk and Ventnor radars and Hawkinge, Lympne and Manston airfields.
Night: Harrassing raids.
Losses: Luftwaffe 31: RAF 22

August 13: Day: 'Eagle Day' postponed to afternoon. Morning raid on Eastchurch. Later, raids on Portland, Southampton; Detling and Andover airfields hit. 1485 German sorties.
Night: Midlands, Wales and West, light raids.
Losses: Luftwaffe 45: RAF 14

August 14: Day: Dover, Kent airfields, Middle Wallop and Sealand.
Night: Small raids, southern England and Wales.
Losses: Luftwaffe 21: RAF 7 (including ground losses).

August 15: Day: Three Luftflotten engaged. Most widespread activity of the battle. Attacks on north east coast, southern airfields, Shorts factory, radars and outer London (Croydon) 1786 German sorties in 24 hours.
Night: Little activity.
Losses: Luftwaffe 75: RAF 34

August 16: Day: 1715 German sorties against airfields in Kent, Hampshire and West Sussex. Tangmere sector station damaged. Ventnor radar again attacked. Heavy damage to aircraft at Brize Norton airfield. Bombs on London suburbs and other civil targets.
Night: Widespread light attacks.
Losses: Luftwaffe 48: RAF 28 (including 6 on the ground).

August 17: Day: Reconnaissance only.
Night: Light raids, South Wales, Merseyside and Midlands.
Losses: Luftwaffe 3: RAF 2

August 18: Day: Very heavy attacks on airfields in south and south-east. Kenley, Croydon, Biggin Hill, West Malling, Thorney Island, Gosport and Ford hit. Severe damage at Ford. Poling radar bombed.
Night: South Wales, Bristol and East Anglia. Minelaying.
Losses: Luftwaffe 69: RAF 43 (including ground losses).

August 19: Day: Reconnaissance. Light coastal activity and some bombers towards London. Pembroke Dock attacked.
Night: Harrassing raids. Minelaying.
Losses: Luftwaffe 10: RAF 5

August 20: Day: Slight activity in morning, Essex and Kent airfields in afternoon. Convoy attacked.
Night: Little activity.
Losses: Luftwaffe 8: RAF 2

August 21: Day: Scattered light bombing on airfields and towns in east and south. Bomber losses at St. Eval.
Night: Slight activity, some in Scotland.
Losses: Luftwaffe 13: RAF 1

August 22: Day: Two Channel convoys plus cross Channel shelling and attacks on Dover and Manston.
Night: Increased activity against Midlands industrial targets Minelaying.
Losses: Luftwaffe 4: RAF 5

August 23: Day: Weather poor, raids limited but London suburbs hit.
Night: Wales, Birmingham and a convoy.
Losses: Luftwaffe 5: RAF 1

208 Luftwaffe meteorological staff assessing the weather map before a raid.

Two German aerial photographs taken on August 12 of **209** the CH radar station at Ventnor on the Isle of Wight and **210** the Brooklands factories of Hawker and Vickers. It was on the 12th that Ventnor was heavily bombed and the station put out of action completely for three days. The Vickers factory, producing Wellington bombers, was hit by Bf 110s of ZG 76 at lunchtime on September 4. Eighty-eight people were killed and six hundred injured. Factory output virtually stopped for four days while the weckage was cleared. Full production capacity was only regained by a major dispersal using small factories in the Weybridge area.

209

210

TIME	DETAILS OF CALLS, MESSAGES, &c.				REMARKS	TIME OF ORIGIN OF MESSAGE
11.43	to through	S	V7625	...S	1+	
11.45	"	S	V7225	W	1+	
11.47	N/c	S	V5628	W	1+	
11.56	Special Watch V.3830 to A.8340					
	2 Watch take over					
12.8	Catk umb	V4332	W.1			
.9	C.D. V.3734	W1				
.24	umb V.2971	NW1				
	new C.J.					
35	C.J V.4842	NW1				
36	Catk 12 Spitfires for Seaham now					
42	Rd 10. X 4025	W	6+ at 35			
42	2 cannon leaving Catterick 12.45 to Acklington					
44	N/ Special watch Relaxed					
52	Catk Rd10. X 1215	SW	20+ @ 20			
57	" Rd10 B.9197	SW	20+ 17			
59	" RD10 W6511	NW	30+ @ 19			
13.04	" RD10 W3409	W	30+ @ 19	220 MPH	
13.07	" RD10 W2203	SW	30+ @ 19		
.09	" RD10 W1603	W	30+ @ 19		
"	" Un No V0790	E	1—		
13.10	" now X26 V4296	SE	1+		
.12	" X26 V1280	S	1+		
.14	" Un No B1054	W	1+		
.14	" RD10 W0400	W	30+		
.15	" X26 V0173	W	1+		
.16	RD10 V7700	W	30+ @ 19	170 MP	
.19	10 V7300	W	30+ @ 19		
.20	10 A6897	W	30+ @ 19		
.25	X30 B5350	W	3+		
.25	Reported to Catk Gunfire + Bombs in Z7135					
30	Un No V7709 — W — 1—					

TIME	DETAILS OF CALLS, MESSAGES, &c.				REMARKS	TIME ORIG MES
13-34	To Catk Gunfire in V2353					
13-34	N/ell told us 47 to be RD.10C					
13-53	To Catk Red Flare seen in Z9903 (22 Post)					
13-53	" Explosion in V1735 from R3.					
14.00	Reported to Catk 1 Hurricane made a forced landing on Hart Station Z9755.				N06 Water	
14.05	To Catk Sound of Hostile Plane in V1551.				Yoke 6	
14.10	To N/ell Explosion in Z9945					
14.12	Catk X13 V7420	W	1—		
14.12	Catk X14 W0014	W	1—		
	X14 V9313	W	2—		
14.15	X14 V8012	W	2@2		
14.17	We told Catk we had picked up a Blenheim which we think might be one of above raids					
14.18	Reported to Newcastle Bombs dropped in Z6129. V4907 — 30+4 dropped by RD 10. Bombs dropped in A4595 by RD 10. one Hostile Plane down in A4995. (Told to Catk @ N					
14.30	Reported to Crash Officer (Yd4824) one Hurricane made a forced landing on HART STATION Z9755.					
14.34	Catk:— CA V4827	SW	1—		
14.40	To N/ell 4 Bombs dropped near Gas Works. Scar 13.25 hr. (Reported to 52 by coastguards)					
14.45	Gave Catk detailed weather report. V0359 — 2 — S, 1 in V1747 N, 2 in V0753 N, 3 V3137 another, 6 in V3339 — N.					
15.07	Catk ask if we can give information on a Blenheim Jet in E9397. we will tell to Catk.					
15.13	Catk said that Their Blenheim had landed					
15.14	N/ell Ask if we can get the name of Pilot who landed at Hart Station + particulars of the condition of his					

211 Two pages of the log book of York 9 Group, Observer Corps, detailing the costly attack by Luftflotte 5 from Norway on August 15. Alerted first by the CH station at Anstruther in Scotland and subsequently by the station at Ottercops Moss, RAF Catterick began to feed radar information to York 9. Twelve Spitfires from Acklington were airborne at 12.36 and at 12.42 'Raid 10' was reported by radar as 6 + at 35,000 ft. Ten minutes later Raid 10 was given as 20+ at 20,000 ft, and by 12.59 it was 30+ at 19,000 ft. It subsequently emerged as 63 He 111s of I and III/KG 26 and 21 Bf 110s of I/ZG 76. Altogether aircraft from five squadrons—Nos. 41, 72, 79, 605 and 607—intercepted and they, plus gunfire (noted in the log), accounted for eight He 111s and eight Bf 110s. The only RAF casualty was Pilot Officer K S Law of No. 605 squadron whose Hurricane crashed into a hedge at Hart station, as reported in the log at 14.00.

		ON TABLE and CONFIRMED					OFF TABLE and/or UNCONFIRMED				
TE	RAID	TYPE	NO down	Sec^n on duty	Grid	Remarks	DATE	NO down	Sec^n on duty	Raid	Remarks.
/40	29	He 111	1	1	V77	Conf. Tangmere	20/11/39	1	2+3	M3 = 52	
/40	47	Do	1	1	Q60	" "	22/11/39	1	1	H7 = 52	
7/40	34	Ju 88	1	2	R17	" Northolt	12/6/40	1	5	X38	1 He 111 K
7/40	44	He 111	1	1	Q51	visual N3	7/7/40	1	3	V15	reported Tangmere
7/40	41	Do 17	1	5	W1197	conf Tangmere					
7/40	61 62 12 R 125	Ju 87 etc	4	1	—	visual P&N	14/7/40	5	1	61.62 12RRS	reported Tangmere. add to 4 conf.
2/40	X52	—	1	6	V74	conf Tangmere	17/8				
7/40	15	Do	1	1	Q571	visual N3					
..	34	He	1	6	Q6407						
7/40	58	Me 110	1	3	Q 32	Post + Mid Wallop					
7/40	X49 X82.8P	Do 17	1	1	V38	Conf Tangmere					
7/40	=X53-53	Ju 88	1	2	R1729						
8/40	115	He	1	3	Q3111	" Tangmere					
..	X22	Me	1	3	Q9525	" K1					
8/40	1 + spuds Do 215 Me 109		6	6	R0929	Arundel Staffs Cish Shoreham Bepton Down					
..	69	He	1	3	Q2515	vis P3					
9/40	8J.K.R 1T U 1S 37 R.S 12.18.23	Ju 88 Me 109 Do. ? Me 110	5	1	Q2515 R0151 0351 Q7763 9747	conf P3 J3 " J3 " T1 " J1					
8/40	22.17-37 19.	Various	14	6	—	rptd T & K					

	RAID	TYPE FWD 43	NO	Sec^n	Grid		DATE fwd	RAID —	NO 9	Sec^n —	
/40											
→	13A 35	Me Ju 87 mostly Do.	9 12	5 1	Q95 Q20.21.32 Q3119 2105(2) 4825 22(4) 4923 2735 R.0541 2107	Conf Bromley + J2 : vis P2 vis. parts	16/8/40	46 50 24 26 44 H6	14	1	4C 50 24 26 44 H6 Remainder claimed by T (26) after deducting visuals.
/40	56	Ju 88	1	3	Q3717	conf P3 + Tangmere	21/8/40	19	1	1	Ju 88. Conf Wallop + Winchester. U85 dam
/40	6.H8 .55 41	..	2	2	Q2317	.. ..					~

212 Pages from an unofficial log book of enemy aircraft shot down, kept by a member of the Observer Corps at No. 2 Group, Horsham in 1940. The diary is not continuous and a number of dates are missing. It is, however, the only document that actually records the grid squares where aircraft crashed, the Posts which saw the incident and confirmation by the Sector Station.

213 The Focke-Wulf 200 Condor was a military conversion of a pre-war airliner. Only one unit, I/KG 40 operated the type during the Battle of Britain. It was used for reconnaissance, meteorological flights and night bombing of British ports. Several aircraft of this type were shot down during the summer of 1940.

214 Britain's first four-engine heavy bomber, the Short Stirling, was in full production in August 1940, and an initial squadron, No. 7, was forming at Leeming. On August 15, Dornier 17s from KG 3 attacked the company's factory at Rochester, Kent, destroying six completed Stirlings and the finished parts store. The whole Stirling programme was seriously delayed.

215 By June 23, 1940, nearly 17,000 employees of the Southern Railway had volunteered for the LDV. At that time they had only 400 rifles for units in Kent, Surrey and Sussex and communications in some cases rested on bicycles taken from the Lost Property Office. In July denim uniforms and all-important American .300 rifles began to arrive. The Southern Railway workers shown drilling here had received some Kennington rifles but only enough for the front rank. It is quite clear from the stance and the way the rifles were held who were the old sweats from the First World War.

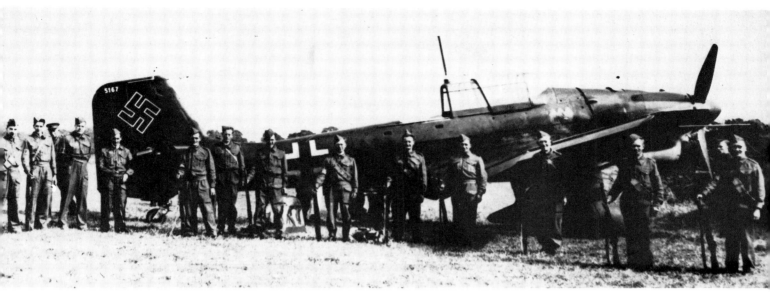

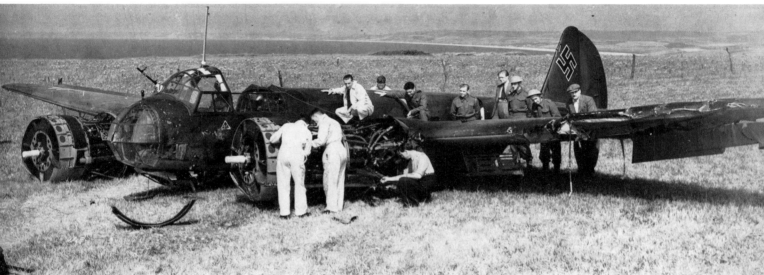

216 A Ju 87 sits, virtually intact, on Ham Manor golf course just north of Rustington, Sussex, on August 18, The aircraft, from II/St G 77, had just bombed the Naval Air Station at Ford when it was hit by a Spitfire of No. 602 squadron piloted by Sergeant Whall. Both the crew were injured and the rear gunner later died. The guard for the aircraft was provided by a platoon of the West Sussex Home Guard.

217 A Ju 88 from KG 54 which formed part of a force of fifty-four bombers which attacked Portland on the morning of August 11. It was hit by anti-aircraft guns and crash-landed at Portland Bill.

218 A Do 17 of 3/KG 2 shot down by Hurricanes at Stodmarsh, Kent, around mid-day on Friday, August 16. British soldiers were removing the crew kit and a machine gun. Clearly visible is the added gun position in the side window, with guard rails to stop the gunner shooting his own aircraft down.

219 Railways were a favourite Luftwaffe target. Here the 4.20 pm train from Southampton had been bombed at St. Denys on August 14.

220 A fighter is burning against a back-drop of five Spitfires at Middle Wallop, August.

221 A dying pilot brought this battered Ju 87 of I/St G 2 into land at Bowley Farm, South Mundham, near Chichester, on August 16. As he touched down he passed between two trees and ripped the outer wings off. His rear gunner was already dead from bullet wounds. St G 2 had been engaged in a heavy raid on Tangmere sector station but were then hit by three squadrons of Hurricanes which shot down seven Ju 87s and damaged three more. The onlookers of various ages were clearly fascinated by this close-up of the enemy; just how the Co-op bakery van got to the site is not clear.

NR.INT/38.   FORM'F' (FROM DUXFORD).
                    ===========================

(A)   G.4.
(B)   NIL.
(C)   19/8/40.
(D)   FLIGHT BEER SECTION GREEN SQUADRON (19.)
(E)   1.
(F)   ME.110.
(G)   1845 HOURS.
(H)   8 MILES EAST OF ALDEBURGH.
(J)   4,000 FEET.
(K)   1 DESTROYED.
(L)   NIL
(M)   NIL
(N)   N/A.
(P)   SEE BELOW.
(R)

THREE AIRCRAFT OF GREEN SECTION 19 SQUADRON WERE ORDERED TO
INTERCEPT RAID X.48. THEY WERE VECTORED ON A COURSE WHICH
TOOK THEM ALMOST DUE EAST OF ALDEBURGH. WHEN THEY HAD CROSSED
THE COAST THEY SAW AN ENEMY AIRCRAFT AHEAD OF THEM AND ABOUT
1,000 FEET ABOVE IT WAS BEING ATTACKED BY A SINGLE SPITFIRE OF 66
SQUADRON. GREEN LEADER ORDERED LINE ASTERN AND AS THE E/A SOUGHT
COVER IN A CLOUD HE HIMSELF WENT ABOVE TO MEET THE ENEMY AS
HE EMERGED LEAVING GREEN 2 AND 3 TO PURSUE IN THE CLOUD.
GREEN 2 FOLLOWED THE ME.110 INTO THE CLOUD BASE WHERE IT WAS
STILL FULLY VISIBLE AND OPENED FIRE AT A RANGE OF 300 YARDS
CLOSING TO ABOUT 100 YARDS WITH A TWO AND HALF SECOND BURST.
LUMPS FLEW OF THE PORT ENGINE AND THE PORT AIRCREW STOPPED DEAD.
GREEN 2 BROKE AWAY TO PORT. THE E/A HAD BY NOW EMERGED
FROM THE CLOUD AND GREEN 3 ATTACKED FROM SLIGHTLY ABOVE DIVING
TO ASTERN BUT FINDING HIMSELF TOO NEAR FIRED A SHORT BURST AND
BROKE AWAY. AS HE DID SO GREEN 1 DID A STRAIGHT AND LEVEL
ATTACK FROM DEAD SX ASTERN. OPENING FIRE AT 350 YARDS AND CLOSING
TO 150 YARDXS WHEN HIS CANNONS STOPPED FIRING. HE NOTICED A
PIECE OF MAINPLANE SHOT AWAY AND PORT ENGINE STOPPED.
GREEN 2 MADE A SECOND ATTACK OF VERY SHORT DURATION AND NOTICED
A GLOW FROM PORT ENGINE. GREEN 3 THEN ATTACKED FROM DEAD ASTERN
OPENING FIRE AT A RANGE OF ABOUT 250 YARDS AND GIVING A BURST OF
2 TO 3 SECONDS , AT THIS POINT THE PORT ENGINE OF THE E/A BURST
INTO FLAME. THREE PARACHUTES LEFT THE MACHINE WHICH TURNED
SLOWLY OVER ON ITS STARBOARD WING AND DIVED IN FLAMES VERTICALLY
INTO THE SEA. RETURN FIRE WAS SEEN TO COME FROM BOTH THE UPPER
AND LOWER GUN POSITIONS WHICH POINTS TO THE FACT THAT THE A/C
WAS AN ME.JAGUAR. ON TURNING TOWARDS THE LAND GREEN 2 NOTICED THAT

222 The Form 'F' from Duxford telexed by No. 12 Group to Fighter Command on August 19, concerning an engagement by No. 19 squadron Spitfires using 20-mm cannon. The poor standard of aircraft recognition at the time is shown by the fact that the machine attacked was not a Bf 110 as stated but a Dornier 17 from 7/KG 2 flown by Ltn. Hamp. The 19 squadron pilot should have been alerted as to its identity by the fire coming 'from both the upper and lower gun positions'. The report indicates the difficulty No. 19 squadron was having with its cannon which suffered continuous stoppages. The No. 66 squadron Spitfire referred to was hit by the Do 17 and the pilot, Pilot Officer J A P Studd, drowned.

223 While air battles were raging up and down the country on one of the most important days of the Battle of Britain, August 15, King George VI visited the de Havilland factory at Hatfield. He is seen here accompanied by Mr Alan Butler with, behind him, Sir Geoffrey de Havilland and (in uniform) Air Marshal (later Marshal of the RAF) Lord Tedder.

224 Göring confers with his senior officers on the progress of the air war against Britain. Laid out on the table is a map of Southern England. Seated on the right is Generaloberst Jeschonnek, Chief of the General Staff of the Air Force while, standing and nervously fingering his uniform, is Oberst 'Beppo' Schmidt, head of the Luftwaffe Intelligence IC.

225/6 A delayed action bomb exploding at RAF Bibury, Glos. All the windows in the Nissen huts have been opened to lessen blast effect on the glass, while two airmen shelter under a lorry. In the second photograph, personnel emerge from shelter and a pilot carrying his parachute, heads for his aircraft. The airman under the lorry is still not certain whether the panic is over!

227 Harmonising the eight .303 machine guns of a Hurricane at the butts at Exeter in August. The aircraft is from A Flight of No. 87 squadron.

228 A group of pilots from No. 92 squadron at dispersal at Pembrey in No. 10 Group. The pilot on the right was obviously a scholar as he was reading that very high grade comic 'Hotspur'.

229

230

229 The hangars and the oil dump at Royal Naval Air Station, Ford, burning fiercely after a heavy Stuka raid at lunchtime on August 18. In the foreground are Blackburn Shark, Fairey Swordfish and Albacore naval biplanes. **230** troops are seen emerging from slit trenches on the eastern side of the airfield with the wrecked hangars in the background. Total casualties in the raid were 28 killed and 75 injured. Five Swordfish, five Sharks, two Albacores and a Proctor were destroyed and 26 more aircraft damaged. Apart from the service types, three other aircraft were destroyed, the Armstrong-Whitworth AW 23 prototype bomber, (the forerunner of the Whitley) and two specially converted Handley-Page Harrows G-AFRL and G-AFRX. All three were equipped for air-air refuelling and belonged to Flight Refuelling Ltd whose base Ford had been since the company's inception in 1934. At the Admiralty's request, Flight Refuelling had moved to the Morgan Motor Works at Malvern, Worcs, in May 1940. Some local people assumed that Sir Alan Cobham had had prior knowledge of the raid and that was why he moved; they accused him of being a spy! **231** The AW 23 on a pre-war trial, refuelling the HP 51, the forerunner of the Harrow. **232** A German reconnaissance photograph taken later on the afternoon of August 18, showing the fires at Ford still burning. The River Arun is clearly visible on the right, while, on the left, is the village of Yapton.

231

232

233 Wrecked and blazing buildings at Tangmere sector station near Chichester, Sussex, after the Ju 87 raid at lunchtime on August 16, 1940. Extensive damage was caused. A total of six aircraft were written off and more damaged. The Blenheims of the Fighter Interception were all put out of action and the first Beaufighter with A.I radar was damaged. Ten service personnel and three civilians were killed and twenty people injured. At the height of the raid, Pilot Officer William Fisk of No. 601 squadron landed his damaged Hurricane and was immediately strafed by enemy aircraft. He was extricated from the burning wreck but died on August 18. Fiske was an American volunteer, the first to be killed in action over Britain. A tablet in St. Paul's Cathedral commemorates him.

234 The fatigue and tension of daily air fighting took its toll, even of the fittest. Here Sergeant G B Booth of No. 85 squadron has fallen fast asleep after the day's operations, his air maps stuffed into his flying boot and his Mae West still on. Sergeant Booth was injured in action on September 1 and finally died of his wounds in February 1941.

235 At a Luftwaffe briefing the target is identified on an illuminated viewer using modified British Ordnance Survey maps.

236 Barrage balloons were favourite coastal targets for German fighters. Here a Bf 109 has finished off a balloon at Dover.

234

236

235

237 An indication of just how many .303 bullets were often required to shoot an aircraft down. This Do 17Z of 9/KG 3 was raked from nose to tail and crew members were injured but it still managed to stagger back to base.

238 3/KG 51 Ju 88s lined up at Etampes prior to a raid.

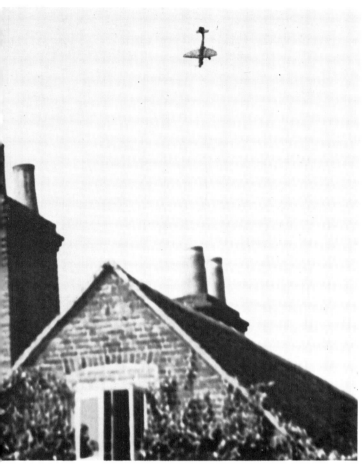

239 A Ju 87 of I/St G 77 diving out of control on August 18, after it had been hit by bullets from a mixed force of Hurricanes from No. 543 and 601 squadrons. It crashed at White House Farm on the northern outskirts of Chichester, Sussex.

240 The remains of a Heinkel 111 bomber lies in the road at Caterham, Surrey, after being hit by anti-aircraft gunfire during the night of August 26. Several houses were wrecked in the crash.

241 Crazy advertisements, totally out of keeping with the seriousness of the time, continued to appear even in technical papers. This advertisement for MG cars, which appeared in *The Aeroplane* for August 9, 1940, probably takes the prize for being the most inappropriate, although perhaps the copywriter did not realise it. It is amazing that new cars were still being advertised at the height of the Battle and with petrol rationed.

243

244

242 A Bf 109E of 2/JG 51 shot down in a Kent field by Pilot Officer B J Wicks of No. 56 squadron on August 24. The unit crest, shown inset, bore the inscription 'Gott strafe England'. The army guard is wearing 1914-18 type uniform and ammunition webbing.

243 Two of the Biggin Hill WAAFs who won awards for bravery during the Battle of Britain. Sergeant Joan Mortimer won the Military Medal and Corporal (in this picture she had been commissioned) Elspeth Henderson. Both won their awards at Biggin Hill. Wherever they were employed. WAAFs earned the lasting respect of their male compatriots for steadfastness and efficiency.

244 On of the oustanding pilots of the period, Flight Lt R R 'Bob' Stanford-Tuck who was posted to No. 92 squadron in July 1940 and to No. 257 squadron in September. He shot down ten German aircraft confirmed during the Battle.

245 Spitfire funds were organised all over the country in 1940, the aim being to buy a Spitfire for £5000. This particular aircraft was paid for by the village of Fairwarp in East Sussex and the name was inscribed ahead of the cockpit. The serial number was P7785.

246 Literally hundreds of bombs rained down on the RAF forward airfield at Lympne in Kent during the early phases of the Battle of Britain. In this Luftwaffe photograph damage points around hangars are ringed and numbered, while arrows indicate various other hits. The white patches peppering the ground show chalk thrown up by the bombs.

248 A Heinkel 111 of 1./KG 26 brought down at Dalkeith, Scotland on February 10, 1940. It was subsequently repaired and flown south during the Battle of Britain by a Royal Aircraft Establishment test pilot, Squadron Leader (later Group Captain) H Wilson. En route for Farnborough, the He 111 lost its Hurricane escort and was only kept alive by the steady plotting of the Observer Corps. **249** The aircraft in RAF markings with the serial AW 177.

Three views of Bf 110s in action. **249** Bf 110C-4 aircraft of 1./ZG 52 preparing for take-off. **250** A Staffel of ZG 26 'Horst Wessel' flying out over the Channel. **251** A badly damaged 110 after crash-landing in France; the injured rear gunner is being removed on a stretcher.

252 A typical group of squadron pilots during the Battle. This line-up of members of No. 87 squadron from left to right: Flying Officer R F 'Watty' Watson, Flying Officer K W 'Harry' Tait, Flight Lt I R 'Widge' Gleed, Pilot Officer R M S 'Roddy' Rayner and Pilot Officer P W Comely.

253 Squadron Leader J S Dewar who commanded No. 87 squadron from November 1939 through to July 12, 1940. He then commanded No. 213 squadron until August 1940, when he was promoted Wing Commander, station commander Exeter. Awarded the DSO and the DFC, he was killed in action in a Hurricane on September 12.

254 Flying Officer R F Watson of No. 87 squadron beside his Hurricane in August 1940. He is wearing his Mae West and the starter trolley is plugged into the aircraft. This photograph gives some idea of the size of the Hurricane which could hardly be described as small.

255 Every squadron had its station 'hack' which was used for communications flights, liaison and illicit visits to girl friends and/or families. This Tiger Moth was on the strength of No. 87 squadron, Exeter and the prop is being swung. The officer on the left is wearing a revolver holster as did many pilots in 1940.

256 Part of circular No. 26 issued by the Commandant Observer Corps from Bentley Priory on August 21.

(d)   At a town I visited in Wales where the windows of a house had been completely shattered by an explosion, an elderly woman was looking out of the window frame when the A.R.P., and Fire Brigade arrived; on being asked what she was looking for, she replied that she was looking for a window cleaner!!!!!

This is typical of the spirit which is prevalent throughout the country.

257

258

259

One of the most daring efforts of the Luftwaffe was the combined low-level/high level raid on the sector station at Kenley on Sunday, August 18. Nine Do 17s of 9./KG 76 set out from Cormeilles-en-Vexin to deliver the coup de grace to Kenley. They flew in over the coast at 100 ft and avoided detection by either CH or CHL radars. They were not, however, proof against the eyes and ears of No. 2 Group of the Observer Corps, which began an extremely accurate track as the raiders approached Beachy Head, Sussex. Post after post picked up the trail as the aircraft 'Bradshawed' up the main London-Brighton railway line. Kenley was prepared and let loose with anti-aircraft guns and the Parachute and Cable (PAC) system fired rockets bearing cables to a height of 600 ft. No. 111 squadron joined in the fray and the slaughter was complete. As the low-level battle abated, the high-level raiders arrived and added their contributions to the chaos. Of the nine Dorniers of 9./KG 76, only one arrived back at base, the others having been shot down over England, ditched in the Channel or crash-landed in France. **258** 9./KG 76 over the Channel and **257** approaching Beachy Head. **259** A view of Cyprus Road, Burgess Hill from the Dorniers, with people running for cover. The building in the foreground is the local cinema and the one with sandbags, the British Legion HQ, used by the Home Guard. A burst of machine-gun fire was put through the International Stores in the town centre. **260** Oberleutnant Lamberty's Do 17 in a field at Leaves Green, near Biggin Hill after the raid. **261** A picture of Kenley taken by the high level raiders just after the low level attack, with a burning Dornier at 2a, bomb craters at 3, and an over-flying Do 17 at 4. **262** The Addington, Surrey, Platoon of the Home Guard, which loosed off more than 180 rounds at Lamberty's Dornier and claimed they had shot it down, despite the fact that it was already a flying wreck and on fire. At Kenley, three out of four hangars were wrecked, there were 19 casualties and the runway was cratered with bomb holes. **263** A German propaganda photograph of Kenley during the low level raid, with the smoke puffs painted in.

261

262

263

264 Adolf Galland (on the right), one of the outstanding Luftwaffe pilots of the Battle of Britain period. He joined the Air Force in 1934 and was prominent in the Condor Legion in Spain in 1937/38. In June 1940 he took command of III/JG 26 on the Channel coast and on August 21 was promoted Geschwader Kommodore. He was appointed Luftwaffe Inspector General of fighters in December 1941 and achieved the rank of Generalleutnant. He is seen here in August 1940 with Generalfeldmarshal Milch.

265 Probably the best known of German fighter pilots during the Battle was Werner Mölders who, like Galland, had gained his spurs in the Condor Legion in Spain. He was appointed Kommodore of JG 51 at the end of July 1940. He was wounded and crash-landed in France the day after he was promoted. He returned to the fight and ultimately, in late summer 1941, he was made Inspector General of Fighters. He was killed while flying as a passenger in a Heinkel 111, on his way to Ernst Udet's funeral in November 1941.

266 The original Luftwaffe target map for raids completed during August 1940. 'Grossangriffen' are major raids with over 100 tons of bombs dropped. 'Störangriffen' are light or harassing raids while the figure 647 refers to other raids not shown on the map. It must be stressed that this illustrates where the Luftwaffe thought it had dropped its bombs and not where, in some cases, they actually fell.

PHASE 3· AUGUST 24-SEPTEMBER 6

During the poor weather from August 19 to 23, both sides drew breath and re-assessed the situation.

For Fighter Command it had been a period of intense activity with very serious attacks on radar installations and airfields. Above all, Dowding had watched his forces suffer continuous losses and undergo severe strain. He continued to rotate his squadrons through to quiet sectors for rest but some had been decimated and the replacements were short on hours, target practice and battle experience.

In his book 'Nine Lives', Air Commodore 'Al' Deere describes meeting a fellow New Zealander who had just arrived as replacement.

'What flying experience have you got?'

'I've got a total of 140 hours approximately, mostly on Wapitis.* I only managed to get twenty hours on Spitfires at O.C.U. and it was hardly enough to get the feel of flying again after a two months' lay-off. As a matter of fact I know damned all about fighters, I was trained as a light bomber pilot'.

'Have you fired the guns on the Spitfire yet?'

'No, I haven't; apart from a very little free gunnery from a rear cockpit, I've no idea of air firing'.

'What about the reflector sight, do you understand it?'

'Haven't the remotest idea what it is, much less understand it'.

The Royal Navy had already provided fifty-eight pilots who fought with conspicuous gallantry and all the other RAF Commands had been combed for likely personnel. Young men were arriving at squadrons with minimum flying-hours and no operational experience. There was no time to teach them the rudiments of their trade and of survival. Many were killed within days of arrival.

The Luftwaffe, too, was beginning to find the experience unpleasant to say the least. Every evening there were unoccupied places in the messes and more battered aircraft to be repaired. The inhospitable Channel was always there and, as the South Coast loomed up, every eye searched for the specks which showed once again that the RAF fighters were waiting and ready. Göring had stated that it would be over in a matter of days but, despite everything, there were the Spitfires and Hurricanes plus the anti-aircraft guns which showed an increasing accuracy.

Some Luftwaffe pilots who crashed told their captors that the German army would shortly occupy London. They were soon to be disillusioned and their views spurred the British

*An ancient 135 mph army co-operation biplane first flown in 1927.

on to greater efforts. Other Germans were only too glad to be alive and adjusted very rapidly to their changed circumstances.

While Göring still vainly hoped to win the war solely in the air, it was becoming increasingly evident that only a full-scale invasion and occupation would liquidate the continuing nuisance of a free and fighting Great Britain.

The German invasion plans as they stood involved vast expense, commitment of most of the best units of the German navy, army and air force and the diversion of Rhine barges and a mass of other shipping. Initially the Wermacht planners intended a landing on a broad front from Lyme Bay, Dorset to Ramsgate, Kent. As the problems of a seaborne assault became apparent, however, the front was narrowed.

About 170 steamers, over 1000 motor boats, fishing smacks and tugs and 1130 barges were in the process of assembly to deliver an all-out assault. Special pontoon craft had been built to provide some measure of seaborne artillery support. Two hundred and fifty tanks were converted for amphibious operation. These PzKw IIIs and IVs were sealed and fitted with fifty feet of pipe connected to a floating schnorkel which allowed them to breathe.

These monsters were to emerge out of the sea off the south coast and form the armoured spearhead for the advance. In 1940 their services were not required but, in June 1941, they proved to be a key factor in river crossings during the invasion of Soviet Russia.

As many Ju 52 trimotor transports and crews as could be found were exercised in towing DFS 230 gliders, mass landings and parachute dropping. By the end of August advance headquarters had been set up in France and the training for air landing units was concentrated upon roads which were considered to be the best transport landing points in England.

However, all of these renewed preparations were still completely dependant on mastery of the air. While Fighter Command still existed as a cohesive force, German air supremacy could not be achieved. Without this the Royal Navy's superiority in warships of all types would have ensured the clearance of minefields and the slaughter of a major part of the invasion fleet before any land action was joined.

Hitler had hoped that Britain would collapse after Dunkirk. When instead Britain fought on, the expectation was that either the Luftwaffe would succeed on its own or it would provide the umbrella for invasion. If Fighter Command was eliminated then the Royal Navy could, by bombing, be driven further and further north away from the landing areas. Bomber Command likewise could be eliminated over the bridgehead by unopposed German fighters.

In the event, all the preparations for and tremendous expenditure on Sealion came to nothing. Fighter Command was not defeated and the invasion fleet sailing at a maximum of 5 knots would have represented one of the most vulnerable targets in the history of warfare.

Apart from potential slaughter at sea, the British army on land was in much better shape by September 1940 to repel invasion troops than it had been in July and it had acquired considerable, although usually antiquated, extra firepower. In addition, thousands of machine guns, rifles, and even tanks in some numbers had been added to the defence. Above all, there could now be no surprise.

It was not the code breakers or the wireless intercept units that ultimately showed the disposition of the German assault units. The task devolved upon a small band of dedicated photographic reconnaissance pilots flying Spitfires at high altitude and ultimately to targets as far distant as the Baltic. Started by Sidney Cotton as a private venture and later incorporated into the RAF, these photographic Spitfires were few in number but invaluable in their results; they played a major part in the understanding of German intentions in 1940.

In the air the crucial phase of the Battle of Britain was just beginning. Göring's aim was to weaken Fighter Command by continuous attacks on airfields in the area around London, by raids on the ground organisation and the aircraft industry and finally by bringing as many RAF fighters as possible into combat.

On August 24 the pattern emerged with attacks on Dover and Manston in the morning, and against Manston and Ramsgate in the afternoon. Manston was little short of being a total ruin and the actual state of the airfield could only be established by No. 11 Group after a member of 1/A.1 Post, Observer Corps, had cycled over to investigate. Although the Post Office, through the most gallant work of the cable maintenance inspector, got Manston back on the air later in the afternoon, it was decided to evacuate the station except for extreme emergencies.

Further attacks developed on North Weald and Hornchurch, while to the west Portsmouth was attacked, killing 100 civilians. Night brought no respite and poor navigation led to widespread raids on outlying London suburbs. For the first time since 1918, London was under direct aerial bombardment.

On the 25th the Luftwaffe reserved its main effort for the afternoon with a raid of 100+ aircraft coming in towards Weymouth. Many places were hit, including the airfield at Warmwell. Then the attack was switched to Dover and the Thames Estuary, the main effort aimed at Hornchurch and Debden. The defending squadrons succeed in breaking up the raid but a handful of bombers got through to Debden.

On August 26, the three main Luftwaffe attacks were aimed at Kenley, Biggin Hill, Hornchurch, North Weald and Debden in No. 11 Group and Warmwell in No. 10 Group. At Debden over 100 bombs exploded, doing extensive damage. A No. 12 Group squadron from Duxford had been sent to patrol Debden but was too late to intercept.

Henceforth, until mid-September, Luftflotte 3 turned mainly to night bombing while the weight of the daylight attack devolved upon Luftflotte 2. This change was, of course, not known to Dowding or his staff and only became apparent as operations went on. The Commander-in-Chief's main pre-occupation on this day was on his mounting pilot losses with four killed and twelve wounded.

Activity was limited on August 27 but night raids were stepped up. Air Vice-Marshal Park, in his instruction on that day, had sharp criticism for No. 12 Group's lack of support over his airfields and he shifted the onus for this, in future, direct to HQ Fighter Command. The No. 11 Group versus No. 12 Group row was beginning to come into the open with Leigh-Mallory using every means to undermine Park's position and get at Dowding—a disgraceful thing to do in the midst of a fight for national survival.

Park was using forward intercept and conservation tactics to break up raids and keep No. 11 Group in being to fight again another day and every day, a concept which had the full approval of Dowding. Leigh-Mallory resented the fact that he did not have the front line glamour Command and his ambition and lack of modern fighter combat experience led him to clutch at any straw which might discredit Park.

It was a godsend, therefore, when Squadron Leader Douglas Bader of No. 242 squadron propounded the big wing theory of assembling three or more squadrons in the air to gain a measure of air superiority. The fact that No. 11 Group was faced with feints and raids coming in from several directions and at different times did not occur to Leigh-Mallory, nor had he the ability to work out the consequences of concentrating a mass of fighters at one point, leaving everywhere else defenceless and then having squadrons caught on the ground.

As was subsequently proved in 'War Games' exercises in 1941, when No. 11 Group was still commanded by Leigh-Mallory, the employment by Park of big wings in the summer of 1940, had it happened, would have led to catastrophic losses, the ultimate defeat of Fighter Command and an invasion. Leigh-Mallory was the armchair critic in the Battle of Britain—Park won the fight but Leigh-Mallory won the subsequent election.

This in-fighting was not apparent to the Luftwaffe, nor, surprisingly, to Dowding who was preoccupied with more immediate matters and, rightly, expected complete loyalty from his subordinates.

Inland, Park was now operating his squadrons in pairs wherever possible. He was getting maximum support from Brand's squadrons in No. 10 Group, and was being given a greater allowance of fully qualified pilots. It could only be a matter of time, however, before the incessant attacks on No. 11 Group sector stations gradually brought Park's organisation to a standstill.

Airfields were again the main targets on the 28th and at night Liverpool was hit by the first of four consecutive night raids which caused a good deal of damage and many casualties.

For the next eight days there was relentless pressure against No. 11 Group airfields. On the 30th the assault on coastal radars was briefly renewed but by far the heaviest damage was done at Biggin Hill and Detling. The German units departing from Biggin Hill left what looked like a ruin with thirty-nine dead and twenty-six injured, while at Detling between 40 and 50 bombs had been dropped.

August 31 saw Fighter Command's heaviest losses, with fourteen pilots killed from the 39 Hurricanes and Spitfires shot down. Once again airfields were the focal points. At Hornchurch one section of No. 54 squadron was blown up on take-off, Biggin Hill suffered severely and Debden was the recipient of about 100 high explosive and incendiary bombs. Somehow the airfields were kept serviceable but this effort could not be kept up indefinitely.

On September 1, there were two damaging raids on Biggin Hill during which the sector operations room was wrecked and had to be transferred to an emergency site in a village shop. September 2 involved four phases of airfield bombing when Detling was hardest hit while, on September 3, North Weald was again a main target. The Luftwaffe achieved parity in losses for the second time. Realising that Britain seemed to have no shortage of replacement aircraft, the Luftwaffe had, on September 1, issued orders for attacks on thirty factories concerned in aircraft, engine and equipment manufacture.

On September 4, Brooklands was very hard hit but the Vickers factory, making Wellington bombers, bore the brunt, not the Hawker factory making Hurricanes which was on the other side of the airfield. Park promptly asked for assistance from No. 10 Group in patrolling over certain aircraft plants.

For the last two days of this phase, the targets were the same—airfields and aircraft plants. Battered and exhausted, No. 11 Group waited for the next assault on its vitals. It never came. At the eleventh hour the Luftwaffe changed its tactics and Fighter Command was granted a reprieve.

DIARY AUGUST 24-SEPTEMBER 6

August 24: Day: Airfields in south east—Manston, Ramsgate, Hornchurch, North Weald. Heavy raid on Portsmouth.
Night: Widespread raids; minelaying; first bombs on City of London.
Losses: Luftwaffe 38: RAF 22

August 25: Day: Morning activity slight; afternoon, Weymouth area and Warmwell.
Night: Widespread; mainly Midlands.
Losses: Luftwaffe 20: RAF 16

August 26: Day: Kenley, Biggin Hill, Hornchurch, North Weald, Debden and Warmwell airfields. Dover, Folkestone and the Solent.
Night: Bournemouth, Coventry and Plymouth.
Losses: Luftwaffe 41: RAF 31

August 27: Day: Quiet except for reconnaissance.
Night: Widespread, Portsmouth to Lincolnshire: factories and airfields.
Losses: Luftwaffe 7: RAF 4

August 28: Day: Eastchurch, Rochford and Kent area.
Night: Heavy attack on Liverpool, small attacks, London, Midlands and north east coast.
Losses: Luftwaffe 31: RAF 20

August 29: Day: Mainly fighter sweeps in south and south-east.
Night: Liverpool and Midlands.
Losses: Luftwaffe 17: RAF 9

August 30: Day: Shipping, then Biggin Hill, Detling and seven radar stations.
Night: Main target Liverpool.
Losses: Luftwaffe 36: RAF 26

August 31: Day: North Weald, Duxford, Debden, Eastchurch, Croydon, Biggin Hill, Hornchurch and six radar stations. Fighter Command's heaviest losses.
Night: Liverpool plus scattered raids.
Losses: Luftwaffe 41: RAF 39

September 1: Day: Heavy damage to airfields, Biggin Hill, Hawkinge, Lympne and Detling.
Night: Liverpool, Midlands and South Wales.
Losses: Luftwaffe 14: RAF 15

September 2: Day: Eastchurch, North Weald, Rochford, Biggin Hill, Kenley, Brooklands, Detling, Hornchurch.
Night: Liverpool and scattered targets: minelaying.
Losses: Luftwaffe 35: RAF 31

September 3: Day: North Weald and attempts on other airfields.
Night: Liverpool, South Wales and Southeast.
Losses: Luftwaffe 16: RAF 16

September 4: Day: Heavy raid on Vickers at Brooklands, also Rochester and Eastchurch.
Night: Liverpool and minor harrassing raids.
Losses: Luftwaffe 25: RAF 17

September 5: Day: Airfields main targets: Biggin Hill and Detling hit. Thameshaven oil tanks.
Night: Liverpool, Manchester, London and other centres.
Losses: Luftwaffe 23: RAF 20

September 6: Day: Several large attacks in south-east broken up.
Night: Light raids only.
Losses: Luftwaffe 35: RAF 23

267 Bombs were no respecters of wealth or title. A large house on the southern outskirts of London, hit during a daylight raid on August 30.

268 On Aug 28, a small two-seat Gotha 145 biplane, the communications aircraft of Stab JG 27, was carrying forces mail to occupation troops in Jersey. In poor weather the pilot lost his way and found himself over the Sussex coast. Acting on plots from the Observer Corps two fighters pursued the Gotha and forced it to land on the South Downs next to Lewes racecourse. The pilot was taken to Lewes police station and a large crowd gathered to see this war prize. The Go 145 was subsequently pressed into RAF service, while military intelligence gleaned a lot of useful information from the

268
269
mail sacks. 269 The Go 145 in RAF colours and used on communications duties.

270 A Heinkel III of KG 27 lies by the road near Lynton, Devon after being shot down on August 25.

271 A Hurricane of No. 303 (Polish) squadron at Northolt in September. The aircraft was flown by Flight Lt (later Group Captain) J A Kent.

272 A flight of No. 87 squadron on route from Exeter to Portland in late August 1940. The pilot is Flight Lt Ian 'Widge' Gleed DFC commanding 'A' flight. He flew this particular aircraft, P2798, in the air fighting over France and through the Battle of Britain. Painted on the starboard side, was a picture of Figaro the cat. The photograph was taken by Flying Officer R F Watson.

270

271

272

273 A Bf 109 of 1./JG 52 brought down at Ramsgate on August 24.

274 The pilot and navigator of a Heinkel III over southern England early in September.

275 Belgians with the RAF, late August 1940. Fifteen of the Belgian pilots who escaped in 1940 joined Fighter Command and fought in the Battle of Britain. They were courageous and able but only four of their number survived to return home at the end of the war.

276 In the summer of 1940 the English Channel became a no-mans' land and the general grave for many aircraft and crews of both sides. Boats, amphibians and seaplanes plied to and fro picking up survivors. Shown here is Sgt C Babbage of No. 602 squadron, Westhampnett (in Mae West) being brought ashore from a rowing boat at Bognor Regis, Sussex. Babbage baled out of a Spitfire after a fight with Bf 109s on the afternoon of August 26. He was awarded a DFM in July and shot down six enemy aircraft during the battle. The Sergeant Pilots of Fighter Command have had their exploits largely over-shadowed by those of the commissioned pilots

277 Two of the crew of a Dornier 17 of KG 3 brought down in flames on the Kent coast on September 1. The original caption to the picture stated 'It was shot down by a Lewis gun whilst it was machine gunning the streets'. Judging by the number of bullet holes the aircraft also met a fighter before it crashed.

but without them Dowding could not have succeeded. After the battle many of them were commissioned and rose to command squadrons.

278 A crew member of a Do 17Z-3 of 6./KG 3 (SK + LP) shot down into the sea off Foreness Point after a morning attack on Eastchurch and Rochford on August 28. Four men were rescued by local boatmen and the Margate lifeboat.

279 Bf 109s of JG 53 on a Belgian airfield in September 1940. In the foreground is the nose of a burned out Fairey Fox biplane.

280 Another section of the private log book kept by a member of the No. 2 Observer Group, showing some of the aircraft shot down between August 24 and September 9 with the raid numbers, grid references and confirmatory notes. It is interesting to note that the Gotha 145 which was forced down intact on August 28 was first reported by L.2. post Lewes, as a Heinkel 45, which was not a bad guess as the members had never seen either type before.

SIGNAL OFFICE DIARY.

DATE 24. 8. 40   STATION Bromley

Watch Times.		REMARKS.	Signature.

'B' Crew.

47	15.14	S1 & S3 post report explosion Q 9381
48	15.18	To L.O. to report explosion in Q 9381
49	15.20	From L.O. Squadron ordered up from Kenley. Inform L.O. when they leave.
50	15.29	S2 & S3 post report explosion in Q 8777
51	15.29	To L.O. to report explosion in Q 8777
52	15.30	To L.O. 12 A/c now up from Kenley
53	16.35	From L.O. "Where are the fighters from Kenley now?" Replied Q 8963
54	15.40	From L.O. "Where are the Kenley fighters now" Replied Q 9965 going N.E.
55	15.41	Z.2 post report parachute descending R1385 " " " plane crashed R0381.
56	15.42	From L.O. Raid X12 is now Raid 12.
57	15.43	From L.O. Where are our fighters from Kenley. Replied no further plots. They have probably gone too high.
58	15.47	To. L.O. Raid 8 is Barking Hornchurch.
59	15.48	Post report Parachute descent in R1177
60	15.52	From L.O. What is B6. Replied we do not know but have passed it to Watford
61	15.54	To L.O. Our post at M3103 reports many aircraft ours & enemy overhead. We think Ken

281 A page from the log book of 19 Observer Group, Bromley for August 24, 1940. The entries show a squadron airborne from Kenley and being reported to No. 11 Group until they were too high to be seen. Item 58 on Raid 8, is a force of Heinkel IIIs and Ju 88s bombing Hornchurch from 12,000 ft. 'LO' refers to the Observer Corps Liaison Officer for 11 Group.

282 The caricature on the side of this German operations van shows Winston Churchill being knocked about by Luftwaffe personnel with hammers. The caption reads 'When we have shut Churchill's big mouth'.

283 Gunners on a Do 17 over England watch out for RAF fighters.

284 Happy to be back! The crew of a Heinkel III of KG 55—force-landed in France after being shot up over England.

285 The famous tower at Croydon Airport shrouded in camouflaged netting and with repairs going on.

286 The Bf 109 of German ace Oblt Franz von Werra, adjutant of II/JG 3 after a fight with a Spitfire flown by Flight Lt P C Hughes DFC of No. 234 squadron on September 5. Hughes himself was killed two days later. As he came into a field at Marden in Kent, von Werra was fired at by a Bren gun team which captured him while he was trying to set fire to the aircraft. Von Werra was subsequently transferred to Canada from where he finally managed to escape back to Germany. He became known as the 'one who got away'. He warned the Luftwaffe that Britain had broken its unit and R/T codes and, as a result, the system was changed. Von Werra was drowned in the North Sea in October 1941 following engine failure.

287 The Czechs like the Poles, were determined to fight and fly with the RAF and they came to Britain in large numbers. This group from No. 310 squadron is shown at Duxford on September 1, 1940. No. 310 the first Czech squadron in the RAF, was formed with Hurricanes on July 10 under Squadron Leader G D M Blackwood and with RAF flight commanders. The squadron became operational on August 17 and fought its first action on the 26th.

289 A Bf 110 of ZG 26 shot down at Stud Farm, Mundon, near Maldon, Essex, September 3. The lumps of turf torn up in foreground resulted from bombs dropped by a Ju 88 in an attempt to destroy the 110 on the ground. In the distance is a row of anti-glider invasion poles.

288 Sgt L Davies of No. 151 squadron, North Weald, crash-landed this Hurricane at Eastchurch after a dogfight on August 28. It was transported to No. 1 Civilian Repair Unit at Cowley, Oxfordshire and completely rebuilt. (Bottom) The machine was later transferred to the Fleet Air Arm. The civilian Repair Organisation performed miracles during the battle and kept up a continuous flow of repaired aircraft to the squadrons.

290 With badly bent wing and propellor and the undercarriage ripped off, this Spitfire of No. 92 squadron had crashlanded at Biggin Hill in September. The nose was dowsed in foam to prevent fire.

291 A high altitude reconnaissance aircraft photograph of RAF Station Northolt, taken on August 31. Running from the middle of the right hand edge down towards the bottom left corner is Western Avenue. The runways have been camouflaged to look like scattered groups of trees.

GB 10 160 bc

Maßstab etwa 1:13400

500m   0   1km

(1cm : 134 m)

Northolt
Fliegerhorst

G B 10 160 bc
Geheim

Kriegsaufnahme:
0853
Nachträge:
31.8.40

Karte:
1:100 000
Blatt 29

Länge
(ostw. Greenw.):
0°25'
Nördl. Breite:
51°33'

Zielhöhe
über N N 37 m

G.B. 10 160   Fliegerhorst

1) Flugzeughallen
2) Werkstätten
3) Unterkunftsgebäude
4) Splittersichere Abstellplätze für Flugzeuge
5) Leichte Flakstellungen ?

Lft. Kdo. 2 . Sept. 1940

133

292 American fighters of 1940, such as the Hawk 75 (Mohawk), Buffalo and Airacobra would not have stood a chance against the Bf 109. As a panic measure, however, Britain purchased large quantities of Hawk 75s and Buffalos which were stored for later use. This Buffalo was part of a batch diverted from a Belgian contract and is shown during flight trials in Britain on September 29, 1940. Buffalos equipped RAF squadrons in Malaya at the time of the Japanese invasion and suffered severely at the hands of pilots flying Zeros.

293 Squadron Leader (later Group Captain Sir) Douglas Bader, commander of No. 242 squadron at Duxford. Having lost his legs in a pre-war flying accident, Bader learned to fly again with artificial limbs. He was a major exponent of the 'Big Wing' philosophy during the battle.

294 Bomber Command's efforts against targets on the continent were mounting at this period. Here a Blenheim 4L of No. 110 squadron is being fuelled and bombed-up at Wattisham, Suffolk. No. 110 squadron carried out the first RAF raid of the war, against warships at Wilhelmshaven, on September 4, 1939.

295 Adolf Galland, Kommodore of JG 26, in his Bf 109, having taxied in after a sortie over England. He has already lit up one of his well-known cigars and the ground crew wait to help him out of the cockpit. The Mickey Mouse emblem is noteworthy.

296 The pilot and his ground crew from No. 92 squadron at Pembrey early in September. This aircraft bore the code QJ-X.

297

299

298

Three pictures of Reichmarschall Göring at work during the battle. **297** With General Bruno Lörzer, commander of II Fliegerkorps and Galland during an inspection of JG 26. **298** With General-Feldmarschall Kesselring (on the right) during a visit to Luftflotte 2's forward headquarters on the French coast. **299** Later in the battle, on a visit to Luftflotte 3, with General Feldmarschall Sperrle, second from left.

300 Spitfires of Nos. 603 and 222 squadrons at dispersal at Hornchurch in September. Code ZD denotes 222 squadron and XT, 603 squadron. In the background is a steamroller carrying out runway repairs.

301 No. 92 squadron Spitfires operating at Pembrey in early September, just prior to the unit being moved to Biggin Hill on September 8.

302 At the height of the battle, on September 6, King George VI and Queen Elizabeth visited headquarters, Fighter Command. They are seen here walking in the grounds of Bentley Priory after lunch. From left to right: Sir Hugh Dowding; the King; the Queen; Dowding's sister, Miss Hilda Dowding; Lady Pile and General Sir Frederick Pile, GOC Anti-Aircraft Command.

303 Frequent incursions by British light bombers and fighters in the summer of 1940 led the Luftwaffe to look to its own airfield defences. Here a Belgian farmer ploughs his field, apparently oblivious of the German crew clustered round their 88 mm anti-aircraft gun.

304 German aircrew of a Ju 88 unit in August 1940 (possibly III/KG 51). Photograph taken by Generalfeldmarschall Milch.

305 Animals are no respecters of aircraft. These sheep being herded on the Sussex Downs in September 1940, had an unexpected obstacle in the shape of a Bf 109 of I/JG 53. The pilot was captured by the Home Guard.

306 Bf 109 Yellow 12 of 3/JG 27 on display in Exeter during the first week of September 1940. The pilot was Uffz Ernst Arnold shot down near Faversham, Kent, on August 30. This aircraft was almost certainly a victim of Squadron Leader T P Gleave, flying a Hurricane with No. 253 squadron. The Exeter exhibition was organised by Mr F Beasley (standing by the aircraft) in aid of the Spitfire Fund.

307 An ignominious end for one of 2./Erp. Gr. 210's Bf **308** 110s—as a London street display to aid recruiting for the RAF and to raise funds at 6d. a time for the Spitfire Fund. This 110 S9 + GK had been shot down by No. 85 squadron near Tunbridge Wells, Kent, on August 31.

On March 30, Squadron Leader Gleave of No. 253 squadron met waves of Bf 109s over Kent. In the space of a few minutes he shot down four of them. Officially he was only credited with four 'probables' but post-war investigation confirmed his claim. On the following day, Gleave waded into a large formation of bombers but his Hurricane was hit in the starboard fuel tank and burst into flames. In the subsequent explosion he was blown clear of the aircraft, came down by parachute and landed just east of Biggin Hill. Although severely burned, he walked to nearby Mace Farm. One of the bombers he hit crashed at Downe village to the north. Gleave became one of the first plastic surgery 'guinea pigs' at East Grinstead under the remarkable Dr Archibald McIndoe. In **309** 1941 he returned to duty as OC Manston and later rose to the rank of Group Captain.

Gleave presumed that his aircraft had broken up and was very surprised, more than twenty years later, to find large sections of the machine and its Merlin engine intact in a thicket near the farm. The engine is now preserved in a museum. Wrecks of aircraft shot down in the Battle of Britain are still being discovered, together with the remains of some of their unfortunate occupants. The photographs show **308** the Merlin engine of Hurricane P3115 as discovered in the thicket at Mace Farm and **309** Group Captain Gleave, in 1967, holding a piece of the aircraft's structure.

<u>WEEKLY ORDERS.</u>

<u>ACTION AGAINST PARACHUTISTS.</u>

It must not be assumed that all men landing by parachute are enemies, as allied foreign pilots are now flying over Great Britain. A foreign accent, or a complete ignorance of English, does not, therefore, always mean that a pilot is hostile. Every parachutist apprehended should, however, be brought to Headquarters immediately.

<u>AIR RAIDS - SAFETY MEASURES.</u>

Experience with recent bombing attacks has shown that many splinters fly with a low trajectory for considerable distances. Persons standing upright are, therefore, in a vulnerable position. When in the open a prone position should be assumed, with hands over the ears, when it looks as if a bomb will fall in the vicinity.

If a ditch or similar cover is available, it should be used.

<u>BADGES.</u>

Royal Berks. Yeomanry badges, probably in cloth, are to be issued to Berks H.Q. Meanwhile, other badges must not be worn.

<u>BOMBING INSTRUCTIONS.</u>

Bombing instructions will be given by Major Broome at 10.15 a.m. on Sunday next, the 8th instant, at Coombe House, Thatcham. As many men as possible should attend.

A. Bond.

Platoon Commander.

<u>NOTE:</u>   It cannot be too strongly emphasised that we are not yet "out of the wood." There must, therefore, be no slackening of our efforts or precautions, and the utmost vigilance on patrols is essential.

310 Orders for the Crookham Home Guard platoon for August 29 and September 6. The reference to 'Action against parachutists' resulted from a number of incidents where pilots descending by parachute had been shot at and some Czechs and Poles had been mistaken for Germans and had been roughly treated after air raids.

German preparations for the invasion of England in August 1940. **311** Feldmarschall von Brauschitsch Commander-in-Chief of the German Army confers on a beach in France during a landing exercise. **312** German troops being trained in cliff-scaling. **313** Mines being loaded onto a German minelayer in a Channel port. Just prior to the invasion, a mine barrage was to have been laid on either side of the route in the hope of keeping the Royal Navy out. In the background are some of the 170 steamers assembled for 'Sealion'.

PHASE 4·SEPTEMBER 7-30

To the Luftwaffe the preceding week appeared to have been very successful, not only in knocking out large sections of No. 11 Group's facilities but also in destroying RAF fighters in the air. It would have been logical to continue the pattern of attacks on airfields and factories and bring Luftflotte 3 back fully into the daylight battle to stretch Fighter Command's resources to the maximum and beyond.

The Luftwaffe High Command under Göring, however, did not work in a logical manner and it never finished any phase of the proceedings even when successful. Outside influences led to a change in tactics. On August 25 bombs had fallen on central London and Bomber Command had retaliated with a series of somewhat abortive raids on Berlin. This only encouraged elements of the senior staff of the Luftwaffe who believed that heavy strikes against capital cities or other major population centres could topple a nation. The examples they cited were Warsaw and Rotterdam.

Göring, who had said that no enemy aircraft would fly over the Reich, was acutely embarrassed and the suggestion that London should be pounded into surrender appealed to his vanity. Accordingly on August 31 the Luftwaffe Command Staff issued orders for a reprisal raid on London to be carried out in daylight.

Kesselring felt strongly that, with a weakened air defence line in the south-east, a massive blow against London would suck in Fighter Command's last reserves and bring them up for destruction by the 109s. This theory was backed up by the completely unreliable information put out by Luftwaffe Intelligence IC suggesting that British fighter forces were on their knees and waiting to be finished off. Kesselring, after strong arguments with Sperrle, won the day at conference in the Hague on September 3. Hitler gave his permission for reprisals against London on September 2 and the Luftwaffe date for this operation was set as September 7.

Across the Channel Dowding faced critical problems. During August the operational training units had turned out 260 fighter pilots while in the last two weeks of that month the total of pilots killed, missing and wounded averaged 120 per week. In addition squadrons replenished with 'green' pilots and cycled back into No. 11 Group after a rest further north very often suffered severely and had to be withdrawn again after a short period in action. For instance, No. 603 squadron came into No. 11 Group on August 28 and eight days later it had lost twelve pilots and sixteen aircraft.

On the other hand, some experienced squadrons that had been in the line continuously were still showing good results and low losses despite fatigue. It was battle hardened know-how that counted. The ground organisation had been badly knocked about and facilities for operating several squadrons simultaneously at some stations were marginal.

The staff at Bentley Priory would have been interested to know that, on September 6, Göring had moved to northern France with his special train and entourage to view the assault against London rather like a Roman Emperor at the circus. His view had, of necessity, to be from the ground as there were only one or two modified aircraft with large doors and seats which the corpulent Reichsmarschall could use. There was also no question of him actually flying anything as his knowledge was far too rusty. He was not like Dowding who flew his own Proctor round the stations, or Park who usually arrived in a Hurricane.

It was not until the afternoon of the 7th that a massive build-up over France began to show on the radar screens. It was expected that the usual tactics would be adopted with the bulk splitting up into several separate attacks aimed at airfields and No. 11 Group prepared accordingly. To the amazement of the controllers, however, the whole force of over 300 bombers and 600 fighters flew at high altitude to the Estuary in two waves and headed for London.

The East End of London and the docks received the main brunt with bombs raining down on the boroughs of Poplar, Woolwich, Barking, West Ham, Millwall, Limehouse and Tottenham. Great fires broke out, factories and warehouses collapsed and whole rows of terraced houses were reduced to ruins.

Both Nos. 11 and 12 Groups hit back as best they could and there were a few very successful interceptions such as that by the Poles of No. 303 squadron against a formation of Dorniers. On the whole, however, the bulk of the attacking force returned to the continent relatively unscathed. The pilots reported heavy damage to the capital and little opposition—Göring was literally jumping for joy—the British were collapsing. From eight in the evening until after four o'clock the next morning a continuous stream of bombers, 247 in all, added to the destruction in east London, the fires leading them like beacons to the target. By dawn, 306 of London's citizens were dead, 1337 seriously injured. No city in the world had ever before suffered air bombardment on such a scale and the process was to go on, with only a few intermissions, for the next eight months.

The threat of invasion also seemed more acute and the

alert warning code-word 'Cromwell' was issued. Many people misunderstood it and thought it was an indication that the invasion had, in fact, begun. Church bells were rung, roads and bridges were mined and everywhere armed Home Guards roamed the streets and the countryside.

On the 8th, the Luftwaffe recuperated and the weather was bad, which brought blessed relief in daylight and much reduced activity. By night, however, it was a different story as 207 bombers again hit the East End and overlapped into the City itself.

Luftflotte 2 had the task of reducing London by day, while Luftflotte 3 undertook the night operations. On the 9th, the Luftflotte 2 efforts were somewhat abortive as Fighter Command had changed its tactics and reacted successfully to the new threat. At night Luftflotte 3 had it all its own way and, as directed by Göring, extended the bombing to the West End and beyond. The 10th was quiet during the day but widely scattered attacks in strength came in on the 11th and on both nights London was bombed. Merseyside also became a 'regular' on the night timetable.

The 12th saw little activity but on the 13th several raiders penetrated to London where Buckingham Palace had its third bombing. Both Hitler and Göring thought that the plan was succeeding and that RAF opposition on the 11th had been scrappy and uncoordinated. In Berlin, on the 14th, Hitler postponed Sealion to September 17 but the build-up continued.

One more big effort was obviously needed against London and it came on the 15th. Now annually celebrated as Battle of Britain day, September 15 dawned with fair weather and a few cloud patches. The first attack formed up at 11 o'clock and moved in with large formations stepped up from 15,000 to 26,000 ft. As soon as they reached the coast, the raiders were attacked and interceptions continued all the way to London. A total of twenty squadrons engaged the enemy.

At lunchtime, the second attack came in, in three waves, and was similarly mauled. A record 185 German aircraft was claimed by the defences which later proved to be an overestimate by a factor of three. To the Luftwaffe, however, the 60 aircraft actually lost on that day, together with 25 damaged, was serious enough and the strength of the opposition came as a complete surprise.

Winston Churchill had been at No. 11 Group on the 15th and he watched as the squadrons landed to refuel after the first wave of attackers left. As had happened on many occasions, there was nothing left in reserve. He was duly impressed with the importance of the occasion.

On September 16, a perplexed and angry Göring met his Luftflotten and Fliegerkorps commanders. He called for a reduction in the size of bomber formations attacking London and an increase in their escorts. Mass raids were only to be used in perfect weather. He even referred to the fact that the aircrews were becoming exhausted after two and a half months of continuous effort.

On his side, Park again revised his tactics with pairs of Spitfire squadrons dealing with high fighter escort and further pairs of Hurricane squadrons to deal with the bombers. A three squadron wing was to be sent to intercept the third wave of any attack like that of the 15th as this section usually contained bombers and the timing would allow for form-up and climb of the separate squadrons.

For more than a week activity slackened except for numerous smaller raids and large fighter sweeps designed to attract RAF fighters. Bomber and Coastal Commands, together with the Fleet Air Arm, kept up a nightly pounding of the invasion ports. By September 18, there were over 1000 invasion craft in the Channel ports and some 600 at Rotterdam. Altogether, 1400 tons of bombs were dropped on or near the ports—a not inconsiderable total which gave the German forces a clear indication of what they might expect if the vessels actually put to sea. On the 17th, Hitler postponed the invasion until further notice. Whitehall of course, was not aware of this. Meanwhile, the Luftwaffe hammered away nightly at London destroying famous landmarks and causing a great many casualties.

On September 25 there was a heavy raid on the Bristol Aeroplane Company's works by Luftflotte 3 and on the 26th, the vital Spitfire production factory at Woolston was completely wrecked. This sort of concentration on supply targets would have stood the Luftwaffe in better stead at the beginning of the battle.

The daylight attack on London was renewed in force on the 27th but was fiercely opposed and the Luftwaffe losses of fifty-five for the day almost matched those for September 15. London was again the target on the 28th, while on the last day of the month the final mass daylight attack took place. The seemingly endless formations of Dorniers, Heinkels and Junkers were not to be seen again.

For those who did not live in the battle zone of the south east in 1940, or who were not alive at the time, it is extremely difficult to understand the atmosphere. One person who succeeded in describing the scene was Freda Tomlin a young woman from Staplehurst, Kent. She wrote a diary in an exercise book which is remarkable, not only for its clarity but also for its powers of observation. It showed that the population in the area below which the battle was fought had learned to accept war as part of the daily round. Work and life in the countryside went on as usual, interspersed with crashing aircraft, parachutes, bombs, machine gun bullets and AA fire.

The following are the entries in her diary for September 13-29, 1940.

Fri. Sept 13th 1940

Some bombs were dropped at Frittenden (On the Biddenden Road) at 4 am. Had air raid warnings nearly all day but did not see anything.

Sat. Sept 14th

At 4-30 pm we saw about 100 light bombers going towards London. George had measured out five bins when we heard machine gun fire, so he got his hat and put it on, because as he says, "You never know what might come down". A few moments later a Hurricane came down in a spin, and crashed about ½ mile to the north of Dunberry. We could see the flames and smoke from it quite clearly. Then we saw a parachute coming down but he had baled out of another British plane. He landed at Hawkenbury, and had been shot through the legs.

The Miss Gibsons said that a plane was caught in the searchlights last night, and it dived and dropped a bomb fairly near where they live.

Sunday Sept 15th

The siren was sounded at about 11.30 am, and we heard terrific machine-gun fire and roarings and zoomings during the sermon. When we came out of church we saw a lot of smoke coming from the station, which was on fire. One of our planes had cut the top off the pear trees which were growing opposite the station, gone right through the station, and then the engine went on through Nolan's shed, and finished up in Sorrell's field.*

One wing landed on the roof of 'Station Cottages'. The pilot, the booking office clerk, and a plate-layer, who was being served in Nolan's shop were killed. The station master was injured, but not seriously.

A Spitfire came down just behind 'Duckhurst', and burnt up, but the pilot baled out.

At 2 pm the siren sounded again. I was walking down the fields to meet Mother, Betty and Bridget, when I saw the smoke rising from a plane which had crashed in the direction of Marden. They found quite a large piece of the plane in the little field. We saw a parachute coming down over the church, and about four minutes later we saw three more parachutes coming down over Marden. Had walked back from the fields and were discussing the latest news with Mr. and Mrs. Brown, when we saw three pieces of plane falling to the south of us.

Suddenly heard a roar and saw a bomber diving straight down over 'Pagehurst'. There was a bang when it came down so we all ran indoors, and had just got in when there was a terrific bang, and we saw a small cloud of black smoke, which looked about a few hundred feet above our ploughed field. After this we saw another bomber come down over Cranbrook and one parachute came down.

There was another bomber flying towards Maidstone, with smoke pouring from it, and anti-aircraft guns firing at it. We could also see smoke from two other planes which had come down.

*The plane which crashed on Staplehurst Railway Station was Hurricane N2537 of No. 229 Squadron, Northolt. It was flown by a Belgian, Pilot Officer G. L. J. Doutrepont

When the all clear went Betty and myself went to view the station and the Spitfire, and there was another terrific bang and clouds of smoke came up over Pagehurst way. It must have been some of the bomber's bombs going up. We went round by the Plain Tavern and saw people picking up pieces of aeroplane for about a mile along that road, so the bomber must have come down near there.

Another warning at about 7.15 pm. This time saw plenty of anti-aircraft fire and one large bomber with three fighters, which looked like Spitfires going round him, but only heard one burst of machine-gun fire, and did not see him come down.

Mr. Moss says that 19 bombs have dropped on Mr. F. Ripples farm (Sweetlands) and they have not exploded yet. Planes over and guns firing from 8.30 pm to 6 am (185 Jerries down).

Mon. Sept 16th

Siren sounded at about 7.35 am, and 30 British fighters circled round here until about 8.10 am, when we saw 10 German bombers coming, but directly they saw the fighters they turned and fled towards the coast.

Heard today that a German airman came down by parachute in Playfoot's field yesterday. Another one came down, but he was killed as his parachute did not open.

Uncle Jack was playing golf at Bearstead yesterday when a German pilot fell on the 13th fairway. He was killed as his parachute did not open. He had a silver Iron Cross and had English money in his pocket.

Single German bombers have been flying over from 11 am to 6 pm but they are all kept above the clouds. One dropped some bombs at Malling.

Went to Frittenden this evening and saw the large bomb crater near the Biddenden road, several houses near had their windows blown out.

A bomber was brought down quite near there yesterday. It had a crew of six, and although it broke in halves, and the engine caught fire when it landed, only one man was killed, and two injured.

Tues. 17th Sept

During the afternoon raid a Spitfire came down on a barn on Folly Hill. The pilot baled out. Also saw a barrage balloon which had broken loose. Only saw small enemy bombers today.

Mr. Wendon told us of how he was feeding his chicken with Antony's help on Sunday morning, when the pilot of the Spitfire which came down at Duckhurst, landed beside them.*

He landed right on top of the hedge and told them not to help him as a plane might come down and machine-gun

*This was almost certainly Pilot Officer R. R. Smith, a Canadian from 229 squadron. The aircraft was a Hurricane.

them. Mr. Wendon said he was covered in oil and had a slight bullet wound in his legs.

Also heard today that a time bomb has been dropped in the camp.

A bomb was dropped about half a mile from the 'Lord Raglan' at 9.15 pm and another dropped in W. Ripples orchard at about 2 am.

Wed. 18th Sept

Had air raids nearly all day. Saw the pilot bale out of a 'Spitfire' this morning. He came down at Munn's, and the plane came down at Bumpstead's, but did not smash up much as it came down in a very slow spin. During the 1 o'clock raid we saw one man bale out very high up and far away to the north. Only saw about 12 heavy bombers. The fighters made 'skid' marks* all over the sky.

Heard terrific machine gunning in a cloud, and soon a bomber came down with 9 of our fighters round it. Three of the crew baled out, but two were killed. The plane came down at 'Collier Street', and the wreckage was strewn over two fields. There were two more raids later when we saw 17 heavy bombers flying through a great deal of anti-aircraft fire.

Thurs. 19th Sept

Finished hop-picking at about 1 o'clock, have finished a total of 579 bushels. There was not much activity in the air until darkness fell, then 'Jerry' kept coming over just above the clouds, and the anti-aircraft guns blazed away at him.

Fri. 20th Sept

Had an air-raid warning at mid-day. Saw a good many planes flying very high above the clouds, but could not tell which were 'Jerries' and which were ours.

Found a bullet clip, which must have dropped from a plane, in the ploughed field this afternoon. Some bombs were dropped at Hunton soon after 9.30 pm and they shook us pretty well.

Sat. 21st Sept

This afternoon Betty, Hylda and Margaret each found a bullet clip in a little field. Did not have any daylight air raid warnings until 6 pm, when we saw a few small planes flying very high in the direction of London. Thirty seven British fighters circled over here for an hour, but they could not find any Jerries. The usual night warning sounded at 8 o'clock.

Sun. Sept 22nd

Was very cloudy and rained all day so did not see anything

*The 'skid marks' were vapour trails.

during the short air-raid warning during the evening. The night warning sounded at 7.30 pm.

Mon 23rd Sept

Had a warning at 9.40 am. Saw some planes making 'skid' marks and heard a good deal of machine gun fire. A plane with white smoke pouring from it came down behind Sutton-Valance and the pilot baled out. We thought another came down somewhere in the direction of Tenterden.

Heard today that four oil bombs, a high explosive and a time bomb were dropped near Vinters Road Maidstone on Tues night but did no damage.

Had a short raid this evening but saw only five German bombers going towards London and two of those had white smoke coming from them.

Tues. 24th Sept

Mother received a letter from Uncle Douglas, which had been burnt in the fire at Staplehurst Station on Sun 15th.

Had two raid warnings this morning. Saw 17 German bombers with a large escort of fighters in the first, and about 20 bombers in the second.

During the second raid we saw a German fighter come down in flames, and the pilot baled out over Tenterden. Somebody saw a bomber come down and three men baled out.

Went to Tenterden this afternoon, and saw where a large part of Sissinghurst Forest had been burned down. The fire was started by incendiary bombs.

Two magnetic mines were dropped there last Wed. night. One blew up an oast-house between Tenterden, and Rolvenden, and the other fell near the Appledore Road, but nobody was killed, and no damage done although it shook Tenterden badly. While we were over there we saw two lone Jerry bombers sailing around, but no warning was sounded.

One of the pullets in the orchard house laid her first egg today.

Wed. 25th Sept

Only had one daylight air-raid warning. Did not see much except a barrage balloon, which was floating towards Hastings (26 down).

Thurs. 26th Sept

Mother's tortoise-shell had five kittens, 1 ginger, 1 black white and ginger, and 3 white.

Had several daylight warnings, but only saw a few planes.

Fri. 27th Sept

Humphries men came to sow the wheat, and Roy Fairway found an unexploded canon shell in the ploughed field.

Saw two stray barrage balloons blowing towards the south early this morning. Soon after a warning sounded, and a few 'Jerry' bombers went over towards London. Then some 'Jerry' fighters saw the balloons and shot both down in flames.

Had another warning mid-day when 17 heavy bombers flew right over us, and then turned in the direction of Maidstone where they unloaded their bombs. The anti-aircraft fire was terrific, and we thought we saw two planes come down.

Another warning sounded this afternoon and we saw about 15 bombers going along over the hills with anti-aircraft shells bursting all round them. Four fighters brought a bomber down over Marden, and we did not see anyone bale out. It must have caught fire as a large cloud of black smoke went up when it crashed. The sky seemed to be full of fighters overhead, but nothing came down although there was a good deal of machine-gunning. Betty counted 78 planes going over at once. (133 down).

Sat. 28th Sept

Had a raid warning this morning and saw one plane come down. The pilot baled out. We counted about 50 of our fighters going round and round but they did not seem to meet any 'Jerries'. Another warning sounded this afternoon, but I did not see anything as I was driving Humphries tractor. A Wellington bomber went over fairly low when we were coming up to tea.

I had three frights today. When I was driving the tractor this afternoon a shadow suddenly came across the field, and I looked up expecting to see a plane coming down, as I knew that the warning had gone, but it was only a Spitfire flying home very low. The second was when the steering of the tractor became disconnected and it charged straight for the pond. Luckily the radiator missed an oak tree by inches and I managed to stop it before it got down the bank. The third was just after I had gone to bed. The 'Jerries were cruising around the chimney pots as usual and there was a little anti-aircraft fire when suddenly there was a deafening bang and the house seemed to lean over to the north and then come back again. Dad got up and mother took Bridget and Margaret down because they were frightened. The rest of us stayed in bed as we could not hear a plane, and the windows still seemed to be in place. Mr. Brown came round to see if we were alright. Dad went along to headquarters where they told him that most of the windows were out up the main street but it was too dark to see to anything so we all went to sleep again.

Sun. 29th Sept

Got up to find that one large pane of glass was shattered in the spare room, the bottom hinge of my window which was open was broken and the stained glass window in the front door was almost sucked out.

Frank and I went up the village to find that windows had been broken and tiles blown off from the station to 'Ely Court'. A magnetic mine had been dropped by parachute in the north-east corner of Mr. F Watkins ploughed field up Bell Lane. It made a huge crater about 12-15 feet deep and the nose cap was found down the Headcorn Road. The houses up Bell Lane lost all their windows, doors and most of the tiles. The houses in the village had windows and frames hanging out and some had lost a good many tiles. One south window and parts of the east windows of the church were blown in. The only casualties were one person cut by glass, three sheep killed and one injured. Betty and Frank found the oxygen cylinder from the plane which crashed on the station in the lily pond this afternoon."

The atmosphere of an average fighter squadron of 1940 is almost incomprehensible to the younger generation of today. The language and attitudes are totally different. In 1940 the RAF had a form of slang exemplified by 'Wizard', 'Hells Bells', 'Bad Show' and 'Tally-ho'. It all came naturally to men of a small and exclusive band who lived life to the full on the ground and faced death daily in the air.

They pumped adrenalin into their systems in combat, their mouths became dry and they sweated profusely. They had to match the stress, in most cases with mad entertainment and hard drinking when off-duty—it was the safety valve.

The squadrons felt themselves a race apart. They had been told frequently on the radio and in the newspapers that all depended on the battle in the air and there was no way that the public could begin to understand the strain of waiting, the apprehension when scrambled and then the tensions of air combat. Pilots died and were mourned—but in a detached way as there was always another raid to be dealt with; being morbid did nothing for squadron morale and such an attitude would have been greeted with displeasure and suspicion by the rest of the fraternity.

'He's bought it' or 'He's got the chop' indicated no lack of feeling, just the appearance of an extra skin that had to be there if the war was to go on. Some broke under the strain and others could not give of their best in combat. They were only a few and they were only human.

Luftwaffe aircrew were strained to an even greater degree. Extremely well trained, they were not supermen. They had been the victors across the continent but each day in the summer of 1940 they had to cross that unpleasant stretch of water which they nicknamed the 'Scheiss-Kanal' (shit-canal). They knew that electronic and human eyes were watching for their approach and that the machinery of Fighter Command was being brought into action to greet them. They craned their necks to detect the first glint or dot in the sky which would indicate the arrival of Hurricanes or Spitfires, or both.

On certain days they felt certain that the opposition had diminished to such an extent that the RAF must be on the verge of defeat. Then on the next day or the day after, there were the fighter squadrons again seemingly as strong as ever. It was depressing in the extreme.

There was also another factor whereby the attitude of the Luftwaffe crews differed from those of the RAF. When an RAF pilot parachuted safely down in southern England he could expect a beer and phone for transport back to the airfield. For the Luftwaffe crew baling out of their burning bomber, the land below was totally hostile and the best to be hoped for was a long stay in a prisoner of war camp.

DIARY SEPTEMBER 7-30

September 7:	Day: Massive daylight attack on London: Defences confused. Heavy damage. Night: East London and docks, dusk until dawn. Losses: Luftwaffe 41: RAF 28
September 8:	Day: Scattered light airfield attacks. Luftwaffe recuperates. Night: All night bombing of London. Losses: Luftwaffe 28: RAF 2
September 9:	Day: Series of raids aimed at London; beaten back. Night: London, including the city and West End. Losses: Luftwaffe 28: RAF 19
September 10:	Day: Small scale airfield raiding in the afternoon. Night: London, South Wales and Merseyside. Losses: Luftwaffe 15 (including 9 write-offs in RAF raid on Eindhoven): RAF 1
September 11:	Day: Raids on London, south-east airfields and Southampton and Portsmouth. Night: London main target. Other harrassing raids. Losses: Luftwaffe 25: RAF 29
September 12:	Day: Poor weather. Small raids in south. Night: Reduced effort over London and scattered raids. Losses: Luftwaffe 4: RAF Nil
September 13:	Day: Poor weather. Small scale raids on London. Night: London. Losses: Luftwaffe 4: RAF 1
September 14:	Day: Probing raids on London, mainly fighters, despite good weather. Night: London, Cardiff, Gloucester, Maidstone, Ipswich and Fareham. Losses: Luftwaffe 14: RAF 14.
September 15:	Day: Heavy attacks on London repulsed by RAF. Heaviest Luftwaffe losses since 18th. Significant effect on German thinking. Night: Heavy attack on London. Losses: Luftwaffe 60: RAF 26
September 16:	Day: Small raids, east London Night: Main target London; small raids Merseyside and Midlands. Losses: Luftwaffe 11: RAF 4
September 17:	Day: Sealion invasion postponed. Luftwaffe fighter sweeps in south-east. Night: Heavy raids on London; smaller raids Glasgow and Merseyside. Losses: Luftwaffe 8: RAF 8
September 18:	Day: Kent, the Estuary and London. Night: London and Merseyside. Losses: Luftwaffe 20: RAF 11
September 19:	Day: Reduced activity: Thames Estuary and London. Night: Light activity over London: minelaying. Losses: Luftwaffe 9: RAF Nil
September 20:	Day: One fighter sweep Kent and Estuary; reconnaissance. Night : London. Losses: Luftwaffe 6: RAF 8
September 21:	Day: Coastal reconnaissance and isolated attacks. Night: Light raids, London, Liverpool, Warrington, Nottingham, Bolton and Colchester. Losses: Luftwaffe 11: RAF Nil
September 22:	Day: Little activity: smallest number of RAF sorties since start of battle Night: Heavy raids on London. Losses: Luftwaffe 17: RAF 9
September 23:	Day: Luftwaffe fighter sweeps. Night: London and Merseyside. Losses: Luftwaffe 17: RAF 9
September 24:	Day: Attempted raid on London, fighter sweeps and fighter-bombers over Southampton. Night: Widespread bombing: main targets London and Merseyside. Losses: Luftwaffe 10: RAF 11
September 25:	Day: Aircraft factory at Bristol and general attacks in No. 10 Group area including Plymouth. Night: London, North Wales and Lancashire. Losses: Luftwaffe 15: RAF 5
September 26:	Day: Spitfire factory at Woolston wrecked. Night: London and Merseyside. Losses: Luftwaffe 10: RAF 7
September 27:	Date: Major efforts aimed at London and Bristol. Heavy German losses. Night: London, Merseyside and Midlands. Losses: Luftwaffe 50: RAF 23
September 28:	Day: Raids on London and the Solent. Night: London. Losses: Luftwaffe 12: RAF 17
September 29:	Day: Several high flying formations in south-east. Night: London and Merseyside. Losses: Luftwaffe 9: RAF 6
September 30:	Day: Raids in south-east and in west. Last big daylight battle. Night: London, East Anglia, Liverpool and Bristol. Losses: Luftwaffe 46: RAF 17

314 A cruiser tank Mk III (A13) waits for the invasion. Like most British tanks of the period it suffered from inadequate armour and gun power, poor transmission and unreliable tracks.

315

316

To counter the impending invasion several strange varieties of aircraft appeared. **315** is the rapidly devised version of the army-cooperation Lysander with twin fins and the mock-up of a four-gun turret in the tail. The aircraft was intended as a ground strafer over the beaches when the Sealion force arrived. On an early test flight of this prototype the observer in the tail-end had the mock-up turret collapse around him and was left sitting on a lonely seat in the fresh air. **316** Nicknamed the 'Pregnant Peach' or 'The Cow', this Lysander (L4673) had an enlarged belly fitted with two 20 mm cannon. It is shown here wrecked in a field in the winter of 1940 following engine failure during a test flight.

Reference No:-
OC/150.

Headquarters, Observer Corps,
Bentley Priory,
STANMORE,
Middx.

Circular No.28.

18th September, 1940.

Dear Sir,

1. Enemy mass attacks towards London by day and more or less continuous attacks by night have given the members of the Observer Corps a very great deal of work under difficult conditions.

2. Enemy formations by day generally fly at a great height and their Fighters are often close to their bombers.
When our own Fighters intercept and the battle commences, continuous tracking of any particular raid becomes extremely difficult especially when plotting is by "Sound" only.
It is of great importance that enemy formations emerging from the battle zone should be tracked and Told forward without delay. The best method of dealing with the battle zone area is under consideration.

3. During intensive enemy action in any particular area Observers in conjunction with members of many other Civil Defence Organisations are exposed to considerable risk, particularly those in the London and S.E. Areas. I feel sure that members in districts which have not experienced intensive bombing wish to join in sending a word of praise and encouragement to those members of the Observer Corps who perform their duty so well under these conditions.

4. With reference to para.10 of Circular No.27, additional methods for assisting Observers to estimate heights at night have been worked out by the Controller and Observer Group Officer in one Group with good results. Details are in circulation.

5. The question of time lag is one that has recently been brought into prominence. When plotting by sound, Posts crews should remember that the aircraft is often well ahead of the direction from which the noise appears to arrive, and that is better to report a square ahead of this direction than behind it.
Plotters at the Centre should be quick in deciding where to place their halma men. Finally, a great deal depends on the Tellers and teleprinter Operators. At the high speeds now flown, the time factor is of very great importance, and all members are asked to pay special attention to this subject.

6. Their Majesties the King and Queen have paid a visit to Fighter Command Headquarters and were much interested in the work of the Observer Corps. H.R.H. The Duke of Kent recently visited an Observer Centre and Post in the S.E. of England and a letter was subsequently received expressing his keen appreciation of the work being performed in this Area and stating that he was greatly impressed by all that he saw.

7. Every endeavour is being made to obtain additional supplies of steel helmets in order that a personal issue can be made to each member. The difficulty is solely one of production caused by temporary factors which are being overcome. The position is improving and a first issue will shortly be made to Centres and Posts in Areas where A.A. fire is most intense and continuous.

8. The following incidents have been reported:-

(1) An Observer out rabbit shooting saw a German plane land ½ mile away. He went towards it and found that two Huns had crawled into a ditch. He covered them with his gun and told them to throw out their revolvers, which they did. At this moment, a farm labourer called out that there was another Hun behind. This one was holding a Tommy gun. The Observer covered him with his gun and the hun then gave his Tommy gun to a soldier who arrived at that moment.

P.T.O ....

- 2 -

8. (Cont'd)

(2) A Lysander crashed in a field and a member of the Observer Corps who was working nearby rescued the pilot from the wreckage. The Aircraft Observer was uninjured but the pilot was unconscious and petrol was pouring on to his face.

(3) A pilot who had some difficulty in finding his aerodrome during a night flight called at a Centre and examined the track. He expressed amazement at the accuracy with which his course had been followed especially when he was circling an aerial lighthouse and again when he made a sharp turn on sighting distant Aerodrome lights.

9. RESERVATION OF "B" CLASS OBSERVERS.
Reference OC/150 Circular 25 Para.9. The following details must be given with every application sent to these Headquarters:-
(1) Name. (2) Address. (3) Date of Registration,
(4) Place of Registration, (5) Registration Number, (6) and Date of

10. ROOF WATCHERS. The advantage of placing watchers on the roof of factories due to the fact that if there are no aircraft within sight or hearing and no gunfire production need not be stopped every time the siren is sounded. Although the R.A.F. is giving assistance in training watchers in recognition of aircraft, it has been made clear that the R.A.F. accept no responsibility whatsoever for the work of the watchers. Members of the Observer Corps are encouraged to give instruction to watchers in their neighbourhood but should not make local arrangements which will enable any responsibility to be placed on them if a factory is bombed without pre warning.

11. SPITFIRE FUND.
The Spitfire Fund is progressing well and £1,000 had been subscribed by September, 16th. One member raised £8. by writing and selling some verses on different types of aircraft. Another raised £11 by making a charge to visitors who wanted to see a bomb crater not far from his Post. It has been suggested that the closing date should be extended to October 31st to enable members to give 6d a week for 10 weeks. I will refer to this in my next circular, but am provisionally extending the closing date to October 15th.

12. For the information of newly joined members it is notified that there is an Observer Corps pattern tie which is worn by many members. These can be obtained through Controllers of Centres and Observer Group Officers who are being informed of the source of supply.

Yours faithfully,

Warrington-Morris

Commandant,
OBSERVER CORPS.

All Controllers
and Head Observers.

317 The Observer Corps Commandants' circular for September 18, 1940. Problems were developing with very large formations at high altitude where it became extremely difficult to sort out friend from foe by observation from the ground. Also, on cloudy days and at night, observer plotting could only be done by sound which was far from easy and often lead to zig-zag tracks and wrong height estimates. The roof watchers or 'Jim Crows' were hastily organised from factory personnel in order to give warning of a raid actually approaching. Many of them later became members of a large organisation known as the National Association of Spotters Clubs which greatly improved standards of aircraft recognition. Finally, the Spitfire fund referred to raised over £10,000 for the purchase of two aircraft which bore the name 'Observer Corps' and the Corps crest.

318 There came a knock on the front door! The rear fuselage of a Ju 88, probably from KG 54, wedged up against a house in Tonbridge Road, Maidstone, Kent on the morning of September 18. The aircraft had been shot down the previous night. The windows of the houses had been criss-crossed with sticky tape to stop them shattering from bomb blast.

319 Ludgate Hill and St Pauls Cathedral stand deserted on the morning of Thursday Sept 12 after 180 bombers had visited the city the previous night. The unexploded bomb was close to St Pauls Cathedral.

320 A scene of desolation in a London street after a heavy raid on the night of September 8. Firemen are working on the blazing ruins.

321 On the night of September 8/9 some 207 bombers raided London throughout the night. This double decker bus and office block in Holborn were wrecked by high explosives.

322 Collecting what furniture and belongings could be salvaged from bombed-out houses in North London after a raid on September 26.

323 Known the world over, the famous sentries beat at Buckingham Palace as it appeared after a delayed action bomb exploded on September 14. The bomb had been dropped during a morning raid on September 13.

324 Heavy bombing of London on the night of September 18 revealed widespread damage when dawn came. This wrecked building was next to St Pancras railway station.

325 Damage done to Peter Robinsons' department store in Oxford Street, London during the night raids of September 18.

327 King George VI, in army uniform complete with revolver holster, surveys bomb damage in London. The King and Queen and Winston Churchill made frequent visits to damaged areas.

326 Clearing rubble in Neptune Street, Rotherhithe near the Commercial Docks after heavy Luftflotte 3 bombing on the night of September 8.

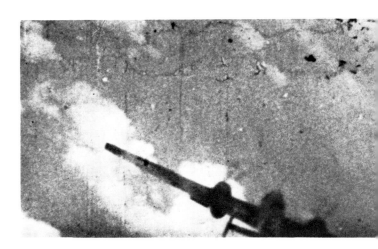

328 Fl Lt Frank Howell, A-flight Commander No. 609 squadron based at Middle Wallop, waits for a scramble call in the cockpit of his Spitfire. The four swastikas denote the shooting down of a Ju 87, a Ju 88 and two Bf 110s. The last kill, on September 15 is shown in official records as a Dornier 17 but Howells' log book contains the camera gun film picture of the interception, shown here. The aircraft (**329**) is quite clearly a Bf 110, seconds before he shot it down near Hastings. Howell was flying Spitfire R6691. Flying Bf 110s in 1940 was an extremely risky business for Luftwaffe pilots and observers as casualties were very heavy. **330** Bf 110s of ZG 26 flying out for a sortie against the RAF. **331** A 110 from the same unit shot down by the main road at Lenham, Kent on September 20. ZG 26 painted the noses of its aircraft white. This particular example's sole claim to fame was that it had shot up a British railway train as shown by the locomotive painted below the windscreen.

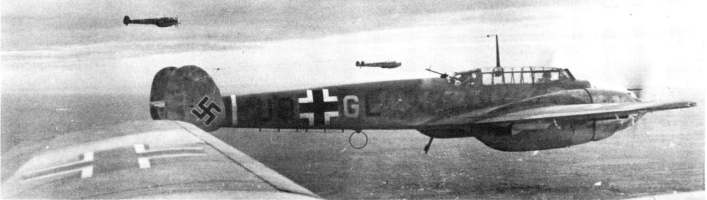

33

33

332 Fl Lt (later Group Captain) Brian Kingcombe of No. 92 Spitfire squadron. He was credited with a total of seven kills in the Battle of Britain but was wounded and baled out on October 15 near Chatham. He won the DSO and DFC as a fighter pilot. The raised fingers below the windscreen typify the general attitude of Fighter Command to the Luftwaffe during the battle.

333 Armourers loading .303 machine gun ammunition belts into the wing of a Hurricane.

334 Three remarkable Americans who fought with No. 609 squadron in the summer of 1940. From left to right: Gene 'Red' Tobin, Vernon 'Shorty' Keough and Andrew 'Andy' Mamedoff. Together they travelled to France in May and saw that country collapse. After getting away on the last ship from St Jean-de-Luz, they arrived in London. The US Embassy thought it would be embarrassing for neutrals to be seen fighting for Britain and tried to have them sent back across the Atlantic. With the help of a Member of Parliament they succeeded in enlisting in the RAF and eventually arrived at Middle Wallop on August 8. All three had had civil pilot licences in America. 'Shorty' had been a professional parachute jumper and was, in fact, the smallest pilot in the RAF. He used two cushions in his Spitfire so that he could see over the edge of the cockpit. On September 26, they were posted north to help form No. 71 (Eagle) squadron composed of US volunteers. Mamedoff is shown here holding the Eagle Squadron badge. All three were subsequently killed. As the late Fl Lt D M Crook wrote in his book *Spitfire Pilot,* 'Shorty was last seen spinning into the sea near Flamborough Head during a chase after a Heinkel. Red crashed behind Boulogne, fighting like hell against a crowd of Me 109s, while Andy hit a hill in bad weather and was killed. As Red once remarked with the usual grin, pointing to the wings on his tunic 'I reckon these are a one way ticket, pal'.' Altogether seven Americans flew operationally in the Battle of Britain and one was killed during it.

335 Major Helmut Wick who became Gruppenkomman-
deur of 1./JG 2 on September 7 and Kommodore of JG 2 on
October 20. He claimed 56 victories in the West at the time he
was shot down on November 28, 1940. He was one of only
three Luftwaffe pilots awarded the Oak Leaves to the Knights
Cross of the Iron Cross in the Battle of Britain (the others
being Mölders and Galland).

336 The German map of raids carried out on Britain in
September.

337 A Dornier 17 of KG 3 takes off from France for a raid.
Several more Dorniers can be seen in camouflaged revet-
ments. KG 3 had been transferred to the Pas de Calais from
Luftflotte 3 early in September.

338 One of the most serious factory raids of the whole battle was that on the Vickers-Supermarine Woolston Works, Southampton, on September 26. Woolston was the main centre for Spitfire production while the line was building up at the big shadow factory at Castle Bromwich. Some 60 He IIIs of KG 55 wrecked the factory with 70 tons of bombs and over 30 people were killed. In August 149 Spitfires had come off the line. Despite the raid, by every form of improvisation, 139 Spitfires were built in October. Work was dispersed all round Southampton. The skeleton of the factory is seen here after the raid with a number of the houses behind it destroyed.

The Evening News

LARGEST EVENING NET SALE IN THE WORLD

LATE EXTRA

NO. 18,301 8 SIXTIETH YEAR LONDON, MONDAY, SEPTEMBER 16, 1940 ONE PENNY

TO-NIGHT'S BLACK OUT
7.41 p.m. to 6.9 a.m.

185 Raiders Down Yesterday in R.A.F.'s Record One-Day Victory

BIG NEW ATTACK BEATEN BACK TO-DAY

RAIDERS CHASED OVER THE CHANNEL: 3 LONDON WARNINGS

Germans Admit That Our Fighters Surprised Them Yesterday

Large numbers of enemy planes crossed the S.E. coast about breakfast time to-day, but were broken up and chased back across the Channel.

London had three warnings before lunch. During the first two there were no reports of enemy activity in the area.

Anti-aircraft fire was heard shortly after the third warning.

GOERING'S Air Force lost 185 planes out of 350, and at least 460 airmen yesterday—a record for one day's destruction, the previous best was 181, on August 15.

The Air Ministry, in announcing the record figure to-day, state that five of our fighters, reported missing, have since turned up.

Yesterday's great success cost us only 25 fighters—and 12 of their pilots are safe. The proportion of losses is therefore more than 7 to one in our favour.

In nine days, since Saturday last week when the air battle of London really began, the Luftwaffe have lost 465 planes and at least 1,100 airmen. The R.A.F. have lost 96 planes and 55 airmen.

SMALL GROUPS AGAIN

Here is an Air Ministry and Ministry of Home Security communique on last night's raids:

"Enemy air attacks on this country were continued during the night by a succession of small groups of bombers. These attacks were directed mainly against the London area and surrounding districts, but a smaller number were also made against other parts of the country.

"In London the attacks were spread over a wide area. Damage was done to houses, commercial premises and other buildings. Once again attacks were directed at hospitals, three of them being damaged by bombs.

"Throughout the country bombs fell in many rural districts, but with little result.

"In the North-West and South-East of England, in South Wales and in some other districts including one town in the South of England, some damage was caused.

"One enemy bomber was shot down during the night.

"Yesterday 185 enemy aircraft were destroyed, seven of them by anti-aircraft guns and the remainder by our fighters. One hundred and thirty-one of the enemy aircraft were bombers.

"Five of our fighter aircraft previously reported as missing have now reported to their bases. Our losses yesterday were, therefore, 25 fighter aircraft. Twelve of the pilots of these aircraft are safe.

There was only one casualty in the three hospitals hit—a doctor who suffered a severe cut. A medical block at one of London's oldest hospitals was wrecked by a high-explosive bomb.

FLED FROM BARRAGE

The bomb passed right through a staircase, but missed wards on either side. Patients were later removed elsewhere.

Yesterday's three attacks by massed raiders—during one of which Buckingham Palace was bombed again—are admitted by the Germans to have met with stiff opposition.

The German Official News Agency stated to-day that there was "an unusual and surprising concentration of British fighters," and that the German fighter escort "had a harder struggle than usual." And last night London's barrage again sent the raiders fleeing to drop their bombs on the outskirts.

BATTLE OUT AT SEA

LONDON'S first warning of the day was sounded at 9.59 a.m. The all clear came at 10.33, after 34 minutes.

It was followed by a second warning, at 10.54; this time it lasted until 11.37, a period of 43 minutes.

At 12.12 p.m. the sirens in the area were sounded for a third time.

A Spotter

The first warning was caused by the approach of a single enemy machine from the direction of the Channel.

It was apparently carrying out a weather or photograph reconnaissance. No bombs were dropped.

The attempted attack by the large force of enemy planes had been made before this.

Making for London

Two formations of German raiders were sighted off the **South-East** coast at one point flying in a westerly direction some hours after dawn.

The first, about 30 bombers, escorted by 40 Messerschmitts, crossed the coast as if making for London.

About half an hour later a second force came inland practically over the same route.

Nine bombers led the way, and behind these came 26 more bombers, spread out in threes or fours. Above and behind them were many Messerschmitts.

Overhauled Them

Anti-aircraft guns drove this formation off their course.

However, within ten minutes this second formation was making its way back to France again, having been intercepted by British fighters.

Spitfires overhauled them while out in the Channel, and fighting was heard in the air out at sea.

During the raid a single bomber flew in from the coast to the east, but it also was driven back by A.A. guns.

Lone Bomber

The formations had passed over S.E. coast towns. One lone bomber glided down to drop a salvo of four bombs in a residential part of one town. Three fell in gardens and the other in a park.

Another S.E. coast town which had had nuisance raiders during the night had a visit from the first formation to-day. No bombs were dropped and there was no gunfire.

Last night's raids: **Back Page.**

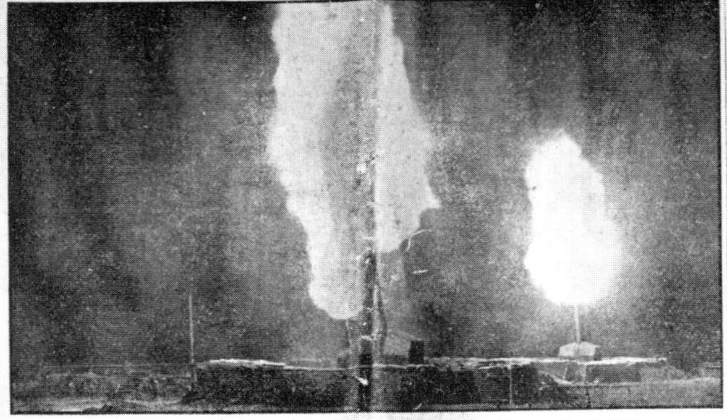

Guns of London's anti-aircraft barrage blazing into the night sky.—"Evening News" picture. A night with a London A.A. battery is described on PAGE FIVE.

BIG BLOWS

Blast from high-explosive bombs dropped in a South London suburb did these strange things:

Wrecked a house, but left every picture hanging on walls with glass intact;

Demolished a schoolroom, leaving only a boy's painting of a British battleship pinned on the wall and an A.R.P. book on a shelf;

Blew apples off tree into bedroom window 100 yards away.

Goering's One-Day Bill

460 Airmen, And About £2,500,000

The 186 machines—178 by fighters, 7 by A.A. gunners and one by the Navy (a trawler bagged it, but it was not included in to-day's Air Ministry communique — which the German Air Force is known to have lost yesterday, cost the German people about £2,500,000.

In addition to the money and machines it is estimated that the German Air Force lost approximately 460 airmen.

The total British losses were 25 machines and 13 men.

131 Bombers

The previous "worst days" were August 15, when 181 German planes were destroyed for the loss of 34 British (17 pilots saved), and August 18, when 153 German machines were shot down, and 22 British machines were lost (12 pilots saved).

These figures show that the proportion of German losses to British yesterday was higher than on the previous days, when large numbers of German planes were destroyed.

The number of bombers shot down yesterday is interesting—131 out of the total of 186 aircraft.

THESE FACTORIES WERE SHUT

The fact that most of Germany's margarine factories have been closed for the past two months was revealed by the German wireless to-day, says Reuter. It was announced that these factories will resume their output this month.

DAVID NIVEN IS TO MARRY

£40,000 FILM STAR WHO IS NOW IN ARMY

DAVID NIVEN, the British-born film star, who gave up a £40,000 a year Hollywood salary to return to England to do his bit, [illegible] Miss Primula Rollo, daughter of Flight-Lieut. William Rollo and Lady Kathleen Rollo, it is announced to-day.

The wedding will take place shortly.

Mr. Niven, who is 30, and younger son of the late Mr. W. G. Niven and the late Lady Comyn-Platt, of Carswell Manor, Berkshire, is now a Captain in the Rifle Brigade.

Miss Rollo is 22. She is a niece of the Marquis of Downshire.

Tried To Join R.A.F.

When war broke out David Niven had reached Hollywood stardom as one of the cleverest light comedians on the screen.

In November last he decided to return to England to join the R.A.F., but his age was against him; he also failed to take up his former commission as a lieutenant in the Highland Light Infantry.

Early this year he was accepted by the Officers' Emergency Reserve and given a commission in the Rifle Brigade.

The remaining five years of his contract with Mr. Sam Goldwyn, the Hollywood producer, will be taken up when the war is over.

He Was Bootlegger

Mr. Niven was at Stowe School before going to Sandhurst and was always the "star" turn at concerts.

Finding he had no time for the Army in peace time, he went to America and tried his hand at many things, including lumbering, fishing, helping to run a race track in Mexico, and a spell of bootlegging.

His ambitions to be an American newspaper man were damped by tough editors and he turned his hand to the laundry business in New York.

The films "Bachelor Mother" and "Eternally Yours" put him in the Hollywood front rank: his final picture before leaving was "Raffles."

Miss Primula Rollo.

£6,000 JEWEL ROBBERY

SILENT THIEVES BREAK INTO MANSION

THIEVES during the week-end broke into Woodhurst, the Maidenhead mansion of Mr. Ernest Dunkels, the London barrister, of Garden-court, Temple, and stole jewellery worth £6,000, belonging to Mrs. Dunkels.

The robbery took place while Mr. and Mrs. Dunkels were in the library after dinner and the maids were having dinner. Nothing was heard.

The thieves got in by climbing a drainpipe to Mrs. Dunkels's bedroom window.

Second in Two Years

The jewellery was taken from her jewel case.

Two years ago £1,000 worth of jewellery was taken from the house.

HINT TO MOTORISTS

Apply Early for Renewal of Licences

The Transport Minister appeals to motorists to apply early for renewal of motor licences which expire at the end of September, to avoid congestion caused in taxation offices by late applications.

Applications may be made from to-morrow. Motorists are asked to see that the renewal order forms, to be had at post offices, are properly filled in. Evidence of third-party insurance must be produced.

PETROL EMBARGO

Secret of Japan's Protest To America Revealed

Discrimination and unfairness are alleged by Japan in a protest to the United States against the American embargo on petrol, the Foreign Office spokesman said in Tokio to-day.

He said that the protest was lodged in Washington four or five weeks ago, and that Mr. Sumner Welles, Assistant Foreign Minister, replied to Mr. Horinouchi, the Japanese Ambassador, in a written Note a week later.

The spokesman would not state the nature of the American reply.—Reuter.

GERMAN CLAIMS

"Aerodrome Attacked, Fires In London Docks"

The German wireless claimed to-day that during an attack "on an aerodrome near Lincoln" in yesterday's raids hangars, barracks, and runways were destroyed.

It was also claimed that four waves of German planes attacked the London docks, "causing fires, especially at the Albert and India Docks.

"A British tanker was attacked by a German bomber north-west of Ireland, several direct hits being registered," said the announcer.—Exchange.

Germans Shell Dover Area To-day

GERMAN long-range guns began shelling the Dover area at 11 a.m. to-day from their emplacements near Cap Gris Nez, on the French coast.

The concussion shook houses and shops in the area, and great columns of black smoke could be seen rising in the distance.

Most people at first assumed [illegible] by delayed action bombs. They did not take shelter until sirens sounded after the firing started.

Sailor Fell Off

A sailor motor-cycling down the main street was so surprised when the first shell crashed that he applied his brakes, skidded violently and fell in the road.

He got up, brushed the mud from his clothes and, with a grin, remounted his machine.

The shelling ceased after 10 minutes. Later the all-clear was sounded.

LONGER PARLIAMENT

A Bill to prolong the life of the present Parliament will be introduced in both Houses shortly.

Consultations are taking place among the party leaders and the Prime Minister will probably make a statement when Parliamentary sittings are resumed this week.

3 LONDON HOSPITALS HIT

EMERGENCY PLANS SAVED PATIENTS

THREE London hospitals were bombed during the night raids.

Carefully laid emergency plans worked so perfectly after a hospital in **Central London** had been hit by a heavy bomb that not one patient was hurt.

The only casualty was a doctor, who received a severe cut.

Four Bombs Fell

Four bombs fell simultaneously on or round the hospital. One fell in a roadway at the side of the hospital and two others fell near the hospital works department.

All the patients—about 100—were in the building that received the damage. Four wards leading off the main staircase were occupied, and it was through the roof above that staircase that the bomb fell.

The entire staircase was demolished, leaving a gaping well.

No one was on the stairs. A ward sister had been there a few seconds before, and had gone into her ward and shut the door. Doors of the ward were blown in and nurses and other staff thrown from their feet.

Doctor's Escape

The doctor who was injured was sitting at a desk in a small medicine room high up in the building. His desk vanished in the crash; his chair was to-day tottering on the edge of a chasm.

The doctor was rescued by a ladder from a window.

It was impossible to move the patients by normal means. Some were taken along a ramp over a low wall and through a window. Others were rescued over a wooden bridge built only two days ago to meet such an emergency.

Meanwhile doctors were dealing with casualties from a town hall in an adjoining neighbourhood which had been hit.

Staff in Shelter

A hospital in **West London** suffered mainly from the effects of blast from a high-explosive bomb, [illegible] casualties.

Women patients had been evacuated and male patients and staff were in a shelter.

The bomb also damaged an in-patients' department.

An official at the third of the bombed London hospitals stated to-day that there were no casualties when an oil bomb fell on the premises.

Damage was caused to a building used as a kitchen and mess room. The maternity home nearby escaped material damage.

"PEACE OFFENSIVE NEXT"

Mr. R. G. Menzies, Australian Premier, in a speech at Melbourne, forecast (says Reuter) a German peace offensive within a fortnight on top of the nerve-racking experiences of the British people. He was sure, he said, Britain would refuse until the evils the Germans had built up had been purged away.

PEOPLE KILLED BY TIME BOMB

Number of casualties, some fatal, when time bomb exploded in S.E. London district to-day.

First demolished some small houses and burst gas main. Second tore away back part of Roman Catholic school. Fortunately parents had been warned and school was empty at time.

BOMB ON A.R.P. CONTROL CENTRE

Members of A.R.P. control staff injured when bomb went through roof of Town Hall in S.E. London borough. A.R.P. system continued efficiently.

A number of casualties, some fatal, when another bomb fell on arches not far away where hundreds of people were sheltering.

THIRD ALL-CLEAR

(See also this page.)

Third all-clear given at 12.50.

LONE RAIDER ON LONDON OUTSKIRTS

(See also this page.)

Lone raider flew over outskirts of London while third warning was in operation, but was quickly driven off by A.A. gunfire. It made off northwards. No bombs were dropped.

TIME BOMB IN LONDON SQUARE

[illegible]

Time bomb exploded during second daylight warning today, shaking business premises over wide area. Water main was burst.

Three adjacent hotels, and raid shelter under another part of gardens were evacuated when bomb fell.

Believed another bomb is near spot where first one fell.

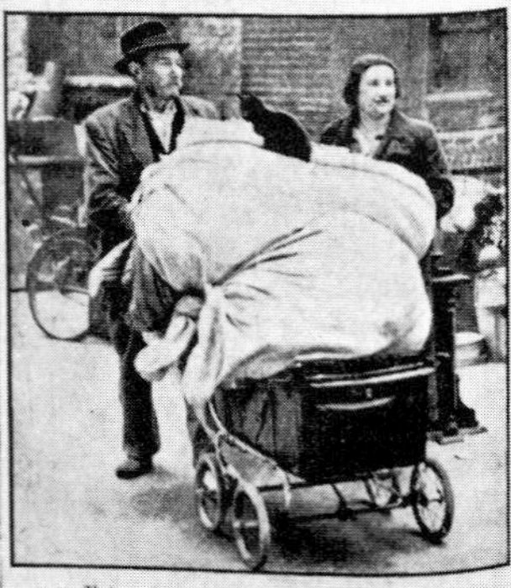

Their most treasured belongings and their cat piled on a baby cart for their journey from a bomb-shattered London home to shelter elsewhere.

339 The front page of the London Evening News for September 16, the day after the big raid on London had been repulsed and the RAF thought that it had shot down 185 Luftwaffe aircraft. Amidst the mass of war news, the only two non-war stories to merit space were a £6000 jewel robbery at Maidenhead and the engagement of film star, David Niven, to Miss Primula Rollo. Niven was at the time an officer in the Rifle Brigade.

340 The fuel storage tanks at Thames Haven, Essex, ablaze during the raid on September 7.

341 A high altitude photograph of London taken by the Luftwaffe during the first big daylight raid on September 7. In the centre are Rotherhithe and Millwall, while on the river from the extreme left are the Waterloo, Blackfriars, South-wark, London and Tower Bridges. The German annotations on the picture are (1) Bomb bursts (2) Anti-aircraft fire (3) German bombers (4) Millwall Dock (5) Grain silos and (7) Fuel depot.

LATEST

GERMANS BOMB "RANDOM"

Many recent Air Ministry communiques have included phrase—"bombs were dropped at random." Germans apparently think "random" is district of London, because this was radioed on Deutschlandsender in German last night: "In the suburb of Random, and also in the East, South and South-West of London, damage has been caused by our bombers."

342 This stop-press item in a newspaper in September shows that the Germans were having slight language difficulties.

344 Vapour trails wove strange patterns across the sky as air battles took place at high altitude during the Battle of Britain.

345 On fire and with its tailplane nearly severed from the fuselage, this Bf 109 dives to the ground and explodes in a hopfield near Maidstone, Kent on September 29.

343 On September 11 a strong force of bombers from KG 26 attacked London. Over the city the bombers lost their fighter escort and were savagely attacked by six RAF squadrons. Altogether KG 26 lost seven Heinkel 111s destroyed and had ten more damaged. One of them burns on the ground at Burmarsh near Dimchurch while the Spitfire that shot it down circles overhead. **346** Two of the crew are being led away by the army.

347 Heinkel IIIs of KG 53 taxi out for take-off across a wheatfield.

348 Approaching London, a Heinkel 111 seen from the nose of another.

349 Whole teams of cameramen were employed by the Luftwaffe during the Battle of Britain. Here a movie specialist was photographing a Heinkel III whilst himself being snapped by a Leica.

350 Radio was of vital importance during the Battle of Britain. Here the TR9 HF set aboard a Hurricane of No. 601 squadron is being tested by the ground crew at Tangmere.

351 Groups of barges being assembled in a French Channel port ready for Operation Sealion. The lack of hundreds of these Rhine barges for a long period put a severe strain on the German home economy.

352/353 A major advantage that Luftwaffe Bf 109s had over Spitfires and Hurricanes in the summer of 1940 was the 20 mm cannon firing explosive shells. The effect of even one hit could be devastating. The RAF was mesmerised by the so-called 'wall of Steel' put up by eight Browning machine guns. The .303 Browning gun fired 1200 rounds per minute at a muzzle velocity of some 2400 ft/second. A gun firing produced a stream of bullets each 120 ft apart from the other and at 1/20th second intervals. If eight guns were aligned on one point, the average gap between bullets at that point would be 15 ft—hardly a wall of steel! A target fighter at 300 mph, crossing the path of the bullets at this point and at right angles would, in theory, receive about seven bullets spaced out at some 3 ft intervals along its centre-line. In fact, gravity,

351

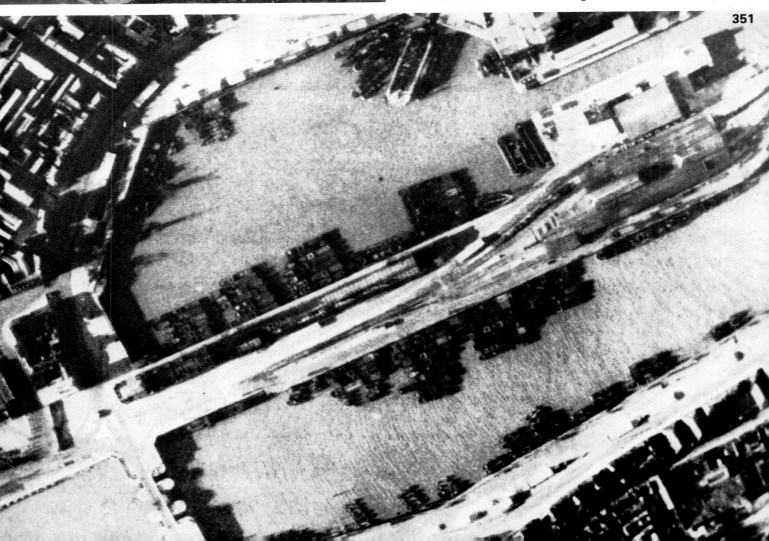

vibration, ammunition variations and misalignment led to increased scatter. Harmonisation, with four gun nests 20 ft apart proved difficult.

Some 16 strikes of .303 ammunition per square foot of enemy aircraft were needed to achieve a lethal density. This could be attained with good harmonisation and a pilot who drew a proper bead and maintained the correct deflection. Many of the young pilots in 1940 however had had little or no practice in deflection shooting and they were supposed to perform in the middle of a dog fight.

The answer lay in the 20 mm Hispano cannon which was being built in Britain. One Hurricane was converted to take two 20 mm cannon in bulges under the wings, while No. 19 squadron at Duxford was equipped with Spitfires fitted with one 20 mm cannon in each wing. Despite all the efforts of the

red to sit around a table and argue. The 'book' said that our .5 ammunition would penetrate the armour carried by the ME 109, so, in their opinion, practical tests were unnecessary. Lord Beaverbrook was by then in the saddle at the Ministry of Aircraft Production, and by appealing to him direct I was able to get a ME 109 fuselage sent to Orfordness for a trial. This trial was boycotted by all Air Ministry officers. Nobody turned up to see it except myself and two junior Army officers who had somehow heard of what was to be done. The first test was on some plates of armour in the open, stated to be similar in all respects to the armour of the Messerschmitts (sic). Some rounds were fired at these from about 30 yards, and the plates were penetrated like butter, thus confirming the verdict of the 'book'. "Now" I said "fire at the armour in position in the aircraft from the same range". This was done,

352 The first Spitfire, L1007, to be equipped with 20 mm cannon in 1939.

353 The first Hurricane with two underslung 20 mm, also in 1939, at Martlesham.

armaments specialists, these proved utterly unreliable and stoppages were continuous. Eventually Dowding went to see No. 19 squadron at the height of the battle and the CO Squadron Leader Lane showed him a minutely detailed analysis of every fault, prepared by the armaments officer. As a result, No. 19 squadron had its cannon-Spitfires replaced by eight machine gun-equipped aircraft.

The 20 mm stoppages occured on the forward action of the gun, due to a mis-fed round or a jam in the empty case ejector chute. The basic cause was that the cannon installation had not been tested with the guns fitted on their sides. This resulted in misalignment of the magazine due to its weight, coupled with a poor fit due to dimensional variations and/or obstructions from the wing structure. Faulty feed alignment resulted in the round jamming in the breech. A combination of effects stopped the spent cartridge case from leaving the ejector chute cleanly. This was aggravated by faulty manufacture of the ejector claws of the gun.

Lord Dowding said after the war 'An incident not related in my Despatch on the Battle of Britain concerned a test of the defensive armour of the ME 109. It was clear from the beginning that the eight .303 guns with which our monoplane fighters were equipped would not be sufficiently powerful when the Germans fitted rear armour to their fighters. In practice our choice lay between the .5 Browning and the 20 mm 'cannon'. Obviously if the smaller gun were powerful enough it would be preferable to the cannon because more of the former could be carried and much more ammunition. I wanted practical penetration tests to be carried out on a captured ME 109 but, as usual, the Air Ministry Staff prefer-

with the result that the armour was only slightly dented and bulged. Nothing approaching to penetration was attained. Once again the value of the practical trial over theoretical argument was demonstrated. Either the armour from which the 'book' results had been obtained was not German armour but something very inferior of our own, or else the passage of the bullet through the frail skin of the fuselage was sufficient to destroy the perfect concentricity of the bullet's spin and so reduce its penetrative power by over 50%. I left that problem for the experts to disentangle—I had learnt that the .5 Browning would not meet our needs."

PHASE 5· OCTOBER 1-31

As September drew to a close, the spectre of invasion faded with the chances of bad weather and a choppy sea in the Channel offering poor prospects for Rhine river barges.

In the air, Göring had decided to concentrate his main bomber forces on night raids where aircraft casualties were few. By doing this, he virtually conceded defeat in the daylight battle. The losses over three months had steadily sapped Luftwaffe strength and aircraft replacements were in short supply. His aircrew were also suffering from battle fatigue.

To maintain a presence over England in daylight and still bring the RAF to battle, one third of the German fighters were converted into fighter-bombers, the 109s with a 250 kg bomb and the 110s with up to 700 kg load. Bomb carrying on both 109 and 110 had been proven with Eprobrungsgruppe 210 but the conversion of some 250 aircraft for use in October represented a major effort.

No strategic result could be obtained by these fighter bombers but they kept Fighter Command constantly on its toes. Since the cessation of major attacks on sector airfields on September 6, No. 11 Group had been undergoing a steady process of recuperation and repair. The high altitude at which the fighter-bomber formations flew (around 20,000 ft), however, meant long climbs for British fighters and plotting and height assessment difficulties for both radar and the Observer Corps.

On October 1, the RAF encountered the fighter-bombers for the first time in a series of waves over Kent and Portsmouth/Southampton. This was to be the pattern for the month, with fighter attacking fighter and the heavily laden fighter bombers jettisoning their loads when intercepted—leading, inevitably, to damage over a wide area.

Fighter Command put up first singly and then in pairs, aircraft to fly at altitude and report the make-up of incoming formations to the Controller on the ground but this was only partially successful.

Some raids did achieve results, sometimes by accident, as was the case on October 3, when a lone Ju 88 caused considerable damage and casualties at the de Havilland works at Hatfield.

Park issued new instructions on October 4 calling for one to three pairs of squadrons to aim at formations going for targets in the vicinity of London. Whenever time permitted he wanted controllers to get readiness squadrons, in company, over sector airfields with Spitfires at 25,000 ft and Hurricanes at 20,000 ft. This, however, was not to stop controllers putting squadrons onto threatening raids even if they had not reached the specified altitude.

At various times, German aircraft did hit airfields but the weight of the attacks did not produce significant damage. Bombs also continued to drop on a variety of targets in London, as for instance October 8, when the War Office, Horse Guards Parade, Adastral House, BBC Bush House and Tower Bridge were hit. Aircraft losses on both sides were nowhere near as high as in August and September.

On October 12, Hitler decided that 'From now until the Spring, preparations for Sealion shall be continued solely for the purpose of maintaining political and military pressure on England'. The invasion fleet had largely dispersed, having lost 21 transports and 214 barges due to British air attacks.

Park, by mid-October, was still wrestling with the problem of dealing with high flying streams and, in an order issued on October 15, he made one telling statement. 'Bitter experience has proved time and again that it is better to intercept the enemy with one squadron above him than by a whole wing crawling up below, probably after the enemy has dropped his bombs.'

Morale in Fighter Command was good and the sense of humour of the time is amply shown in a letter written by Flight Lt Frank Howell of No. 609 squadron on Sunday, October 12, to his brother, in which he describes with masterly understatement one air fight in terms of a bogus cartoon character:-

Middle Wallop, Sunday (*Oct. 12 '40*)
"I just feel in the mood to write you a couple of pages, to tell you of my latest adventure! The powers that be, as you probably already know, dished out the odd gong—all very pleasing.[1] Our C.O. has been posted, and he got the D.S.O.,[2] which is tres bon.
'Fritz the Fearful' by Fearless Frank the frightful fighter floogy[3]—or something.
Chapter 1. Two squadrons there were, two squadrons, twelve Hurricanes[4] and 13 Spitfires, winging their way through the cold (bloody cold) blue sky, to defend the shores of Britain against the fearful invader.[5]

---

[1] Howell had been awarded the DFC
[2] Squadron Leader H S Darley
[3] Floogy came from a popular song of the period which began 'The flat foot floogy . . .'
[4] 238 squadron
[5] The incident took place on October 7 when Ju 88s of KG 51 escorted by fifty Bf 110s of ZG 26 raided Westland Aircraft at Yeovil. ZG 26 lost seven 110s in the engagement which involved five RAF squadrons. Some thirty Bf 109s took part in the later stages of the fight.

They were coming up from the south, we were told, over 200 of them—and the fearless (?) fighters (all 25 of them) flew on to meet the foe, to do battle for England's sake (or because there were others behind me and I couldn't run away). There they were! Little dots in the sky—above us, below us, suddenly all around—109's diving down out of the sun. Me 110's circling around in a huge circle—bombers below with a "beehive" of fighters above them. The Hurricanes split up in all directions, some diving for the bombers, others to engage the fighters. F. Frank was getting *very* frightened, when word came to split up and cop the buggers. Just then, a very obliging Me 110 came round in front of me, guns spitting flame and smoke, blasting his way through the air in a shower of lead and flame (I didn't see all this, but I expect he was doing it, and it sounds good). But wait! as he turned away F. F. was on him like a flash, his eight guns spitting a shower of death in front of him, and into the raider. Was he dismayed? No—the rear gunner, with his one gun stood up like a man, and returned bullet for bullet (divided by eight) with the eight gun one place pursuit ship of the British Royal Air Force. The battle was on—long and fast did it wage—it was over in 4 seconds when with a mighty report (I expect) the starboard petrol tank burst into a raging furnace, and that ended well—that.

With a smug expression on his face, F. F. screamed away with a vertical dive for 4000′ with who knows what on his tail! He pulled the stick back, and with chin out and eyes blazing, flew back into battle!

Back he went, but suddenly with one tentative sniff, and another big one, the smug expression was wiped off his face quicker than if the airscrew had stopped—But what had happened—the prop was trying to stop anyway—hold yourself together—maintain an icy calm and look at your instruments! The oil, my God, the oil—pressure at zero—the engine was crying out in agony, the airplane shaking as if a giant hand was throwing it about. Shall I take to the silk—no no—there was land below, and good friends, besides, why waste the best part of a good aeroplane? The ground seemed very close—good God which way was the wind blowing—icy calm chaps icy calm. Ah, the cloud shadows, and a lovely bonfire (I hope I remember to thank the farmer) showed the way. My God, what about a field—yes there was one—only one, oh dear, oh dear, and with a fearful side slip between an avenue of trees, he crashed—he crashed—would the bloody thing never hit the ground—he CRASHED down, skidded along—turned right over—yes—no yes no no—whew, and landed 2 yards from the hedge.

Flight of foot, F. F. nimbly nipped out, and within 2 minutes the farmer was on the spot with hot cocoa, a local with brandy, and another dear soul with a nicecupertea. 2 minutes later the police arrived in a neck to neck race with the army and proceeded to fight as to who should take possession of me! I decided by going with the police, for I knew there would be some good beer around the corner! *And* there was."

The night Blitz, nevertheless, continued unabated as the day fight diminished and the provincial cities began to get their share of attention. Liverpool, Coventry, Manchester and Birmingham were attacked several times in October and the net widened in November and December. On the night of November 14/15, for instance, Coventry received over 500 tons of bombs, 554 people were killed and 865 seriously injured.

London, meanwhile, continued to absorb the main punishment. The first raid-free 24 hour period, after September 7, only came on November 25, Living with air raids became a way of life. After a night in the shelters or in the cellar, the citizens would pick their way to work through the fires, rubble and broken glass, mingling with the commuters using such stations and railway lines that still operated. The firemen, rescue squads, police and wardens dug out the living and the dead from the ruins and life went on with some semblance of normality. Morale was not broken and, with Britain fighting alone, this represented a contribution equivalent to many combat divisions.

For Dowding, the night bombing of September and October was a matter of sheer frustration. Ground Control Interception (GCI) radar was not yet ready and A.I. radar on the Blenheim night fighters was crude and unreliable. He spent night after night watching the efforts to make a dent in the bomber streams, without success. His successor, Sholto Douglas, reaped the benefit of all the earlier work, in 1941, when the Beaufighter with A.I. Mk 4 combined with GCI to cause the Luftwaffe heavy losses in the hours of darkness.

To those who daily and nightly watched for and listened to the Luftwaffe and its effects on the approaches to London, the only difference between July to September and September to December lay in the size and shape of the enemy forces and the times of maximum effort. Extracts from Freda Tomlin's diary accurately record the period:-

Fri 4th Oct

Had air raid warnings nearly all day. Saw a bomber being chased by three Spitfires in the morning. Went round Staplehurst Plain to get some leaves and berries for Harvest Festival this afternoon and heard some of the longest machine-gun bursts that we have ever heard but only saw one or two of our fighters as visibility was very bad. We think that ground machine guns must have been firing at a Jerry bomber. Some bombs were dropped at Cranbrook station in the afternoon and at about 8.30 pm six were dropped at Folly Hill.

Sun 6th Oct

We all went to Church as it was Harvest Festival. Had very few Jerries over during the day, and it was the first night for over a month that there was not a warning between 10 pm and 6 am. Hylda left.

Mon 7th Oct

Had Jerries over nearly all day. Betty saw a fighter brought down over Headcorn. The pilot baled out but his parachute did not open. One of our planes came down but the pilot baled out safely. Some bombs were dropped at Coxheath during the day, and some more during the night. Mother had a letter from Uncle Douglas posted on Sept 5th.

Wed 9th Oct

It was a wet cloudy day. During the morning we heard bombs dropping in the direction of Linton. Then we heard a terrific burst of machine-gun fire almost overhead and a German bomber came out of the cloud with one of our fighters after it. The bomber went off towards Ashford with black smoke coming from it.

Fri 11th Oct

Was a lovely day so had raids pretty well all day. Mother had the dining-room and lounge chimneys swept. Quite a number of army lorries and cars went by this afternoon. At about 4.30 pm we saw a Spitfire coming towards here from Sutton Valance when suddenly its engine spluttered and smoke came from its wings. The pilot did not bale out and the plane seemed to turn towards Marden and glide down.[1]

Sun 13th Oct

Was a glorious day but we only had air raids during the afternoon. Auntie Evelyn and Peter came down. I spent the afternoon wandering in Rocks Hill woods with Miss Fox and then had tea with her. During the evening we went round to the old emergency landing ground at Pagehurst to see a Spitfire which had landed upside-down because it is now ploughed. The pilot escaped with only a cut thumb.

Sun 20th Oct

Jerries have been over pretty well continuously lately but we have not seen much fighting until today as it is mostly over Maidstone or Ashford. Saw a M.E. 110 brought down at Collier Street this morning[2] and we thought another came down this afternoon. Yesterday a Hurricane fired at one of our Blenheims but it did not come down.

Fri 25th Oct

The last three nights and two days have been very quiet. Today Jerry has been over all day and we had two terrific air battles overhead. This morning two planes came down at Stylebridge and two at Headcorn.[3] This afternoon we saw three more come down. One came down in the field next to the Hurricane which came down in Grave Lane. Some bombs were dropped in Maidstone.

Sat 26th Oct

Jerries were over nearly all day but we did not see much fighting. Went for a bike ride this afternoon and found one wing and the back half of a M.E. 109 in a field near Marden so we suppose it must have been part of the one which exploded in the air yesterday. Had just got back and fed the chicken when we heard an explosion and then cannon fire. Then a Spitfire came sideways out of the clouds and crashed in an orchard up Craddocks Lane.[4] The pilot baled out

[1]Probably from No. 605 Squadron
[2]An aircraft from LG 2 shot down by No. 66 squadron
[3]All four were Bf 109s.
[4]Probably from No. 605 squadron.

above the cloud. Mr. and Mrs. Brown, Miss Fox and I cycled up to see the remains of the plane and then we went and saw a bomb hole in the same field as a Spitfire crashed in sometime ago at Mann's. The bombs were dropped at 10 am this morning and had made a large round hole with a large lump in the middle.

Mon 28th Oct

Went into Maidstone and was just coming home when the siren sounded, and a few minutes after heard some bombs whistling down. On the way home we saw three of the bomb craters, one was in the middle of the road and the others were in gardens. Italy declared war on Greece at 6 am this morning.

Wed 30th Oct

Bombs seemed to be dropping all round last night. Some fell at Hawkenbury and 19 at Marden Thorn. This morning we heard terrific machine-gun and cannon fire overhead, and then saw a plane come down in flames over Marden. Have heard since that it was a Jerry.

Sat 2nd Nov

Five air raid warnings sounded this morning, and we heard crowds of planes zooming about overhead but did not see them all as they were flying so very high.
Went to a confirmation service conducted by the Archbishop of Canterbury this afternoon. Had tea at the Rectory and was introduced to His Grace the Archbishop.

Fri 8th Nov

There was a ground mist this morning so we could not see Jerry but we could hear planes zooming and machine-gun fire. Mother and I were talking to Mrs. Brown when some machine-gun bullets came down plop, plop, plop, in the yard. So far we have only found one and that fell just outside the gate.

Sun 10th Nov

Jerry has been chucking out bombs somewhere around nearly every night lately. This morning I went to the 8 o'clock service and just as the service finished we heard bombs whistling down and most of the congregation disappeared under the pews. There were 18 bombs and they fell from Craddocks Lane across to Munns but did no damage. We saw a lot of barrage balloons over towards the North West. Today was the first day for weeks that we have not had a daylight air-raid warning.

Sat Nov 23rd

Saw some Jerries being chased home this morning. Two crashed between Frittenden and Biddenden. We have not had many raids during daylight lately, and when we do, we do not see many Jerries; as there are generally about 30 of our fighters up on patrol and the Jerries don't seem to like meeting them.

Sun Nov 24th

Was a beautiful day so we had a few raids. Saw six yellow-nosed M.E.s go over about 1.30 pm. Went for a bike ride with Mary through Sutton Valance and Melcombe this afternoon. We heard two loud bangs when there were some Jerries overhead but did not know whether they were bombs or guns.

Wed 27th Nov

Was a beautiful clear day and we saw a grand fight between some M.E. 109s and our fighters. Saw one plane come down over Ashford, another somewhere in the direction of Maidstone, and another went right overhead with smoke and flames pouring from it and two Spitfires giving it burst after burst. It went into a dive and came down at Benenden.

Thurs Dec 12th

Except for Sunday night when the gunfire was terrific and Jerry unloaded once or twice pretty close we have not had much excitement until today.

This morning we were working down the fields when there was a sudden whistling sound pretty close overhead, and two loud cracks. As there were planes fighting overhead we thought one had come with its engine full on and then exploded especially as we saw a great puff of brown smoke or dust just the other side of the railway. Since we have found that what we heard was two bombs falling. One fell in a corn field round Newtown and the other in an orchard down Clapper Lane. Both fell close to houses but did not break any windows or do much damage except kill a few chickens. The craters must have been at least 30 ft across.

A few minutes after the bombs fell we heard a plane come down and saw the pilot coming down by parachute.

A few seconds later we heard terrific machine gun and cannon fire over Marden and saw two planes fighting. They gave each other burst after burst until at last one crashed at Cranbrook. Both the planes we saw come down must have been Jerries as none of our planes were lost today.

Christmas Day 1940

Jerry did not come over at all during the night. Either he has got a little sense of decency left, or else the weather must be very bad for flying over there.

The R.A.F. did not go out on any bombing raids.

Mr. and Mrs. Brown came in to tea and supper.

It has been very cold lately and it tried to snow this afternoon.

I could hardly realise that it was Christmas in spite of the cold weather. No carol singers came round this year. I was unable to go to church as I shall not be free from the whooping cough until the New Year. This is the first year I have missed since I was quite small."

As 1940 drew to a close, the people of Britain in particular, and the rest of the free world in general, realised that the islands had managed to stand alone for over six months and survive everything that Göring could throw into the arena. The population was becoming battle hardened and capable of absorbing still more punishment as the night bombers moved from city to city.

Before this momentous year was ended, however, Dowding handed over his Command, on November 25, and was followed by Keith Park. Between them they had stopped the Luftwaffe in its tracks and averted an invasion. In four months over 1700 German aircraft had been lost; Fighter Command was still intact and expanding.

In any other country, honours and promotions would have been the order of the day. Not so in Britain where two other brooms were waiting to sweep up and exploit the victory.

DIARY PHASE FIVE, OCTOBER 1-31

October 1:	Day: Portsmouth and Southampton. Large scale fighter-bomber streams over south-east. Night: London, Liverpool and Manchester. Losses: Luftwaffe 12: RAF 6
October 2:	Day: Fighter/fighter-bomber sweeps, London and Biggin Hill. Night: 100+ again attack London. Smaller raids, Manchester, Usworth and Aberdeen. Losses: Luftwaffe 17: RAF 2
October 3:	Day: Small scattered raids, London and south-east. De Havilland works, Hatfield, hit Night: London, mainly suburbs. Losses: Luftwaffe 9: RAF 1
October 4:	Day: Convoys and single raiders in a stream over south-east. Night: 100+ raiders over London. Small raid Liverpool. Losses: Luftwaffe 12: RAF 1
October 5:	Day: Waves of fighter-bombers over Kent and London. Luftflotte 3 against Southampton. Night: South London and airfields in E. Anglia. Losses: Luftwaffe 15: RAF 7

October 6: Day: Light raids London and East Anglia.
Night: Only seven raiders over London.
Losses: Luftwaffe 9: RAF 3

October 7: Day: Heavy raid aimed at Westland, Yeovil.
Fighter-bombers over south-east.
Night: Widely scattered raids. Main targets,
London and Merseyside.
Losses: Luftwaffe 21: RAF 17

October 8: Day: Main targets London and suburbs.
Night: London.
Losses: Luftwaffe 14: RAF 4

October 9: Day: London and heavy damage to Kent
airfields.
Night: Whole country covered; main raid,
100+ on London.
Losses: Luftwaffe 11: RAF 5

October 10: Day: East Kent, London suburbs and
Weymouth.
Night: London, Liverpool, Manchester and
15 airfields.
Losses: Luftwaffe 7: RAF 8

October 11: Day: High fliers over Kent, Sussex and
Weymouth.
Night: London, Liverpool, Manchester,
Tyne-Tees.
Losses: Luftwaffe 7: RAF 10

October 12: Day: London and south-east.
Night: Light raids, London.
Losses: Luftwaffe 6: RAF 12

October 13: Day: London and Kent again.
Night: London, Wales, Bristol, Liverpool,
Birmingham and Birkenhead.
Losses: Luftwaffe 4: RAF 3

October 14: Day: Small attacks on wide front.
Night: Very heavy raid on London, 500 killed.
Raid on Coventry.
Losses: Luftwaffe 3: RAF 1

October 15: Day: London, the Estuary and Kent.
Night: Heavy raid on London at full moon,
400 killed. Birmingham hit.
Losses: Luftwaffe 15: RAF 18

October 16: Day: Bad weather, activity low.
Night: Small attacks on London.
Losses: Luftwaffe 12: RAF 2

October 17: Day: Continuous streams to London, also
Kent.
Night: Liverpool, Birmingham and targets in
11 Group.
Losses: Luftwaffe 15: RAF 6

October 18: Day: Few raids.
Night: Reduced scale.
Losses: Luftwaffe 13: RAF 6

October 19: Day: Few patrols and reconnaissance.
Night: London, Liverpool, Midlands and
Bristol.
Losses: Luftwaffe 4: RAF 1

October 20: Day: Fighter bomber streams over London
and south-east.
Night: 300 bombers over London; Midlands
attacked.
Losses: Luftwaffe 11: RAF 4

October 21: Day: London, West Country and Liverpool.
Night: London, Wolverhampton, Birming-
ham, Coventry, Liverpool and south coast
radars.
Losses: Luftwaffe 6: RAF 3

October 22: Day: Fog; effort reduced.
Night: Small raids on London, Coventry and
Liverpool.
Losses: Luftwaffe 10: RAF 5

October 23: Day: Reconnaissance and small raids,
quietest day of the battle.
Night: London and Glasgow; minelaying.
Losses: Luftwaffe 3: RAF 1

October 24: Day: Nuisance raids.
Night: Mainly London and Birmingham.
Losses: Luftwaffe 11: RAF 4

October 25: Day: London and Kent throughout the day.
Night: Italian raid on Harwich.
Losses: Luftwaffe 21: RAF 16

October 26: Day: Continuous fighter-bomber raids in
south-east.
Night: London, Manchester, Liverpool and
Midlands.
Losses: Luftwaffe 10: RAF 9

October 27: Day: London, Southampton and convoys.
Night: London, Liverpool and Bristol; also
airfield attacks.
Losses: Luftwaffe 12: RAF 10

October 28: Day: London and shipping.
Night: Widespread attacks.
Losses: Luftwaffe 12: RAF 2

October 29: Day: London and Portsmouth. Italians attack
Ramsgate.
Night: London and the Midlands.
Losses: Luftwaffe 27: RAF 10

October 30: Day: Nuisance raids.
Night: Few raiders.
Losses: Luftwaffe 8: RAF 7

October 31: Day: Fighter bombers and fighters over
south-east.
Night: Little activity.
Losses: Luftwaffe 2: RAF 1

354 Two No. 32 squadron Hurricanes wrecked in a ground accident at Acklington in the autumn of 1940. One aircraft was being run up by a fitter when it jumped the wheel chocks and cut clean through the Hurricane in the background.

355 The Defiant turret fighter was roughly handled by the Luftwaffe in the daylight battle. It had a new lease of life, however as a night fighter. Flying Officer D C Williams and Flying Officer G F C Pledger (air gunner) of 141 squadron at Gravesend in the autumn. Both officers had fought through the Battle of Britain but were killed before the years' end.

356 The pilot of this No. 141 squadron Defiant misjudged his take-off and hit the road embankment at Gravesend in November. The aircraft code was TW.W.

Reference No:-
OC/15

Headquarters, Observer Corps,
Bentley Priory,
STANMORE,
Middx.

Circular No.30.

16th October, 1940.

Dear Sir,

1.   As the war progresses, new problems arise which tax the ingenuity of the
Royal Air Force, and Observer Corps.   For instance:- The Germans frequently employ
Fighter Squadrons by day for bombing.   These Fighters can gain their height before
crossing the Coast, and they fly very fast at heights of between 20,000 and 30,000
feet.
        It is difficult for the Observer Corps to maintain continuous tracks when
they are hidden by cloud or haze, and to separate their tracks from those of our
own Fighters by "sound" alone.
        Nevertheless, the problem has to be tackled and can in many instances be
overcome by close co-operation between Posts and Centre crews, and between Centres.

2.   Efficient inter-centre Telling is of the greatest importance for maintaining
continuity of tracks and all messages passed must be short and to the point. Lengthy
conversations will delay some other Inter-Centre Teller from getting his message
through.

357 The Observer Corps Commandants' circular to members for October 16. The problems of tracking high flying fighter-bomber raids in mixed weather were becoming apparent.

358 The Observer Corps Commandants' circular for October 30. The 'Alarm' within the 'Alert' system for giving direct warning to vital factories via the Observer Corps worked extremely well.

Reference No.OC/150.

Headquarters, Observer Corps,
Bentley Priory,
STANMORE, Middx.

CIRCULAR NO.31.

30th October, 1940.

Dear Sir,

1.   The organisation and development of a system whereby an "Alarm"
message can be issued to certain control points from Observer Centres is being
developed.   From these control points the message will be relayed to Factories
etc., in the vicinity.

2.   This message is for the purpose of giving a short warning of the
approach of enemy aircraft and a "release" when the raiders have passed. It is
obvious that only a limited number of control points can receive this message
from any one Observer Centre and that any message sent to a particular control
point can only apply to factories etc.,in the vicinity of the control point.

3.   "Alarm" message will be issued by Alarm Controllers and Assistant
Controllers responsible to the Ministry of Home Security.

359 Every night the London Underground stations were filled with men, women and children who sought shelter from the bombing. This became a way of life for many thousands of Londoners.

360 Even postmen were issued with the steel helmets. This one is searching for residents in a bombed street. Letters for wrecked houses were specially marked and then returned.

On the morning of October 3 a Ju 88, 3Z + BB from Stab 1/KG 77 at Laon, set out to bomb Reading but lost its way in poor visibility and found the de Havilland works at Hatfield instead. Four high explosive bombs killed 21, wounded 70 and destroyed 80 per cent of the materials and a lot of work in progress for the Mosquito bomber. The Ju 88 was hit by anti-aircraft fire and subsequently crashed at Hartfordbury. **361** Damage at Hatfield. **362** The target the Luftwaffe would have given a great deal to hit, the prototype Mosquito nearing completion in a hangar disguised as a barn at Salisbury Hall five miles west of Hatfield. The Mosquito went on to become one of the most potent military aircraft of the Second World War.

363 The mainstays of the Luftwaffe daylight offensive in October 1940 were bomb-carrying adaptations of the Bf 109 and Bf 110 fighters. Bombs are shown here being loaded on a Bf 109 E-4/B.

Mussolini, in July, offered to take part in the air battle over Britain but was fobbed off by Hitler. The Führer had a change of heart later and during September the Corpo Aero Italiano built up in Belgium under Luftflotte 2. The force consisted of fifty Fiat CR-42 biplane and forty-eight G-50 monoplane fighters and eighty Fiat BR 20 bombers. The outfit was not trained for the tough air fighting in north-west Europe and its equipment was sub-standard. Several small excursions towards England were made in late October with poor results. The one real attack made by Corpo Aero Italiano came on November 11 when six bombers and three fighters were brought down. Thereafter the Italian effort faded away. **364** A group of Italian personnel being shown damage to a Heinkel III by their Luftwaffe opposite numbers. **365** A Fiat CR-42 of 56 Stormo shot down in East Anglia.

362

363

364

365

366 During one of the October night raids, part of the Whitehall Treasury offices was wrecked. This view of the scene was taken from a window in No. 10 Downing Street.

367 No. 242 squadron led by Squadron Leader Bader, airborne from Duxford on October 4.

368 Pilots of No. 616 squadron relax at Kirton-in-Lindsey on October 15.

369 A Bf 109E being towed away by a team of plough horses after being shot down in Kent in the week ending November 30, 1940.

370 Quite clearly the York 9 Observer Group was not over-impressed with the efforts of RAF Catterick. They produced this magnificent card for the station in December 1940, the sentiments of which need no explanation.

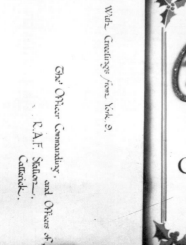

Ode to a Fighter Station.

Who is it we Observers serve
By plotting raids, straining each nerve
To keep informed of every curve
In every track that we observe?
Why, Catterick!

Who is it, when we do our best
To tell them an unwelcome guest
Is bombing York, is not impressed,
But treats our plotting as a jest,
And sends their fighters off North-West?
Why, Catterick!

Who is it, when we phone relating
That Jerry's over Dishforth waiting
To catch our Whitleys' emigrating,
Just simply sends a message stating,
Sorry, but we're not operating"?
Why, Catterick!

Who is it, when their Spitfires race,
By accident, towards the place
Where some bold Heinkel's shown his face,
Sends out the call "Return to base"?
Why, Catterick!

Who is it that is so adept
At promising to intercept —
A promise that is seldom kept?
Why, Catterick!

Who makes our tellers curse and swear
On hearing the DC declare –
"You've just been telling to thin air:
They haven't had a plotter there"?
Why, Catterick!

Who is it, when the Blitzkrieg starts
Round here, will surely play their parts,
OR ELSE BREAK ALL OUR RUDDY HEARTS?
Why, Catterick!!

Christmas Greetings to CATTERICK from YORK 9

With Greetings from York 9.

The Officer Commanding, and Officers of, R.A.F. Station, Catterick.

371 Bombers and bombs were painted with matt black distemper in order to cut down reflection at night. This bomb, loaded on a Heinkel III, had written on it 'Greetings from' . . . on the nose and 'Heil London' on the side.

372 'Winter comforts for England' reads the message on the tail of this He III during the night blitz.

W.H.W. für England.

373 Balloon Command of the RAF had a difficult and unglamorous role to play in 1940 but its work was vital. The balloon barrage was something all Luftwaffe aircraft tried to avoid. This He III was fitted with a massive fender intended to push balloon cables out of the way.

374 German map showing raids completed in October 1940.

375 A large bomb crater in the Strand at the corner of Aldwych, London, in October 1940. Car wings and bumpers have been painted white so as to show up in the blackout.

376 Re-arming a No. 19 squadron Spitfire at Fowlmere, October 9, 1940.

377 Pilots of No. 92 squadron at Biggin Hill in December 1940.

378 Some observers posts in the far west and far north belonged to 'Observer Groups in the back areas'. These operated with simplified forms of plotting. Posts did not have instruments, only a map chart with a white wooden arrow on it. This is one such 'Back Area' post, 21/C.1 Lynton, Devon., deep in snow in December 1940. The post reported to the Centre in Exeter. It was eventually fully equipped with instruments etc.

379 Squadron Leader Peter Townsend and pilots of No. 85 squadron at Kirton-in-Lindsey, in October.

Bentley Priory, the heart of Fighter Command, was not hit by German bombs but it suffered a near-miss from an RAF aircraft. At midnight on 16/17 October 1940 a Wellington bomber of No. 311 Czech squadron based at East Wretham, Norfolk, was returning from a raid on Bremen. The weather was very bad and the aircraft had suffered a wireless failure. Groping in the dark, the Wellington hit the lawns in front of the Priory. It caught fire and was completely destroyed, only the tail gunner surviving. **380** On the morning of October 17, shows the burnt-out wreck being examined by Flight Lieutenant Robert Wright, PA to Lord Dowding. In the background is the familiar tower of the Priory.

381 The ARP services made a great contribution to Britains' survival in 1940. The Wardens watched over the streets, reported incidents, helped clear rubble, rescued trapped victims, dealt with incendiary bombs and assisted the fire services and the salvage workers. Shown here is a typical group of ARP men outside a bombed building. Well in evidence are stirrup pumps and water buckets.

382 Caves, tunnels and a variety of underground structures were used as shelters. A typical group of civilians is shown here in the tunnels at Northfleet, Kent in mid-October 1940. Beds have been put up, candles provide some light and one woman has her inevitable knitting to while away the hours. The second photograph illustrates the communal atmosphere with a whole family in bed and the parents drinking the British salvation liquid—tea. Blankets strung on posts provided the demarcation line between one family and the next.

383 Lifeboats operated continuously in the summer and autumn of 1940 picking up British and German aircrews. Here the wounded pilot of a Bf 109 who crashed in the Channel on the afternoon of October 7 is being brought ashore by the Dungeness lifeboat. It is believed that there was an argument between the lifeboat and a Heinkel 59 as to which should pick him up.

384 Members of a bomb disposal section, Royal Engineers, wheeling away an 1100 pounder which fell next to the railway line at Brentford, London, on October 7, 1940. The bomb had been defused and hauled up by the crane in the background. If it had exploded it would have smashed the line and wrecked all the houses.

385 By October convoys were sailing with barrage balloons winched up from ships. The man in the foreground is operating a Lewis gun.

H O M E   G U A R D.

NO. 3 (CROOKHAM). PLATOON.

PATROLS. "WITHDRAW"

As from Monday next, the 3rd November, Patrols will be discontinued, the last Patrol being the First Watch on the Sunday evening.

The Runner at Headquarters will, however, still be maintained every night, and his general duties will remain as hitherto. There will be no published weekly Roster, but each man will be warned for duty well beforehand.

During the Winter months, Section Leaders should do everything possible to keep their men together, and give them the maximum Instruction practicable.

The C.W. members will be paraded in uniform by their Section Leaders once a week for Drill or Instruction.

The local Sections should also be similarly paraded once a week, if possible, even if this is done on Sunday mornings.

The Weekly Rosters and Orders will be discontinued for the time being:-

Any Special Orders will be circulated to Section Leaders, who will be responsible for passing them on to their men.

The Fortnightly Orderly Room will also be discontinued, but Meetings will be called from time to time.

Platoon Commander.

1st November, 1940.

ORDERS
Uniform.
A set of 5 sizes of Serge Battle Dress will be available at H.Q. on Thursday evening between 6 and 7p.m. for the purpose of obtaining the local men's fittings. All men are requested to attend.

Enemy Aircraft.
Small ballons (10 to 20 ft. in size) with attachments, containing leaflets, and small explosive clockwork charge to scatter them, are being dropped. If any are observed great care should be exercised in handling them.

Instructions.
The attendance at last Wednesday's instruction was very disappointing. Unless there is a considerable improvement during the Winter months, the spring will find No. 3 Platoon as ill trained as they are now, in which event they would make a very poor show. Members must make an effort to attend these Instructions and drills.

A. BOND
Platoon Commander.

25th October, 1940.

386 Orders for the Crookham Home Guard Platoon for October 25 and November 1, 1940. With late autumn and winter weather the threat of invasion receded, only to return in the spring of 1941.

387 Winter 1940; a group of pilots from No. 92 squadron.

388 A Spitfire of the same unit, flaps down, coming in to land.

Appendix I · Invasion

As German preparations for the invasion of England moved into high gear at the end of August, so did the German printing presses. Hundreds of thousands of handbooks on Britain were produced for the use of the invading forces and large numbers of a publication entitled 'Militargeographische Angaben uber England'—Military-Geographical Data on England. This was virtually a mini-encyclopaedia with a welter of information ranging from the location of airfields and military sites down to to the details of gas works, power stations and buildings of interest.

German military cartographers of the period were kept hard at it day and night, marking pirated Ordnance Survey maps with every pill box, gun position, road block, trench and length of barbed wire they could find on the Luftwaffe's reconnaissance photographs.

So many of these maps were printed that, when the end of the war came, the RAF impounded them. The word 'cancelled' was marked over the German map and the clean side was used for the printing of RAF air maps.

Far more sinister, however, were the publishing efforts of the Gestapo/SS who were licking their lips at the thought of controlling the heart of the British Empire and its people. A 'Black List' was issued, which contained names and addresses of men and women from every walk of life and, of course, all the prominent British Jews.

Pages from Informationsheft GB, the Reich Security Head Office's secret handbook on the United Kingdom giving information on British institutions and photographs of those people on the Gestapo arrest list.

— 20 —

rellen Gesellschaften und Vereinen in allen neutralen Ländern und versorgte sie gelegentlich mit Material und mit Rednern. Als Anhaltspunkt für ihre Aktivität mögen ältere Daten und Zahlen Aufschluß geben: Das Komitee verfügte im Weltkriege über 250 Vortragsredner, die auf insgesamt 1500 Versammlungen eingesetzt wurden. Es verteilte 850 000 Flugschriften an Schulkinder und 900 000 an die Arbeiter der wichtigsten Industriezentren. Rund 250 000 Pamphlete, Traktate und Bücher wurden allein in die neutralen Länder versandt.

Besonderes Augenmerk erfordert weiter das „Institut Français" in Kensington. Dieses Institut ist die Zentrale der französischen Kulturpropaganda in Großbritannien. Es steht mit den britischen Hochschulen in Verbindung.

Von großem Interesse ist in diesem Zusammenhang das „Public Record Office" (Staatsarchiv), London W. C. 2, Chancery Lane, gegründet 1838. Es enthält seit 1902 ein eigenes Museum.

Eine Sammelstelle für die Emigranten aus Deutschland, die auch an der Herstellung des 1937 erstellten Emigrantenverzeichnisses beteiligt sind, ist der „Academic Assistance Council", 12, Clement's Inn Passage, Clare Market, London W. C. 2 (Notgemeinschaft deutscher Wissenschaftler im Ausland). Er entspricht der hiesigen deutschen Forschungsgemeinschaft und finanziert Forschungsaufgaben und propagandistische Arbeiten der deutschen emigrierten Wissenschaftler.

Das Informations-Bureau der City of Birmingham im Council House ist ein sehr wertvolles, in der Öffentlichkeit wenig beachtetes Institut. Das Büro entspricht etwa unseren statistischen Ämtern, hat öffentlich-rechtlichen Charakter und verfügt über Unmengen statistischen Materials über alle in Birmingham betreffenden Fragen. Propagandamaterial in deutscher Sprache wird dort veröffentlicht.

Schul- und Erziehungswesen

1. Public-Schools

Die in der Welt bekanntesten englischen Schulen sind die Public-Schools. Sie verdienen insofern besondere Beachtung, als dort die politische Führerschicht Englands seit Jahrhunderten in ihrer Jugend Erziehung und politische Ausrichtung erfuhr. Wesentliches Propagandamaterial gegen Deutschland und politisch und historisch wichtige Dokumente und Sammlungen sind dort vorzufinden.

Es gibt etwa 150 Public-Schools, von denen dem gesellschaftlichen Rang nach folgende als die vornehmsten gelten: Eton, Harrow und Winchester als die drei besten, dann Westminster, Rugby, Charterhouse, Malborough, Clifton u. a. Kaum 1 % aller schulpflichtigen Kinder Englands besuchen heute eine der Public-Schools, und sie besetzten etwa 80 % aller politisch und gesellschaftlich bedeutsamen Stellen. Es sind die Schulen der führenden englischen Oberschicht. Eine dieser alten Schulen besucht zu haben, ist heute noch der Stolz jedes Engländers der führenden Oberschicht. Väter melden ihre Söhne oft schon bei der Geburt in ihrer alten Schule an (Eton-College ist bis zum Jahr 1949 ausverkauft). Reichtum allein genügt nicht für die Aufnahme, er muß politisch oder gesellschaftlich bedeutsam geworden sein. Die erste Generation der englischen Arbeiterführer stammt durchweg aus einfachen Verhältnissen, die sich meist als Gesellschaftssekretäre eine politische Stellung errangen. Die heutigen Sprecher der Arbeiterpartei, Major Attlee, Arthur Greenwood, Dr. Dalton, Sir Stafford Cripps, sind Public-School-Boys. Chamberlain ist Rugby-Schüler, wie auch Minister Lord Hankey, Halifax, Eden, Oliver Stanlay, Duff Cooper kommen aus Eton. Dort wurde auch der jetzige Vizekönig von Indien, Lord Linlithgow, und Sir Robert Vansittart, außenpolitischer Berater der Regierung, erzogen. Sir Samuel Hoare hat Harrow-College besucht;

More significant was 'Informationsheft GB' an expensively produced bound volume which had no reference to its source (the Gestapo) but was marked 'Geheim' (secret) on the cover and each copy of which was individually numbered.

The book contained an extraordinary assortment of information including a large pull-out which was a reproduction of a wall poster listing the officials of the Metropolitan Police in 1937. The main emphasis, however, lay on hated British institutions such as the Public Schools, the Churches, the Trades Unions, Jewish organisations, the Boy Scouts and even the Church Lads Brigade. The last written section concerned British Intelligence, which the Gestapo found extremely difficult to understand but for which it had great envy and respect. There were numerous errors in the text but also a lot of uncoordinated facts, names, addresses, etc. which were correct. This information was obtained from two Secret Intelligence Service (SIS) agents, Stevens and Best, who were captured by the Gestapo in a raid across the Dutch border in November 1939, which became known as the 'Venlo Incident'. The head of Air Intelligence is given in the book as 'Winter-Bottom (Whing-Commander?)'. Group Captain F W Winterbotham was, in fact, in charge of security for the top secret Ultra-decoding system based at the Government Code and Cypher School at Bletchley.

The following extracts come from Informationsheft GB and deal with aspects of British Society understanding of which would assist the conquerors in subduing the nation.

SECRET
INFORMATIONSHEFT GB

SCHOOL & EDUCATION SYSTEM

1. Public Schools

The type of English schooling known throughout the world is the English Public School system. It merits special consideration in as much as the foundations of English political leadership, for generations past, have been laid in the education and political guidance of her youth. Considerable anti-German propaganda material and important political and historical documents and archives are lodged in the Public Schools.

There are about one hundred and fifty Public Schools. In order of social precedence among them, the following rank foremost: Eton, Harrow and Winchester come first; then follow Westminster, Rugby, Charterhouse, Marlborough, Clifton, etc.

Of all school-age children in England today, scarcely 1% goes to the Public Schools; and about 80% of all political and socially important jobs go to the 1%. These are the schools of the English governing upper class. Upper-class Englishmen are still proud to have been to one of these old-established schools. Fathers put their sons' names down at birth on entry lists for their old schools (Eton is fully booked for as far ahead as 1949). Wealth of itself is not enough to ensure the acceptance of a candidate, he must also have the required political and social background. The first generation of English Labour Party leaders all came from simple backgrounds; they mostly achieved political status through being workforce representatives. However, today's Labour Party leaders, Major Attlee, Arthur Greenwood, Dr Dalton, Sir Stafford Cripps, are all Public School educated. Chamberlain was at Rugby, just as Ministers Lord Hankey, Halifax, Eden, Oliver Stanley (sic) and Duff Cooper were at Eton. The present Viceroy of India, Lord Linlithgow, was at Eton too and also the Foreign Secretary, Sir Robert Vansittart. Sir Samuel Hoare was at Harrow, as was Winston Churchill. Hore Belisha went to Clifton in Bristol, whereas Sir John Simon was at Fettes in Edinburgh.

These are all boarding schools, and they were founded as far back as the fourteenth century. They exist on old-established endowments and are, by and large, independent of State control and finance.

They have been of the greatest service to England in maintaining uninterruptedly, via the younger generations, the imprint of English upper class traditions. Within their orbit the English gentleman was formed. A man who never gave thought to political problems, who knew hardly anything of foreign cultures, and who considered Germany the living embodiment of all evil and thought England's might unassailable. The whole public school system is geared to producing men of iron will-power and dedicated energy to whom abstractions are a waste of time; men who, nevertheless, know how to deal with other men and who understand the art of ruthless mastery. They were not the nurseries of individuals capable of contributing their own special talents to the old established values, but rather they produced men who deemed the whole object of their lives to be a stern adherence to English ideals of leadership and to the interests of the English hierarchy.

2. The International Boy Scout Movement

The International Boy Scout Movement was founded in 1907 by Lord Baden-Powell, the defender of Mafeking in the Boer War.

At first this movement only existed in England, but later on, thanks to advised propaganda on the part of the Government, it spread to Europe (1911), and eventually the movement spread throughout the whole world. The Boy Scout movement in the British Dominions was built up primarily under the aegis of the British authorities.

Lord Baden-Powell, as 'Chief World Scout', is the overall leader of the international Scout movement. Its Headquarters is in London at the so-called I.B. (International

Bureau), which, until recently, was run by the half-Jew, Mr Martin. Martin was also in charge of the British Passport Office. The present Chief of the I.B. (a Mr Wilson) is also employed in the Passport Office. Eight years prior to this he was Chief of Police in Calcutta. Possibly someone called Lunt is now his successor. The I.B. is a means of establishing communication between the Scout movement in the different countries. Each country's section has its international representative, who is the only person of that country authorised to maintain contact with the I.B. in London. It is the duty of the different international representatives to furnish the I.B. in London with monthly and quarterly reports on the economical, cultural and political state of their section of the movement. Moreover personal contact and correspondence between Scouts must go through their international representative. The individual national Scout sections in the different countries have a set-up similar to that of the I.B.

Given that the different Scout sections are outwardly engaged, almost exclusively, in training in the primary military arts of the young of their different countries then it follows that the Boy Scout movement is a powerful instrument of British cultural propaganda and an undercover source of information for the British Intelligence Service. During the First World War Lord Baden-Powell himself was posted as a spy against Germany. The disbandment of the Austrian section of the Scouts proved, among other things, the connection of the Boy Scout movement with the Secret Service. From the point of view of ideals, by and large, the English Boy Scout movement shows the same trend of thinking as exists within the German youth associations, but naturally in the former case orientated towards the English way of life. There are, therefore, very close personal links between the German groups and English Scout circles.

The Kandersteger Agreement on Minorities of 1926 is of special importance with regard to international relationships, since by this agreement, all countries with a national Scout section were guaranteed the right to establish Minority Scout Sections abroad.

It is well known also that the 'German Youth Front', acting on behalf of combined emigré youth leaders, maintains strong ties with the International Bureau. Therefore the strongest suspicions exist that the International Bureau, in view of these numerous connections abroad, operates on behalf of the British Intelligence Service.

THE BRITISH INTELLIGENCE SERVICE

In reply to a question raised in the House of Commons concerning the state of the British Intelligence Service, a member of the Government explained: "The essence of the Intelligence Service is to be a secret service. Therefore one cannot discuss it. Any raising of the subject only endangers the maintenance of this secrecy."

Consequently, the British Intelligence Service abides by this principle in all things. At the very start, no one knows exactly what its official designation is. Indeed, with the silent concurrence of the authorities, all novels, films and publications produced by outsiders or technical experts connected with the service, have, as far as we can make out, contributed towards causing ambiguity rather than clarity on this point, as indeed on general matters connected with the British Intelligence Service. Captain Best and Major Stevens, who fell into the hands of the German Service, explained that there was no 'Intelligence Service' functioning as a simple overall organisation, nor was there a 'Secret Service' in the sense that we could use this nomenclature for classification purposes. At best the term 'SIS' ('Secret Intelligence Service') could be used. However, they called their Chief, Admiral Sinclair, 'CSS' initials stand, for 'Chief, Secret Service'. vice'.

This lack of definition is as characteristic as the purposeful decentralisation of the sections of the service, which, for technical reasons, are not concealed or intended to be concealed. These are: the Offices of the Central Authorities (sic), the Passport Offices (PPCO's, ie Passport Control Offices), the Embassies and Consulates General. Often lack of cover is preferable, as this of itself constitutes a deception and satisfactorily deflects the attention of the enemy from the real activities of the organisations concerned.

If we wish to penetrate the very essence and the structure of the British Intelligence Service, then, from the outset, let us rid ourselves of all the usual preconceived ideas of a tightly knit organisation based on that tendency peculiar to the Germans towards exact divisions, parameters and definitions. Until now they have been able to prevent all insight into the running of the Service, its real machinery, its nerve centre, and the assembly point of the various branches from whence impulses for all new undertakings emanate. Until now no-one could state categorically that the Service was organised in such and such a way, that it had its headquarters here or there and was staffed by so-and-so or so-and-so who held this or that office. If any details regarding the British Intelligence Service were indeed known, or were even divulged by the British, then it had to be assumed that only those authorities or administrative offices which could not be kept permanently secret had been publicised. The brains and the brawn of that entity we call the Secret Service are kept secret, from the top directorate to the lowest field unit. Any information published about it must be treated with the utmost caution as being a red herring put out by the British—of which more will be said later. As a general rule such revelations should be regarded as manoeuvres intended to deceive. The real enterprises are kept secret and to remain silent about them is indeed an acquired art."

Appendix 2

From 1933 onwards with constant up-dates, Air Ministry Publication 1480 provided the services and the Observer Corps with a basis of recognition material and by 1940 had reached a comparatively high standard. These pages from 1940/1941 illustrate many of the major types engaged in the Battle of Britain.

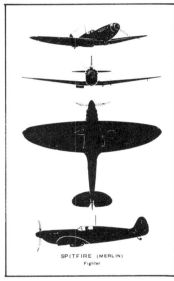

SPITFIRE (MERLIN)
Fighter

MESSERSCHMITT Me 109E
SINGLE-SEAT FIGHTER

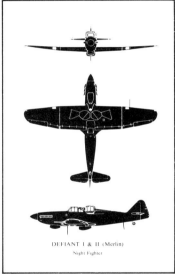

DEFIANT I & II (Merlin)
Night Fighter

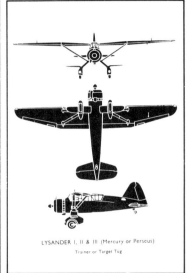

LYSANDER I, II & III (Mercury or Perseus)
Trainer or Target Tug

HEINKEL He 111 (2-Jumo)
Bomber

HURRICANE I (MERLIN)
Single-Seat Fighter

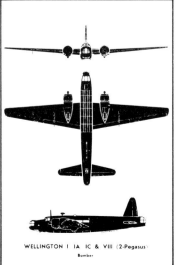

WELLINGTON I, IA, IC & VIII (2-Pegasus)
Bomber

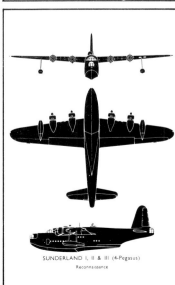

SUNDERLAND I, II & III (4-Pegasus)
Reconnaissance

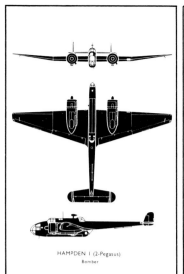

HAMPDEN I (2-Pegasus)
Bomber

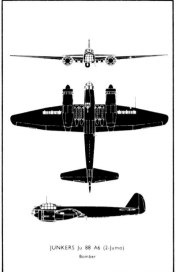

JUNKERS Ju 88 A6 (2-Jumo)
Bomber

DORNIER Do 17Z
Bomber

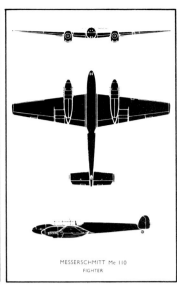

MESSERSCHMITT Me 110
FIGHTER

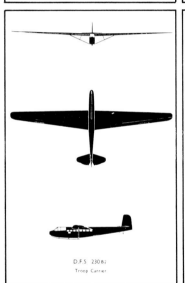

D.F.S. 230 B2
Troop Carrier

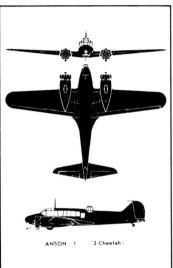

ANSON I (2-Cheetah)

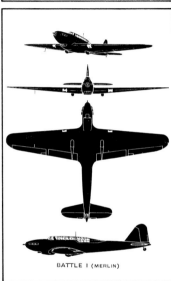

BATTLE I (MERLIN)

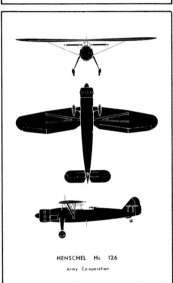

HENSCHEL Hs 126
Army Co-operation

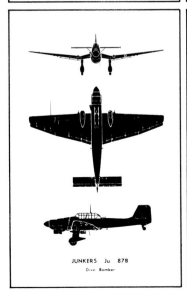

JUNKERS Ju 87B
Dive Bomber

BLENHEIM I (2-MERCURY)
BOMBER
BLENHEIM IF (2-MERCURY)
MULTI-SEAT FIGHTER

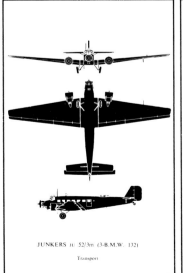

JUNKERS Ju 52/3m (3-B.M.W. 132)
Transport

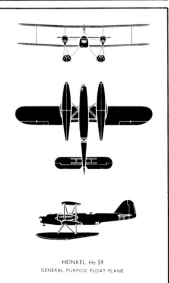

HEINKEL He 59
GENERAL PURPOSE FLOAT PLANE

Appendix 3: Order of Battle

R.A.F. Fighter Command and its subsidiary formations at 0900 hours.

September 15th, 1940

Air Officer Commanding-in-Chief: Air Chief Marshal Sir Hugh Dowding
Headquarters: Bentley Priory, Stanmore, Middlesex.

FORMATIONS UNDER COMMAND

No. 9 Group

Headquarters: Barton Hall, Preston, Lancashire.
Stations and Squadrons: None.

No. 10 Group

Air Vice-Marshal Sir Christopher Brand
Headquarters: Rudloe Manor, Box, Wiltshire.

Stations	Squadrons	Type
Pembrey	No. 79	Spitfire
Filton		
Exeter	No. 601 (County of London)	Hurricane
	No. 87 ('B' Flight)	Hurricane
Bilbury	No. 87 ('A' Flight)	Hurricane
Colerne		
St. Eval	No. 234	Spitfire
Roborough	No. 247	Gladiator
Middle	No. 238	Hurricane
Wallop	No. 609 (West Riding)	Spitfire
	No. 604 (County of Middlesex)	Blenheim
	No. 23 ('A' Flight)	Blenheim
Warmwell	No. 152	Spitfire
Boscombe Down	No. 56	Hurricane

Operational Training Units		
Aston Down	No. 5	
Sutton Bridge	No. 6	
Hawarden	No. 7	

No. 11 Group

Air Vice-Marshal Keith Park
Headquarters: Hillingdon House, Uxbridge, Middlesex.

Stations	Squadrons	Type
Debden	No. 17	Hurricane
Castle Camps	No. 73	Hurricane
Martlesham	No. 257	Hurricane
Heath	No. 25 ('A' Flight)	Blenheim
North Weald	No. 25 ('B' Flight)	Blenheim
	No. 249	Hurricane
Stapleford	No. 46	Hurricane
Abbots		
Hornchurch	No. 603 (City of Edinburgh)	Spitfire
Rochford	No. 41	Spitfire
	No. 222	Spitfire
Manston		
Kenley	No. 253	Hurricane
	No. 501 (County of Gloucester)	Hurricane
Croydon	No. 605 (County of Warwick)	Hurricane
West Malling		
Biggin Hill	No. 72	Spitfire
	No. 92	Spitfire
	No. 141 ('B' Flight)	Defiant
Gravesend	No. 66	Spitfire
Redhill	No. 600 (City of London)	Blenheim
Hawkinge		
Lympne		

Tangmere	No. 607 (County of Durham)	Hurricane
	No. 213	Hurricane
	Special Unit	
	The Fighter Interception Unit	Blenheim/Beaufighter
Westhampnett	No. 602 (City of Glasgow)	Spitfire
Ford	No. 23 ('B' Flight)	Blenheim
Northolt	No. 229	Hurricane
	No. 1 (Canadian)	Hurricane
	No. 303 (Polish)	Hurricane
	Special Unit	
	The Air Fighting Development Unit	
	No. 264 ('B' Flight)	Defiant
Hendon	No. 504 (County of Nottingham)	Hurricane

No. 12 Group

Air Vice Marshall Trafford Leigh-Mallory
Headquarters: Watnall, Nottingham, Notts.

Stations	Squadrons	Type
Duxford	No. 19	Spitfire
	No. 310 (Czech)	Hurricane
	No. 312 (Czech)	Hurricane
Coltishall	No. 74	Spitfire
	No. 242	Hurricane
Wittering	No. 1	Hurricane
	No. 266	Spitfire
Digby	No. 151	Hurricane
	No. 611 (West Lancashire)	Spitfire
	No. 29	Blenheim
Kirton-in-Lindsey	No. 616 (South Yorkshire)	Spitfire
	No. 264 ('A' Flight)	Defiant
	No. 307 (Polish)	Hurricane
Speke	No. 308 (Polish)	Hurricane
Ringway	No. 64 ('B' Flight)	Spitfire
Church Fenton	No. 85	Hurricane
	No. 306 (Polish)	Hurricane
Leconfield	No. 302 (Polish)	Hurricane
	No. 64 ('A' Flight)	Spitfire
Yeadon		

No. 13 Group

Air Vice-Marshal Richard Saul
Headquarters: Blakelaw Estate, Ponteland, Newcastle-on-Tyne

Stations	Squadrons	Type
Catterick	No. 54	Spitfire
	No. 219 ('A' Flight)	Blenheim
Usworth	No. 43	Hurricane
Acklington	No. 32	Hurricane
Turnhouse	No. 65	Spitfire
	No. 3	Hurricane
	No. 141 ('A' Flight)	Defiant
Drem	No. 111	Hurricane
West Freugh		
Prestwick	No. 615 (Auxiliary)	Hurricane
Dyce	No. 145 ('B' Flight)	Hurricane
Montrose	No. 145 ('A' Flight)	Hurricane
Wick	No. 804	Sea Gladiator
Castletown	No. 808	Fulmar
Sumburgh	No. 232	Hurricane
Aldegrove	No. 245	Hurricane

No. 14 Group

Air Vice Marshal Malcolm Henderson
Headquarters: Drunmossie Hotel, Inverness.

Stations

Castletown
Skaebrae
Squadrons: None
Other operational fighter units in Fighter Command: No. 421 Flight, No. 422
Flight.

Battle casualties. RAF, UK, July 1—October 31, 1940

Cat. 2 = repairable by depot or contractor
Cat. 3 = missing or wrecked beyond repair (i.e. total loss)

Cumulative totals at dates shown

| Date | Total | Bombers | | Fighters | | Other | | Op. | Types |
		Cat. 2	Cat. 3	Cat. 2	Cat. 3	Cat. 2	Cat. 3	Cat. 2	Cat. 3
July	1	82	358	56	517	16	104	154	979
	11	87	386	78	565	20	108	185	1059
	18	92	396	100	588	23	112	215	1096
	25	95	413	113	623	26	116	234	1152
Aug.	1	102	435	130	650	29	120	261	1205
	8	106	448	143	685	31	128	280	1261
	15	124	487	211	807	35	137	370	1431
	22	133	510	272	897	37	145	442	1552
	29	144	534	314	1017	38	147	496	1698
Sept.	5	153	563	423	1184	39	153	615	1900
	12	161	595	487	1293	41	161	689	2049
	19	167	611	532	1362	43	164	742	2137
	26	176	624	568	1406	49	169	793	2199
Oct.	3	179	648	628	1488	51	178	858	2314
	10	183	661	662	1537	56	184	901	2382
	17	185	689	701	1587	58	189	944	2465
	24	192	701	726	1607	63	190	981	2498
	31	198	725	766	1657	66	200	1030	2582
Grand totals for period		116	367	710	1140	50	96	876	1603

German battle casualties during the Battle of Britain

Claimed and definite (all reasons)

Date	R.A.F. claimed Destroyed	Actual* Destroyed		Damaged
10 July—7 August	188	192	(63)	77
8 August—23 August	755	403	(213)	127
24 August—6 September	643	378	(243)	115
7 September—30 September	846	435	(243)	161
1 October—31 October	260	325	(134)	163
Total	2692	1733	(896)	643

Figures in brackets denote losses publicly admitted by the German High Command at the time of the battle, i.e. just over half the actual total.

*The figures are taken from the German Quartermaster General's returns.

Appendix 4· Maps

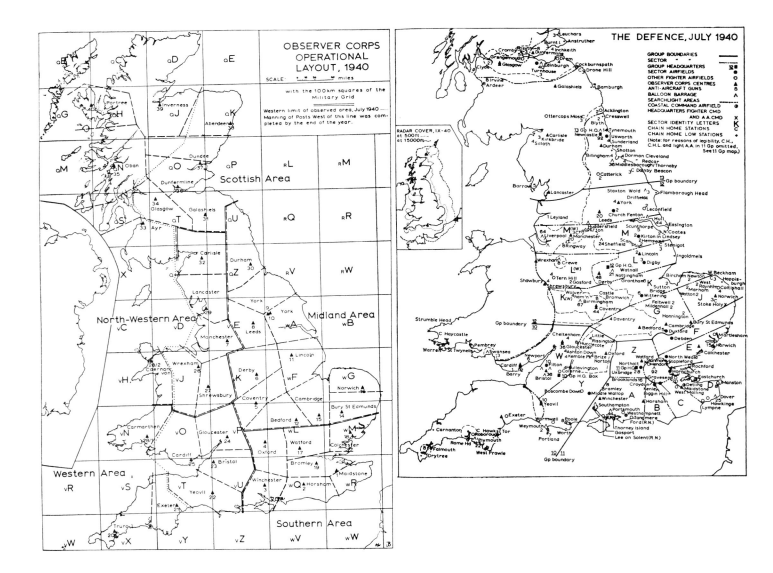

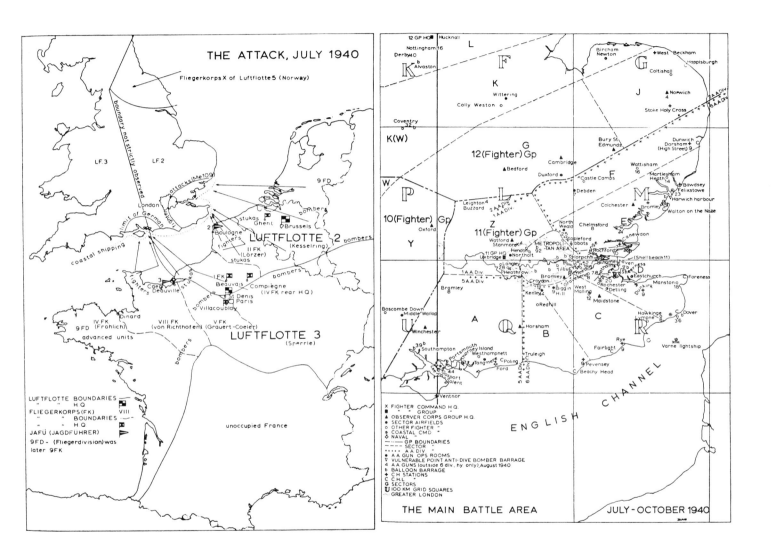

THE ATTACK, JULY 1940

Fliegerkorps X of Luftflotte 5 (Norway)

LF.3   LF.2

boundary not strictly observed

limit of German attacks(Me109)

9 FD

London

coastal shipping

fighters

attacks(Me109)

stukas   Ghent   bombers

2   Boulogne   Brussels

fighters   stukas   LUFTFLOTTE 2
II FK   (Kesselring)
(Lörzer)   bombers
stukas

I FK   bombers
3   Beauvais
Caen   Deauville   stukas   Compiègne
(IV FK rear HQ)
bomber   St Denis
Villacoublay   Paris

Dinard
IV FK   VIII FK   V FK
(Fröhlich)   (von Richthofen)   (Grauert-Coeler)
9 FD

advanced units   LUFTFLOTTE 3
(Sperrle)

unoccupied France

LUFTFLOTTE BOUNDARIES
"   "   HQ
FLIEGERKORPS (FK)   VIII
"   "   BOUNDARIES
"   "   HQ
JAFÜ (JAGDFÜHRER)
9 FD - (Fliegerdivision)was
later 9 FK

---

12 GP HQ   Hucknall
Nottingham 16   L
Derby40   b   Alvaston   F   Y   Bircham   +West Beckham
Newton   Happlsburgh
K   Coltishall
K   Wittering   Norwich   G
Colly Weston o   4
Coventry   Stoke Holy Cross   7 A A Div
32 b   6 A A Div
K(W)   Bury St   Dunwich
G   Edmunds   Darsham +
12(Fighter) Gp   (High Street) 9
W   Cambridge   Wattisham
P   Bedford   Duxford   Castle Camps   16
Debden   Martlesham
10(Fighter) Gp   Leighton   L   Heath+
Buzzard   1 A A Div   Colchester   Bawdsey
Y   Oxford   North   Chelmsford   Felixstowe
Z   Weald   Harwich harbour
11(Fighter) Gp   Watford   Stapleford   Walton on the Naze
Stanmore   METROPOLI-   Abbots   E
11 GP HQ   Hendon   -TAN AREA
Uxbridge   Northolt   (Shellbeach11)
Langley   Tilbury   Rochford   D
1 A A Div   Heathrow   Croydon   Eastchurch   Foreness
Bromley   5 A A Div   Biggin   West   Rochester   Detling   Manston o   18
Hill   Malling   12   Maidstone   K
Boscombe Down   Kenley   o Redhill   C   Hawkinge   C Dover
Middle Wallop   A   Horsham   B   Lympne   36
Winchester   Q   Truleigh   Rye   R
U   C Poling   Fairlight   Varne lightship
Southampton   Westhampnett   5 A A Div   Pevensey
Portsmouth   Tangmere   Ford   6 A A Div   Beachy Head
Gosport   Solent
Ventnor   ENGLISH   CHANNEL

X FIGHTER COMMAND H.Q.
"   "   GROUP
OBSERVER CORPS GROUP H.Q.
SECTOR AIRFIELDS
o OTHER FIGHTER   "
COASTAL CMD
NAVAL
– – GP.BOUNDARIES
– – – SECTOR   "
• • • • A.A. DIV
A A GUN OPS ROOMS
VULNERABLE POINT ANTI-DIVE BOMBER BARRAGE
4 A A GUNS (outside 6 div, hy. only), August 1940
b BALLOON BARRAGE
CH STATIONS
C C.H.L.
G SECTORS
U 100 KM GRID SQUARES
GREATER LONDON

THE MAIN BATTLE AREA   JULY - OCTOBER 1940

191

Index